"*Drawing on the testimony of those trapped in the quicksand of poverty,* Broke *is an overdue wake-up call for anyone who still thinks Britain is a normal, fair or 'civilised' country.*"

Darren McGarvey, BBC Reith lecturer, Orwell Prize
winner and author of *Poverty Safari*

"*A devastating portrait of modern poverty,* Broke *is urgently reported and beautifully written, with humane and empathetic accounts of what it feels like to be caught in a 21st-century poverty trap. This collection of essays sets out in disturbing detail the true impact of a decade of austerity policies and should be required reading for politicians and policymakers.*"

Amelia Gentleman, award-winning journalist
and author of *The Windrush Betrayal*

"*I grew up at a time when poverty was rife but governments of right and left were committed to its eradication. In this book, Tom Clark conducts an orchestra of experts to demonstrate that poverty is rife once again, and the only thing that's been eradicated is government's determination to deal with it.*"

Alan Johnson, former Cabinet minister and author
of the Orwell Prize-winning *This Boy*

Broke

Edited by Tom Clark

Broke

Fixing Britain's
poverty crisis

\B^b\

Biteback Publishing

This paperback edition published in Great Britain in 2024 by
Biteback Publishing Ltd, London
Selection and editorial apparatus copyright © Tom Clark 2023, 2024
Copyright in the individual essays resides with the named authors
Unless otherwise attributed, photographs copyright © Joel Goodman 2023, 2024
April 2021 Deliveroo protest photograph (pages 216–17) copyright
© Guy Smallman/Getty Images

ISBN 978-1-78590-829-3

10 9 8 7 6 5 4 3 2 1

A CIP catalogue record for this book is available from the British Library.

Set in Minion Pro

Printed and bound in Great Britain by
CPI Group (UK) Ltd, Croydon CR0 4YY

FSC
www.fsc.org
MIX
Paper | Supporting
responsible forestry
FSC® C171272

CONTENTS

A NATION DISTURBED: WHERE THINGS STAND IN 2024

Nobody who has walked around a British city in recent times can have missed the proliferation of street tents. In the past fifteen months, since the first edition of this book was published, I have myself seen them in many places, including the centres of Bristol and Liverpool and right beside the Ritz in London.

Compassion is one natural reaction. Another is curiosity: how on earth is it that so many people who, presumably, used to sleep with roofs over their heads are now bedding down under canvas? In *Broke* we make efforts to find out, hearing for example from Zhcnya (Chapter 7), who lives in a tent near Great Yarmouth and quietly explains how severe back problems had ruled out work at just the same time as a bit of botched paperwork had locked him in a Kafkaesque limbo in which where he was unable to cash in any notional rights for protection against destitution.

Sadly, we have recently witnessed a third reaction, very different to both compassion and curiosity: namely, callousness. Seventy-year-old Anthony Sinclair gave me a first-hand account of what happened to him in his tent in late 2023, as the nights drew in. Anthony had become homeless after the heavy weight of London rent became too great. Although he receives a modest pension, a twenty-year career as a bus driver had ended with a costly three-year employment dispute; he explained it was 'either drop the case or stop paying rent'. But, remarkably, he had latterly achieved a certain stability as a self-described 'urban camper', using some of his savings on rent to pay for a gym membership which allowed him to keep showered and fresh.

But then, on 10 November 2023, the police descended from out of the blue and disturbed him in his tent on a street in north-central London. In his unbowed Mancunian tones, still unmissable after forty years in the capital, he recalls how officers had turned up 'demanding my details: name, date of birth. But I stood my ground and refused because I'd done nothing wrong.' The officers said they were enforcing a 'Section 35 dispersal order', which Anthony thought couldn't be used without notice, nor to move someone 'away from their home – and this was my home'. But whatever the rules said, the authorities would soon ensure it was not a home he would have for much longer.

The police handcuffed Anthony, searching his pockets and inside his tent, even as he declined permission. They soon found his driving licence, forcibly extracting and confirming his details from it. After briefly releasing him, the officers talked in general terms about rough sleepers begging and defecating in the street (offering nothing to challenge Anthony's avowal that he had never done either of these things in his life), and then ordered him to leave the area. Again he refused, and again he was arrested, now put in cuffs so tight they were painful, taken to the police station and held for several hours, being released that evening.

He then went home to the tent, to find it wasn't there. His tent and those of another ten or so neighbours had been thrown into rubbish lorries and crushed up – destruction captured in footage that immediately went viral online.[1]

'We had no sleeping bags and we were freezing,' he recalls. Hastily erected barriers and patrolling security guards had taken over the small patch of ground alongside University College Hospital where he and others had been based for some months. Fortunately, the police had agreed to bag up and take Anthony's most important possessions with him to the station. Even so, he returned to find that his mattress and toiletries had been destroyed along with his tent.

Others in neighbouring tents, who were mostly elsewhere when the police had arrived, were altogether less fortunate: 'One guy who'd been nearby had mental health problems; I think he was bipolar. His tent and everything went in the bin.

We couldn't get hold of him for a long while after that.' When Anthony and the other rough sleepers eventually did make contact, the man was inconsolable: 'He told me, "There was my dad's watch in there, which he gave me just before he died; there was twenty-three years of my life in that tent."'

So the security operation broke hearts as well as make-shift homes. And it is perfectly possible that it also ended up shortening lives and, perversely, trapping more people out on the street for longer. Anthony underlines what the notorious footage had already suggested: that the tents and everything inside went into the Veolia rubbish-crusher truck. He knew first-hand how practically as well as emotionally devastating this could be, because once before his own tent had been sin-gled out and swept away by local security guards.[2] That time, all the contents had been binned: 'Everything: my clothes, my asthma pump and even my passport.' His asthma, unsurpris-ingly, had been aggravated by homelessness, so the sudden loss of that pump could have been dangerous. And it's only too easy to imagine the grim potential consequences of the loss of ID documents, if they are needed to access housing, benefits or any other crucial support.

The Camden affair betrayed a nation disturbed by the penury in its midst and yet entirely unsure what to do about it. Beyond, that is, the age-old trick of dealing with 'vagrancy' by trying to turn the people at the sharp end into someone else's problem by moving them along. The neighbouring Uni-versity College Hospital acknowledged that it had wanted the sleepers dispersed but let it be known that it had never meant for the tents to be destroyed;[3] an anguished Camden Council very publicly looked into its role in the matter;[4] and, eventually, the police admitted they had acted unlawfully.[5] No one came out of the incident proud.

A certain cognitive dissonance enables many to treat the likes of Anthony Sinclair with contempt without facing up to what they are doing. Others are more straightforwardly cynical. On 4 November 2023 – just six days before the Camden tents were cleared – the then Home Secretary Suella Braverman had tweeted: 'We cannot allow our streets to be taken over by rows of tents occupied by people … living on the streets as a lifestyle choice.'[6] Anthony didn't hear about those words until the following week, but he has 'no doubt' they emboldened the authorities locally: 'That's why they felt bold enough to go for everyone at once, not just pick off one tent like they did with me before.'

But at Westminster, just as in the communities confronting the unsightly reality of street squalor, a strange doubleness besets the politics of destitution. No political approach, whether cruel or compassionate, is for long sustained. For her part, Braverman was almost immediately out of office, after a backlash against her merciless words on rough sleepers was compounded by a separate row involving the policing of Palestine solidarity protests.[7] Her plan to create a new penalty for charities that issued homeless people with tents bit the dust. And yet, into the spring of 2024, the government was still attempting to criminalise rough sleepers, introducing provisions akin to those in the 200-year-old Vagrancy Act, and actually increasing the (surely uncollectable) fines for people who can't afford a roof over their head. Under the legislation, those deemed to be 'nuisance' rough sleepers were to be stung for up to £2,500[8] (with 'nuisance' being spitefully defined in terms of things like 'smells').[9] A month of prison was even threatened. It soon ran into a parliamentary rebellion,[10] and ultimately the whole bill the plans were contained in fell victim to the dissolution for the general election.

But irrespective of the fate of this particular government shin-kicking stunt against vulnerable people, what's needed is a complete reboot of the whole discourse that leaves the powerful dreaming such things up. My hope is that *Broke* can contribute to this process, by allowing people on the sharp end, with the help of skilled and compassionate reporters whom they know they can trust, to share their stories and have their voices heard.

The first step, as I wrote in the original edition, is to face up to the ugly realities of the poverty crisis – and then find the right policies and build the right politics to fix it. I will use the remainder of this update to look at how things have evolved on each of these fronts in turn. The picture is inevitably somewhat mixed but, overall, it has if anything darkened since early 2023. The 2024 general election, a few weeks away as I write, could be a chance to change direction – but only if that chance is seized by the politicians who emerge from it.

THE SHIFTING FACTS: FROM CRISIS TO CHRONIC CONDITION

The past fifteen months have witnessed a great gust of relief blowing through the corridors of power, as headline inflation slowly returned from a forty-year high (11.1 per cent in October 2022) to something much more ordinary (2.3 per cent in April 2024).[11] If the problem of poverty in our country really could be reduced to a 'cost-of-living crisis' then, you might think, the stabilisation of living costs should clear the way for that crisis to pass.

Unfortunately, what matters for securing those absolute basics in life which are our focus in *Broke* – food, shelter, heat and so on – is not the general price index, which is also affected by prices in fancy restaurants and the bill for domestic staff, but the costs of precisely those necessities. After an extremely painful delay, headline benefit rates finally caught up with general inflation in April 2024: the rise over the period from April 2021 was about 20 per cent. And yet, in parallel, food prices had risen by about 30 per cent and energy bills by 75 per cent.[12] Consequently, the return of some sort of order to the summary cost-of-living statistics has not translated into much let-up in the struggle to keep body and soul together. Indeed, the very latest data from the Trussell Trust food bank network, covering that disinflationary financial year 2023/24, showed the number of emergency parcels it had issued had not fallen but risen yet again, to set a new record of 3.1 million.[13]

Still, it is in the nature of 'crises' to culminate in a particular moment – and indeed some aspects of the recent crunch, notably fuel costs, are now finally easing.[14] But a raft of chilling new evidence in the past year suggests that the very phrase 'cost-of-living crisis' may have been something of a misnomer: Britain's problems with poverty are curdling into the sort of chronic condition that has long dogged, and shortened, life in large parts of the United States.[15]

The latest headlines are provided by an appalling new batch of official data released in March 2024, which covered the period (financial year 2022/23) when life was returning to some sort of normal after the pandemic.[16] Everything was moving the wrong way: real incomes were down and inequality up. Child poverty is now not only rising on the 'relative' measure preferred by campaigners but also rocketing on the 'absolute' gauge, which Rishi Sunak and his Chancellor had previously reached for to suggest that all was well.

Also out in the past year, and particularly pertinent to *Broke*'s focus on the most brutal privations, is the giant Joseph Rowntree Foundation-backed 'Destitution in the UK' report.[17] Run out of Edinburgh's Heriot-Watt University, this study supplements ordinary household surveys by heading into crisis services the breadth of the country – soup kitchens, emergency housing offices, refuges and more – to count the queues and find the people whom the routine data misses. It deploys an extremely stiff definition of 'destitution', related to basic physical needs: the ability to keep warm, dry, clean and fed. It found some 3.8 million Britons had had a brush with destitution during 2022, including a million children. These figures, respectively, represent a near two-and-a-half-fold increase and a virtual tripling over the mere five years since 2017.

So much for the headlines; let's consider how things are looking in respect of the distinct aspects of hardship around which the chapters of *Broke* are arranged, starting with housing. At the most acute and visible end, official figures confirm what our own eyes have been telling us: rough sleeping is on the rise. It continues to break new records in London[18] and is now up by 60 per cent in just two years in the latest England-wide count.[19] In other words, the problems faced by the likes of Anthony Sinclair in Camden, as well as Zhenya in Norfolk and 'Mary' in Leeds (whom we will encounter in Chapter 7) are becoming more common.

Rough sleeping is only ever the small visible tip of a huge submerged iceberg of hidden homelessness: the official tally suggests only around 4,000 English street sleepers against well over 100,000 households (containing many more individuals) who are shunted into (frequently terrible) temporary accommodation. This broader category includes, at points in her story, the likes of Tracy Benson and her son Dan in Bideford, Devon, whom we meet in Chapter 1, and also the young Kerry Hudson, who in the foreword recalls her experience of 'bed and breakfast' digs in which there was no breakfast. This temporary housing tally has more than doubled since 2010,[20] with a particularly rapid rise for families with children evident in the past year.[21] A careful recent *Financial Times* analysis of OECD data established that this recent rocketing was unmatched in peer countries, where homelessness had often fallen or stalled, and concluded that the rise had now left Britain with 'by far the highest rate of [broadly defined] homelessness in the developed world'.[22]

Turning to food, hunger and missed meals, our first edition supplemented frank personal testimony – from the lonely stomach cramps of 'Yvonne' in Tottenham to Blackpool single mum Lowri's terror of keeping her daughter fed through school holidays (Chapter 2) – with operational data from the food banks and worrying surveys produced by charities including the Joseph Rowntree Foundation.

Only after we went to print did the first set of official poverty data containing information on food bank use emerge, the government's own statisticians having recognised they could no longer ignore such a major plank of the survival system of poorer people. The first official tally, covering 2021/22, suggested a considerable 2.1 million people were living in homes that had turned to food banks for help in the previous twelve months; the next, which emerged in March 2024, showed this figure had grown to 2.3 million by 2022/23.[23]

These are pretty big numbers, edging towards the scale of the notorious '3 million unemployed' that was seen as the defining blight on British society in the 1980s. Other indicators in the same official dataset point to hunger that is not merely big but rapidly escalating. In the numbing bureaucratic parlance, some 7.2 million Britons are in 'food insecure' households, of whom more than half (3.7 million) are in the most exposed 'very low' security category.[24] That damning second number had shot up by a full two thirds (68 per cent) over the past year alone, bearing out *Broke*'s branding of our unfolding decade as 'the Hungry Twenties'.

Not everything is getting worse: early 2024 saw falling energy prices translate into lower bills, with the price cap for a house with average use dropping by an annualised £238 between the first and second quarter of the year.[25] But the picture is clouded by the exhaustion of various emergency relief schemes, and special problems for those dependent on unusual fuel sources, including some of the Highlanders we meet in Chapter 3, or those with particularly high energy needs. All told as of 1 April 2024, National Energy Action calculates that 6 million are still living in fuel poverty on its definition, which is up by a third on late 2021.[26] Just a few months earlier, an NEA survey shed harsh new light on exactly how the struggle for warmth was playing out across an even wider swathe of society: it found that 10 million Britons had been closing curtains in the day or covering windows with newspaper, and as many as 19 million UK adults had gone to bed early to keep warm.[27]

Over the past fifteen months, interest rates first rose and then remained at a perilously high plateau. In light of this, it is a relief to report that the aggregate picture on debt is more mixed than disastrous, although Citizens Advice warns that this overview is concealing growing problems at the bottom end.[28] Certainly, the form of unregulated 'buy now, pay later' credit in which Phoebe and friends in Manchester (Chapter 4) are heavily immersed has become more salient: its overall scale is estimated to have grown as much as four-fold since 2020, and political anxiety about its unregulated nature is rapidly building.[29]

Some of the financial consequences of the new poverty for business and wider society which were not apparent by the time of our first edition have become starker since. In particular, both official numbers[30] and retail industry figures[31] are recording an astonishing surge in shoplifting, something industry insiders have linked to a black market for food that has burgeoned during the big squeeze.[32] The most recent figures from multiple sources point to store theft and violence against staff not merely creeping up but doubling – or on some counts much more than doubling – year on year.[33]

The latest developments in the labour market have been mixed. After unprecedented stagnation, real wages finally began to edge up after mid-2023.[34] Around the same time, at least one marker of job insecurity – zero-hour contracts – stopped growing and edged down.[35] But against this, it's become evident that the expanded number of people entirely locked out of work by long-term sickness was not some passing post-pandemic problem but a dark structural shift.[36]

Another big, underlying material shift is exceptionally strong immigration, which – post-Brexit – increasingly comes from further-flung parts of the world, from which newcomers arrive without the rights regarding work and welfare that used to be automatic for EU nationals.[37] While the overwhelming majority of destitute UK residents remain British-born (72 per cent), the 'Destitution in the UK' report documented 'an especially rapid increase in the size of the destitute migrant population since 2019'.[38] All this means more of the very particular problems of being stony broke that arise when permission to work and welfare are simultaneously denied, as for people like Zhenya and 'Mary' in Chapter 7.

But perhaps the darkest batch of indicators of all come in relation to health. After the long petering out of progress in life expectancy, highlighted in reportage from in and around Glasgow in Chapter 5, another year of UK-wide data saw life expectancy dip for both men and women, with the result that, as the official statistics sum things up, life expectancy at birth for 2020 to 2022 is back to the same level as 2010 to 2012 for women and slightly below that benchmark for men; a whole decade, in other words, in which things have, if anything, slipped backwards.[39]

This isn't normal. Barring war or revolutionary convulsions, lives have always got longer, not shorter, in industrial societies. Admittedly, the Covid pandemic colours the picture for part of the period covered by that most recent release, but as I highlight in the conclusion, there are inextricable links with poverty: women specifically in poorer postcodes were already dying earlier than they used to before the virus arrived, and then the heavily male deaths caused by Covid piled up disproportionately in the same poor neighbourhoods. Moreover, the perennial inequality in *healthy* life expectancy has grown. The most deprived areas of England, government demographers report, registered a significant decrease on this count in the second half of the 2010s. In the case of women from poor neighbourhoods, this was matched by another significant drop in the distinct quota of disability-free years of life.[40]

Looking ahead, analysts at the University of Liverpool and the Health Foundation have just unveiled predictions for an increase of some 700,000 in the number of working-age Britons living with a major long-term illness, overwhelmingly accounted for by developments in poorer communities, where already-heavy rates of chronic pain, diabetes and anxiety/depression are set to rocket faster than elsewhere.[41] Irrespective of any moral concern about poverty, purely in terms of employment and productivity, that sounds like a very expensive problem in the making.

This past year has also provided some arresting new evidence regarding the precise routes by which poverty can get underneath the skin. After our first edition highlighted the small but rapidly growing number of malnutrition diagnoses in English hospital patients, *The Guardian* used hospital data to chart the incidence of other markers of poor diet that can spell trouble ahead – deficiencies of iron, vitamin

B and other nutrients – and found they had also been rocketing.[42] Meanwhile, the plunging relative height of British five-year-olds came into the spotlight after new interrogation of academic data from 2019 and 2020, which found the UK tumbling down the international table, leaving young British children far shorter than many European counterparts.[43] One of the country's pre-eminent public health experts, Michael Marmot, pointed to a potential link with austerity.[44] New evidence also emerged on the mortal dangers of poor housing, reinforcing the anecdotal link that was apparent in tragedies like the death of toddler Awaab Ishak, which we described in the original edition. ITV News trawled official records of child deaths since 2019; it identified that problems with temporary accommodation were a contributing factor in the deaths of fifty-five children – forty-two of them babies.[45]

When I began commissioning the essays in *Broke*, I quickly realised that however strict the editorial intention of focusing on the different elements of deprivation – cold, squalor, hunger, disease and so on – in the end, the idea of neat divisions between them are a distortion. A marauding giant of Want runs across the entire terrain; and as 2023 gave way to 2024, the trouble wrought by that giant only became more pervasive. The question for our generation, as for William Beveridge and the generation that came through the war, is once again how to devise the policies and summon the political will needed to slay it.

GOT TO GET POLITICAL

We close the book with a list of charitable and other resources, both to provide pointers to any readers who may need support and to provide others moved to action with suggestions about where they can help. The impulse to make a difference runs deep, and a very personal dedication from just one person can sometimes entirely turn another life around: witness the story of how Glasgow charity worker Cally Archibald gave Kevin Buchanan a life worth living (Chapter 5). Moreover, through the right coordination with voluntary organisations and other people, especially those on the sharp end themselves, concerned individuals can do even more good.

In this dark hour for so many, we must look to get the most out of every available avenue of altruism. At the same time, however, we must remain clear-eyed about one blunt reality: the problem of impoverishment in 2020s Britain is systemic, and it will ultimately need systemic solutions. There is, in other words, no ducking the need for politics.

I spent the early months of 2024 working with former Prime Minister Gordon Brown (who has had no involvement with or sight of this update chapter) writing a pamphlet on the potential contribution of a new partnership against poverty, in which the state could offer itself up as a 'node' to connect the increasingly indispensable poverty relief efforts of charities with those companies best placed to support them – for example, by supplying the charities with essentials that the companies are producing at cost-price, or even donations of surplus stock for free distribution.[46]

I refer readers to this pamphlet for some really inspiring stories of the difference that determined cross-sectoral working can make. And, indeed, also to the detail of our argument that, in a world of rapidly rising expectations of business in regards to corporate social responsibility, the pressure on executives to pinpoint the particular positive contributions they can most effectively make is bound to grow. Redirecting good food that would otherwise be left to rot or essential durables that would otherwise pile up in landfill to meet desperate social needs makes obvious sense. The pamphlet also highlights links that anti-poverty initiatives are already occasionally making with a whole range of businesses, including the odd enlightened property developer and utility company, as well as manufacturers and chain hotels that can cheaply supply the toiletries and furnishings so many people can't currently afford. We highlight, too, the huge potential to forge many more such links if only the government would create a modest and time-limited partnership fund. And we suggest that this could be funded by reforming the rules on the reserves that the commercial banks hold at the publicly owned Bank of England, which could yield savings for the state on interest payments – payments that have come to operate as an unintended subsidy for the banks.

Putting some energy behind these sorts of initiatives could ensure food banks and other charities have the resources they need to provide more of the emergency relief that is, as things stand, the last line of defence against destitution. But as with strong pain relief in medicine, one must never mistake emergency treatments, which over time will create their own serious problems, for a sustainable cure. Recognising the inherent uncertainty of relying on a charitable impulse to supply life's essentials, as well as the warping effects of free grocery distribution on the dignity of the recipients, Britain's food banks, including the largest network, the Trussell Trust, are now united in their ambition to put themselves out of existence.[47] They demand, rightly, that we look beyond the inescapable task of managing symptoms and start to grapple with root causes.

Perhaps it's because I find myself writing in the immediate run-up to a general election that I feel impelled to suggest litmus tests to establish which politicians are serious about this challenge. If we can identify the right tests, however, they should continue to be instructive way beyond polling day for assessing how much, or how little, the incoming government is doing to turn the corner on poverty over the course of the next parliamentary term. I group the tests under three broad headings: economic regulation, the welfare state and, more nebulously but just as importantly, civilising the conversation about poverty. For reasons of space, amid what feels like an unusually binary election year, I will restrict myself to the government and the main party of opposition, though it must of course be acknowledged that other parties are available.

SECURING PROGRESS

Of the various problems exposed by *Broke*, those where our politics currently edges closest to solutions concern the insecurity flowing from mis-regulated or under-regulated markets. The easily uprooted tenancies of people like Tracy Benson (Chapter 1), the perennially unreliable shifts of gig workers such as Ian Morrison (Chapter 8) and the impossible energy bills of the likes of Lindsay in Orkney (Chapter 3) are things the national conversation is, at least, beginning to grapple with.

On the homes front, both front benches are, in principle, agreed that no-fault evictions need to go in England, although shameful drift on the part of successive recent governments makes it impossible to give the Conservative Party much credit here. By the time the election was called, five years and three Prime Ministers had passed since Theresa May first acknowledged reform was needed. Campaigners have recently identified a new way to tally the consequences of that long stasis: the Renters' Reform Coalition reports that 84,650 households have contacted their council asking for support to avoid homelessness after receiving a Section 21 eviction notice since it was accepted that these no-fault notices should be abolished.[48]

The outgoing Communities Secretary Michael Gove has let it be known that he had fought hard to keep the reform alive, and yet in spring 2024 a leaked letter from one of his deputies, Jacob Young, revealed that the government would be amending its own legislation to actually impose a new lock on renters to stop them leaving tenancies early, and make the abolition of no-fault evictions conditional on an official assessment establishing that the creaking court system is ready to deal with it.[49] Then, finally, the Renters Reform Bill was simply shelved in the parliamentary 'wash-up' when the general election was called.[50] On the government side of the House, at least, it seems that the 'landlord interest' of MPs directly profiting from the rental system has the sort of distortionary grip on parliamentary outcomes in the 2020s that, say, the 'East India interest' might have had in the 1820s.

The opposition attaches much more urgency and fewer caveats to abolishing no-fault evictions and more generally seems keen to engage with the housing crisis, including by using planning reform to boost supply, and thereby curbing costs. As the 2019 parliament ground on, however, Labour, too, became notably more cautious on broader questions of renters' rights. The landlord lobby boasted about a big win when the party quietly dropped its plans for rent controls in 2023.[51] While Keir Starmer is happy to nail himself to quantitative targets for overall housebuilding, and still stresses 'affordability', at the time of writing, Labour's previous specific promises on creating particular numbers of the council and social homes that can most straightforwardly guarantee realistic rents seemed to be yielding to vaguer ambitions.[52]

When it comes to ensuring genuinely affordable new

housing, a great deal now turns on reforming the way councils acquire land for themselves or others to develop. It is heartening to find at least a measure of cross-party interest here, with Gove having already pursued some reforms to extend the scope for local authorities to compulsorily purchase land,[53] and Labour floating wider reforms to reduce the valuations paid to landlords.[54]

Labour has stuck its neck out a bit on debt, too, demanding new protection for customers,[55] which is all of a piece with shadow Chancellor Rachel Reeves's wider 'securonomics' pitch.[56] Although that phrase is very much hers, it encapsulates a slowly growing cross-party understanding, which has falteringly developed since many marketopian delusions were dispelled in the credit crunch.

The evolution of the approach to energy price regulation is a telling case study. When the then opposition leader Ed Miliband first floated the idea of price caps, they were denounced by David Cameron as a product of 'a Marxist universe'. Later, however, a very similar scheme was embraced by Theresa May,[57] before being supplemented with a vast energy price subsidy by – of all people – Liz Truss.

There is a similar story with the labour market and low pay. In 2016, George Osborne began the recent ramping up of the minimum wage, even though it had been introduced in the teeth of Conservative opposition almost two decades earlier. That process has continued into April 2024, with a rise of 9.8 per cent for most earners and more than 20 per cent for the very youngest.[58] Cross-party concern about the insecurity, as opposed to insufficiency, of earnings in the gig economy age also dates back to at least the May premiership and the Taylor review.[59] The Supreme Court ruling that granted sick pay and maternity rights to Uber drivers suggested that the judges, too, accepted the need for limits on the power of businesses to wriggle free of their obligations to the workers they rely on.[60] A change of government looks likely to further advance these shifts. Even if endless media briefings and counter-briefings about slowing the pace of the prospective employment law reforms make it hard to know exactly what new rights Labour will entrench when,[61] there is enough detail in its New Deal for Working People to suggest that many pay packets could soon be better protected from the vicissitudes of unreliable shifts.[62]

This could soon make a real difference to the hardships of people like Ian Morrison in London and Bora Radu in Swindon that are described in Chapter 8. But it's important to temper expectations about the effects on the broader poverty crisis. After all, the various steps towards 'securonomics' already taken in recent years – such as that higher minimum wage, the energy price cap, those selective employment rights for some gig workers and even the abolition of no-fault evictions in Scotland described in Chapter 1 – haven't yet achieved a society that feels any more secure overall, nor even kept destitution at bay. The principal reason why not is that these progressive regulatory changes have arrived in tandem with deep benefit cuts.

BENEFITS AND THE DOUBT

Any government truly serious about security against destitution must reach for the surest (and most obvious) foundation stone for building it on – decent social security. The privations revealed in *Broke* have many causes, including malfunctioning markets for housing, labour and energy. But the single issue that runs through more of our chapters than any other is the systematic shredding of our safety net through the long austerity years. Sadly, this is the area where deep doubts set in about the resolve of our politicians to act.

Now, there is of course a serious – and potentially transformative – agenda about reducing the need for social security over the decades ahead, by ensuring more people enjoy the good health, the right training and the necessary support first to start earning something and then to get on in a career. But many of the steps involved here – such as changing diets to check the onset of diabetes in poorer communities, or overhauling tertiary education so that the rising generation enter the workplace with better skills – would take a long while to come to fruition at any time and a very long while to do so at a moment when virtually all our public services are creaking. When it comes to our concern in this book – fixing the current poverty crisis – much more immediate relief is required.

The list of austerity cuts, restrictions and freezes on social security is so long that it can be hard to distil in a comprehensible way. It never seems to stop. Since our first edition, for example, the government has announced, among other things, new restrictions on the so-called Work Capability Assessment.[63] Even more recently, it has reported that these will have the effect of exposing 457,000 people with mobility problems and particular health risks to either new harsher strings attached to their benefits or reduced rates of payments, or even both, all in the expectation that a tiny fraction of them – around 15,000 – will be jolted to move into work as a result.[64] And even since I started writing this update, Rishi Sunak has announced a consultation on an 'overhaul' of Personal Independence Payments – a financial lifeline for both 'Sandra' and Becca in Chapter 6 – which aims to curb costs, with strong hints that claimants with anxiety and depression could be denied similar help in future.[65]

So it is hard to keep up. But Gordon Brown has usefully highlighted four main 'holes' torn into the traditional protections that have recently left so many falling through the old net and onto the rocks below: stiff deductions from benefits which leave claimants heavily out of pocket; the capping of benefits without regard for costs, such as housing; particularly punitive reductions in support for children; and reduced basic benefit rates.[66]

I might identify a fifth driver of the destitution on our streets: the brutal treatment of asylum seekers and many other migrants documented in Chapter 7. But there is an obvious fix for most of the people we meet there that wouldn't incur any extra social expenditure: namely, allowing more people to work while their paperwork is processed. So let's put that to one side and consider each of Brown's four headings.

The first two are doing such abject damage that even in pre-election, tax-cutting season, the Conservative Chancellor Jeremy Hunt was recently moved to offer a couple of easements: a somewhat longer repayment period for those requiring Universal Credit budgeting loans; and a temporary restoration of the old link between so-called local housing allowances and the actual cost of low-end private rentals.[67] This is better than nothing, but neither move is remotely adequate. Under existing spending plans, the dangerous decoupling of benefits from basic rents will soon set in again. We need to restore a systematic link. Slower repayments, meanwhile, may help some with relatively modest debts to the Department for Work and Pensions, but the maximum rate of repayments out of workless claimants' very low incomes remains an eye-watering 25 per cent. That figure needs to be reduced and – more fundamentally – Universal Credit needs to be reformed so that new claimants don't immediately sink into debt during the ludicrously long wait through the initial processing period.

Amid the slings and arrows of the election build-up, the Labour opposition, which understands most of these problems full well, has mostly been quiet about them, fearing any firm commitment to action will be translated in the time-honoured fashion into a 'tax bombshell'. Sometimes it has talked about a comprehensive review of Universal Credit, but little was heard about even that suggestion in the first half of 2024.

Hopes that Labour was serious about poverty took a huge hit in July 2023, when Keir Starmer pointedly told the BBC that 'we're not changing' the government's two-child welfare limit. This is the defining austerity policy as regards support for children, and the most fundamental of all the recent attacks on old ideals of social security.[68] In an unprecedented manner, this 'reform' wilfully breaks a link embodied in social policies since the Elizabethan poor laws: namely, the connection between the support a family receives and the number of mouths it has to feed. It declines to regard children born with more than one sibling as people with their own rights and needs, and reimagines them instead as bad consumer choices made by their parents.[69] Even if thought of as a populist dash of collective punishment for 'workshy' families, the policy is misdirected: the majority of families affected are earning something.[70]

Biting on children born after April 2017, the two-child limit will cast ever more children into penury as the next decade goes by and the effect is felt ever further up the age range. It is, therefore, not only a very damaging policy but a policy that is getting more damaging. Already, a stark connection to the warning flags for hunger is evident: the government's own data records that homes with three or more children are twice as likely to have turned to a food bank over the past year, compared to those with two children.[71] Looking at more recent food-bank use, the Resolution Foundation reported an even bigger differential, as well as a more than doubling of the risks of 'food insecurity' for larger families.[72]

In sum, it is hard to imagine any serious version of social progress where this policy is not changed. Inevitably, there are questions about a lack of commitment from Starmer, who proactively issued a 'when resources allow' pledge for very substantially raising defence spending[73] but brushed off Mishal Husain's sharp BBC questions about abolishing the two-child cap by saying, 'In an ideal world, of course, but we haven't got the resources.'[74] Campaigners I speak to are left hoping that the refusal is part of some cunning (if less than democratic) plan for stakeholder management, whereby the resources to axe the two-child limit are suddenly found in office, giving supporters reason to keep the faith through the first couple of thorny years of a Labour government. But it hardly seems reasonable to ask families on the edge and losing hope right now to wait for such a political scheme to play out, even if it exists.

While Westminster nods through hugely expensive cuts to National Insurance rates worth most to people on decent pay – the hole blown in the public finances by these cuts since our first edition will soon tot up to £20 billion a year – the £3 billion or so needed to end the two-child limit remains taboo.[75]

Compounding these warped priorities are arbitrary accounting conventions, which in some specific settings build deepening impoverishment into the financial 'baseline'. Most of the social security system is assumed to adjust automatically with inflation, but a few of its parameters are fixed in cash terms, including a couple which leave disadvantaged children particularly exposed whenever prices rise. One is the cap on a family's total benefits, imposed by George Osborne for the sake of an easy headline in 2013. Over the years since, it's rarely budged: once being cut in cash terms (in 2016) and only once adjusted for inflation (in 2023), leaving its real value plummeting and the number of affected families increasing by an order of magnitude.[76] To insist there is an affordability issue with adjusting this cap for prices automatically is to argue that the *only* way of balancing the books is to make Britain's poor continually poorer. That is absurd.

Even more so is another fixed cash threshold that directly and continually reduces the number of poor children we can collectively 'afford' to keep fed. Namely, the mere £7,400 limit on parental net earnings, after which free school lunches are snatched away from pupils. The value of that fixed figure has tanked since it was entrenched in 2018. Way back in 2013, the government-commissioned School Food Plan produced devastating data showing that while 70 per cent of eligible children ate their free school meals, for youngsters in the poorest postcodes who weren't eligible for free lunches, the figure eating school meals dropped to just 20 per cent.[77] One very positive commitment from Labour at the moment is to answer the need for children to start the day well fed by supporting breakfast clubs across England's primary schools.[78] But the dwindling real value of the earnings threshold for school lunches is still going to lead to more hungry pupils in the afternoon.

Campaigners often argue that 'the question is not whether we can afford to do X; the question is whether we can afford *not* to do X'. And the typical response from officials is a world-weary sigh: everyone thinks their pet project is important, and if the government yielded to all of them, it would soon be deep in the red. There's something in that, but when it comes to making sure that the next generation are decently fed, then for reasons of health, learning and the work-readiness of the next cohort of workers, skimping must surely rank as a false economy.

And without denying the parlous immediate state of the public finances, there should also be room – over time – for a more expansive attitude towards steadily raising basic benefit rates. Consider the basic allowance available to those made unemployed. Having drifted ever-further behind wages since the 1970s, the proportion of average earnings covered has long slid beneath the 'replacement rate' offered elsewhere in Europe and even the United States.[79] And after the past decade, during which supposedly automatic inflation adjustment has been suspended more often than not, the basic replacement rate has now fallen to a lower share of average wages than at any time since the creation of the modern welfare state eighty years ago.[80] We cannot allow the poor to become continually poorer, and – fortunately – we can afford to get on to a different track.

In 2023, I worked with the Resolution Foundation on its flagship Economy 2030 Inquiry. The final report emphasised that, factoring in the demographics of our ageing society and assuming the continuation of existing uprating practices, the share of GDP devoted to working-age benefits is actually on track to decline from around 4.6 per cent in 2026 to roughly 4.1 per cent by 2031, with a further decline to below 3.3 per cent by a decade later.[81] In principle, this easement of approaching 0.1 per cent of GDP every year should release meaningful resources for repairing social security before the 2020s are through. Indeed, the weight of these benefits within the economy would fall *even if* they were linked to earnings, so that the workless were not condemned to fall ever-further behind. Of course, the state would be giving up some savings by not continually squeezing these people tighter. But a large offsetting gain for the Exchequer could be found if the costly pensions 'triple lock' were replaced by a more conventional, and perfectly robust, earnings link. A government that was prepared to tax some portion of the riches of those who have done best in recent times could, of course, act even sooner.

WORDS AS WELL AS DEEDS

These are all perfectly practical choices open to any politicians who are serious about poverty, although the lack of airtime most of them devote to the subject suggests little confidence, or even interest, in grappling with the emergency.

That dangerous silence underlines the need to reframe the whole discussion, creating a mood in which serious action first becomes thinkable and then inevitable.

As it is, the past year has seen the discourse hemmed in between reactionary tropes in the press (with slurs against the growing numbers of long-term sick being particularly fashionable just now) and either outright indulgence or timidity in challenging those tropes from politicians.[82] The story of 'Mike' and 'Sandra' in Chapter 6, unwilling to be interviewed under their real names because of having once been hounded as benefit scroungers by the local paper during an earlier bout of moral panic, is a reminder of the human toll that the ugly caricatures take.

But it's not just about feelings. The atmosphere of suspicion whipped up against claimants when politicians talk about 'crackdowns' leads to warped practices by officials, as seen in the growing scandal about the DWP's merciless pursuit of carers for disabled people. Vivienne Groom, sole carer for her late nonagenarian mother, was one. After unwittingly stumbling over the bureaucratic cliff edge of 'allowable earnings' that is attached to the (uniquely stingy) Carer's Allowance by somewhat increasing the hours she worked at the local Co-op, she was served with a notice to repay many years of the money in full. She was ultimately hounded using the Proceeds of Crime Act, designed for use against mobsters.[83] The Guardian's exposure of her case brought other similar stories to light, and before long politicians from the hardline former Tory leader Iain Duncan Smith to Keir Starmer were agreed that something had gone badly wrong.[84]

In such cases, the political overlords create an environment in which officials act in ways that everyone – politicians included – can eventually see is indefensible. In others, politicians lead themselves into perversity with their own rhetoric. Ahead of his November 2023 Autumn Statement, Jeremy Hunt, who as we have seen has been prepared to soften some of the rough edges of poverty elsewhere, nonetheless felt a need to trail 'tougher sanctions' on supposed layabouts.[85] When he set out the detail in his speech, it transpired that what this meant was that Britain's vanishingly small number of long-term unemployed people would have their benefits entirely cut off if they declined unpaid work placements.[86] Unfortunately, the government's own figures showed that the bureaucracy involved in this show of toughness on behalf of 'hard-working taxpayers' would actually cost the Exchequer money.[87]

What's needed instead is, as much as anything, a new generosity of spirit. One of the most positive recent suggestions from a frontbench politician has come from Labour's Alison McGovern when she proposed we call time on the DWP's 'any job' culture, whereby claimants are very rapidly frog-marched into any available post, on pain of losing their benefits, without any regard for their skills or experience or even the potential public cost of the means-tested support they may need to top up low wages.[88]

The background to this proposal was the government cutting to just four weeks the time unemployed people could search for jobs in their own line of work, rather than taking any available position. The statutory Social Security Advisory Committee had rung the alarm bells about both the lack of any evidence for the original change having a positive impact and the lack of regard shown for potential negative effects, such as 'claimants potentially having career paths hindered'.[89] If the change had turned out to save any money, it would have been the duty of the bean-counters at the Office for Budget Responsibility to record that; they never did so.[90] Nonetheless, DWP Secretary Mel Stride was able to call on loyal stenographers at *The Sun* to report as fact that McGovern's assumed reversal of the rule change would cost taxpayers a chunky £450 million a year.[91]

It seems plain that, absent a reset in 2024, the way Britain discusses social security will not change. And that really matters. Because, ultimately, it isn't so much financial arithmetic as the stories we tell ourselves about poverty – and our ability to understand that it is something that we all need protection against – that determines whether we fall for the lie that the old ideals of decency can no longer be afforded. If, on the other hand, this does prove to be a year in which Britain changes direction, it's still unclear whether or not there will be a serious effort to reset the discourse from the top. So far, as I've tried to describe here, the messages have been mixed. A great deal is still going to be contested, even under a new regime. So whatever outcome the election produces, campaigners concerned to fix all that is broke in Britain are going to have work on their hands.

FOREWORD

I've known the reality of being broke ever since I first walked across my primary school classroom and sweatily collected my green free school dinner token, tucking it covertly up the sleeve of my secondhand jumper. Experiencing a new self-consciousness, and a sick, itchy feeling that I would come to know was shame, I was watched by other girls in school uniform with blonde pigtails who, the teacher announced, 'PAID'. My soon-to-be no-longer pals had, until that moment, thought that I was 'normal' and not poor.

There is a spectrum, of course, a vast multitude, a sweeping wide register of exactly what it means to be broke. One person's bones of their arse is another's doing pretty good actually. My '80s single-parent family, for various 'time and place', intergenerational and individual reasons, was at one of the most extreme ends of poverty.

I didn't immediately realise that we were broke, and indeed broken, in a different sort of way from the many other poor local families when we arrived in a deprived area of North

Shields in Teesside. I was eight years old and had tumbled off a National Express from Lanarkshire smelling of my own stale, travel-sick vomit, hoisting my sturdy toddler sister on my hip while my five-foot-nothing mum dragged two laundry bags stuffed with all our worldly belongings behind her. We had nowhere to go that night. Mum was thrilled when a 'B&B' that accepted 'DSS' (the old Department of Social Security) had a 'family room' for us. But 'Bed & Breakfast' was a euphemism for a halfway house for the newly homeless, usually men freshly out of prison remand or mental health facilities.

Needless to say, there was no breakfast. The beds, in our room at the very top of the old house, were iron bunk beds, icy to the touch. The space was deemed suitable for families because it had 'cooking facilities' behind a thin plaster partition: a plug-in frying pan, tabletop freezer, kettle, aluminium sink. Showers were available communally – if you had a 20p piece for the meter. We didn't. 'We aren't made of money, Kerry,' said Mum as she guarded the bathroom door and I ran through the steam across wet tiles to catch the last of someone's credit. Soon my meandering stepdad joined us, a giant in a doll's house, constantly bumping himself on the sloped ceilings and the additional single bed somehow crammed into the room. We lived on drop pancakes and frozen sausages. I learned to like mustard that year.

I might not have known this was a bad way to live – though I often had a sore stomach for no reason at all, it seemed – if the kids at school hadn't tried to follow me home to see if I lived in a 'homeless shelter'. I walked up the path of a fancy-looking house (in reality, just a regular pebble-dashed semi), my face burning, their laughter hitting my back, lingered at the white PVC door and then sneaked into the back garden to wait until they had given up. The full understanding of exactly where we landed on the spectrum, the second part of the one-two punch of realisation, came soon after when the housing association man in his nice suit came to see if we qualified for rehoming. He had a gentle Northumbrian accent and a clipboard and, God love him, he just could not keep *it* off his face. '*It*' being profound pity. I don't blame him. Anyway, he found us a home, a rural red-brick flat in a village with ponies roaming by the swing set who'd snuffle a Polo mint from your sticky palm if you were prepared to sacrifice one.

People can say that not all problems are related to money, but I would counter that in my own experience, social problems, mental and physical poor health and addiction very often stem from the sheer imbalance caused by trying to do too much, or even the bare minimum, without the resources. The 'Help' section at the end of my memoir, *Lowborn*, reads like a chunky, sad chapbook given out by the Citizens Advice Bureau: domestic abuse and poverty charities; debt, addiction and mental health advice; support for homelessness and sexual violence. It's a shopping list nobody wants to write, a catalogue of problems that are made so much worse, so much more common and so much more inescapable by being skint.

My family – my mum, my sister and I – continued to move up and down the country constantly looking for a never-to-be-found fresh start. From Aberdeen, where fish houses were on their way out and oil was sloshing its way in but somehow never to the poorest enclaves, down to the Norfolk seaside town of Great Yarmouth, where the pink lights and arcade music were fading on British tourism, to a village in Durham already hollowed out by the closing of the mines.

Of course, I grew up in the '80s and '90s and you would be right to think, 'Well, different times. That was Thatcher, riots, "loadsamoney" and a heroin epidemic.' In the years that followed, there was lip service to eradicating poverty, even a few wobbly steps in the right direction, but since then, the pendulum has swung again, full force, smashing any progress even further back.

So while I wish I could agree that the years of my child-hood were the 'bad old days', my belief is that if I was growing up now in the same conditions – with a single parent with mental health problems, the latest body in a long family line of extreme poverty, with a gamut of issues directly connected to that hardship – my experience would be far worse.

A punitive welfare system designed not to elevate but to trip up, push over, gag and bind has forced many who might have succeeded back into poverty. An out-of-control housing market compels those deemed unable to afford mortgages to pay double this amount in private rent while paying some-one else's mortgage (can someone make that make sense for me?). Added to the continuing erosion of social housing and income-related inequality in education, I think there is today instability that is far greater than in my childhood and teens.

The reasons for this are many and are explored with nuance, skill and craft in this book by journalists who've been working on the front line of austerity for decades now. Some have direct experience of hardship or the system turning a cold shoulder, but all are equally committed to closely listening to and faithfully reporting the voices of those at the hard end of an unfolding crisis. The chapters in this collection highlight both the perilous cliff edge of problems that poor people in the UK are teetering on and, equally vital, the absolute importance of grassroots organisations, local communities, unions and solidarity in tackling these issues. As with *Lowborn*, a list of charities and other support organisations is included at the end for those seeking help and those who feel able to contribute.

I believe this book represents hope. In the pages that follow, the writers and their subjects together redress the lazy, seemingly inevitable, narrative peddled out again and again: that to be poor is an individual failing due to fecklessness, uselessness or stupidity rather than collective political, national and historical flaws. This book challenges the insidiously negative stories about those who are broke, and about how they end up and stay broke, stories that have been used to justify cuts to crucial social benefits and services, and stories which – most damagingly of all – persuade a majority that it is acceptable to look the other way while millions of our fellow citizens, and untold children, go hungry.

This book can be used as a tool, as a point of connection, as a challenge. Those who know what it is like to be truly broke will see themselves reflected in these pages, and I hope they will feel heard. Just as important, those readers who have until now had little understanding of what it is like to struggle might read this and see that they have a fundamental part to play in fixing this crisis, too – that they should not look away but instead make themselves part of the movement to change things for the better for future generations.

Kerry Hudson
February 2023

FACE TO FACE WITH BRITAIN'S NEW PENURY

TOM CLARK

I was mulling pulling together a volume of reportage on Britain's unfolding poverty crisis in spring 2022 when 77-year-old Elsie unwittingly convinced me that it really had to be done.

We were a dozen years into austerity, and the cost of living was starting to soar. Various statistical warning lights were flashing to suggest a return to types of deprivation that we once fondly imagined we had consigned to the history books. NHS Digital numbers were recording that diagnoses of malnutrition in hospital patients had more than doubled since 2010.[1] The official count of rough sleepers had also doubled during the decade before lockdown,[2] while dependence on food banks had swelled by an order of magnitude.[3] All this was despite long years of strong jobs growth, but now – post-pandemic – the economic forecasts from the likes of the Bank of England were altogether dicier, pointing to another big squeeze on incomes, which would surely make everything worse.

And yet as the swallows flew in that spring, Downing Street lockdown parties were looming larger than anything else in the UK news. So the question remained: how to wake the country up to the rapidly worsening hardship?

This is where Elsie came in, revealing the power of individual testimony in the conversation. The widow asked ITV's *Good Morning Britain* to solicit any advice that the Prime Minister might have about dealing with her plight. It was duly explained to Boris Johnson that Elsie only ate one meal a day, and passed her hours going round and round on the local bus, so as to avoid having to turn on the heating at home. Squirming, the PM commented that it was only thanks to government decisions that she enjoyed a freedom pass for bus travel – and jaws dropped nationwide.[4]

Six months later, an inquest verdict on a single lost life abruptly forced Britain's politicians and journalists to face up to a slow-building problem which it's fair to say is usually an awfully long way from the top of the agenda in SW1. Namely, untreated mould in social homes. An experienced social affairs reporter once told me that her first news editor had urged her to investigate something other than rampant damp in local flats on the basis that mould 'doesn't photograph'. True enough, but the smiley and gorgeous toddler Awaab Ishak certainly did. And so when senior coroner Joanne Kearsley ruled that the respiratory crisis that killed the two-year-old from Rochdale was 'due to prolonged exposure to mould' and action 'not taken' to fix it, parliamentarians, hardened hacks on newspaper desks and voters a long way away from run-down estates at least briefly found themselves worrying about all those communities where under-investment is breeding squalor.[5]

We should not be surprised that an individual trauma cuts through in a way that no amount of frightening numbers ever could. After all, as Stalin is supposed to have said, where the death of one man is a tragedy, the death of a million is a sta-tistic. Over two centuries of the methodical collection of data on social conditions, it has never been any official number but rather the individual human stories – from the fictionalised accounts of Dickens to the faithful factual reporting of Orwell and Priestley – that have seared the reality of hard times into the public imagination.

This is not just a British but a universal human phenom-enon. What lodges in the American mind is not the dread-ful data on Depression era unemployment or statistics on 21st-century working poverty but rather the travails of John Steinbeck's Tom Joad in *The Grapes of Wrath* or the exploita-tion revealed undercover by Barbara Ehrenreich in *Nickel and*

Dimed.[6] Nor is this a truth that applies only in connection with deprivation. Much more generally, it takes confrontation with the fate of an individual human being to force a reckoning with an emergency. Back in 2015, for example, the terrible photograph of two-year-old Syrian boy Alan Kurdi, washed up on a Turkish beach, lifeless and face down in his shorts and red T-shirt, jolted the continent of Europe into finally understanding the scale of its migration crisis.[7] All manner of stories, poems and films have brought home the reality of war through the prism of a single family or individual.

But there is, perhaps, a particular failure to find similar stories that can make vivid the frightening realities of contemporary want. What is sneeringly dismissed by some as 'the poverty industry' – the campaigners and researchers concerned with exposing deprivation – too often relies on dry and impersonal facts at the expense of personal testimony. If the grim data is leavened at all, it might be with a few quotes from focus groups or so-called qualitative research studies, hardly sufficient to humanise the hard facts about life at the bottom of the heap.

What this book does instead, with the help of Joseph Rowntree Foundation resources, is send a cast of exceptionally skilled reporters and gifted storytellers deep into our most distressed communities, to seek out those on the roughest edges of life, and commit serious listening time to the voices society so often ignores. Bespoke photography from Joel Goodman, who has toured the country to produce portraits of the people telling their stories, allows readers to look many of the characters in the eye.

The team of writers have all the National Press Award commendations, Orwell Prize nominations and Royal Society of Literature endorsements you could hope for. But what's just as important is that, as you will read, from the housing list to the benefit office, some also have first-hand experience of the issues raised. That matters, because if there is one thing that is missing from the political discussion that has led us towards today's privations, it is empathy. The politicians whose austerity cutbacks have corroded the foundational promises of social security – that basic rent would always be covered, that payments would keep up with living costs, that account would be taken of the number of mouths a family must feed – justified their decisions through devious wordplay that set 'workers' against 'shirkers' or 'strivers' against 'skivers'.[8]

For a while, this worked well enough politically, but the eventual result of shredding the safety net was, inevitably, growing numbers falling through it and into destitution. That is now on a scale that can be tallied at the doors of crisis services, and at a speed that is becoming impossible to miss.[9]

SOMETHING OLD

There is no point in trying to summarise the chapters that follow. each is a powerful piece of writing that stands on its own and deserves to be read in full. But it is just worth highlighting a few common threads that emerge across them, suggestive of certain specific features of poverty as it is experienced in Britain today.

At one level, the new poverty that emerges is very much like the old. The street urchins in Dickens's London and the impoverished mill workers in Engels's Manchester would be well familiar with the sense described in 2022 by 'Javed', an undocumented migrant with good reason to fear a return to Pakistan would mean persecution, in relation to his homeless life in Leeds: 'You feel dirty, you think everything around you is dirty.' The brute effects of material privation – the bite of the cold, the gnawing of hunger, the terror of ending up without a roof over your head, all of which pulse through these pages – have not changed. What has is the regularity with which they are being felt.

A generation ago discussions about poverty in Britain would often lapse into debates about whether it is best captured by relative measures, which gauged how far poorer people were falling behind the more prosperous, or instead by absolute privations, where progress always used to be easier to show. That argument is heard less often today. The question of measurement seems beside the point when outright destitution is palpably rising.

Efforts to silo off different aspects of the poverty problem are also increasingly hard to sustain. I tasked each of our writers with examining a distinct issue – cold, hunger, shelter, ill health and so on – but honest reporters, however disciplined, could not help but notice the way all the other problems intruded onto their patch.

Take hunger, the topic for Samira Shackle, who introduces us to London teacher Emma, whose pupils sometimes let slip they have eaten nothing all day. And yet 'I only eat one meal a day' is a refrain that also echoes through several other chapters: we hear it from 'Mary' in Leeds (in Daniel Trilling's piece on the plight of migrants); from 'Mike' in High Wycombe (in Frances Ryan's chapter on disabled people); and, again in Dani Garavelli's dispatch from the Glasgow neighbourhoods where people die earlier than anywhere else in Britain, in which David in Drumchapel adds the twist that at least once a week this one daily meal 'will be cereal'. Likewise debt, the dedicated subject of Jennifer Williams in Chapter 4, crops up in most of the others, including in those on disability and migration, as well as in Jem Bartholomew's exposé on the realities of toiling in the gig economy.

Shame and exclusion are other decidedly familiar features of Britain's new penury. A hundred and fifty years after George Eliot likened poverty to leprosy in *Middlemarch*, on the basis that 'it divides us from what we most care for',[10] we hear how hungry 'Yvonne' in Tottenham refuses to let her four adult children know that she is struggling, how eviction from her home in the Isle of Lewis left Jo feeling 'like I've failed as a

mother' and how destitute Javed in Leeds cut short his stays
on friends' sofas out of the great fear of becoming unwelcome.

We read, too, about the steady destruction of self-worth
which eventually led Javed to fling himself into the River
Aire in an attempt to end it all. It was an extreme act, but
the thought processes that drove him to it are shared with
many of the hard-pressed people we meet: Becca in Glasgow
confides that 'it crossed my mind that there was little reason
to want to be here'; church-going but penniless Mary in Leeds
concedes that, given the way she has to live, 'sometimes I feel
like I should have died'. And as Cal Flyn chronicles the battle
against the cold that so many face in Scotland's Highlands
and Islands, she introduces us to Dieter, whose recent trials
amid the chill winds of Lewis have sometimes left him feeling 'suicidal'. Further south in Scotland we meet Lorna, who
works in the GP practice in Drumchapel, and affirms how
often such thoughts turn into deeds in her part of the world:
overdoses and suicides are materially contributing to the gro-
tesquely truncated average local lifespans.

SOMETHING NEW

The real shock of the privations and shame that we highlight
is not that they are new phenomena but rather that they have
returned to haunt a 21st-century society that is incomparably

richer than the cruel early industrial society with which they are more often associated. There are, however, a few truly novel features to poverty as it is found in the Britain of 2023. The first is an unsettling sense that the boundary between the supplicants of life and their supporters is beginning to get blurry, as the big squeeze of the moment pushes privation up the social scale. Thus it is, for example, that we hear how food bank volunteer 'Sophie' in Manchester one day found herself with no choice but to become a food bank client. Just up the road in Salford, we find Phoebe energetically running a support group on financial problems while at the same time battling with her own very serious problems of debt from buy-now-pay-later deals.

Another big twist in our times concerns age. In the past, from the Elizabethan poor laws through the Victorian poorhouse and on to the ground-breaking studies of Charles Booth and Seebohm Rowntree, poverty was in hugely disproportionate measure a problem of old age.[11] The truth is closer to the opposite today.

There are still ways in which people are especially exposed as they age, particularly when it comes to keeping warm: the sorts of indignities faced by Elsie, highlighted at the start of the chapter, remain a stain on society. But at least until very recently, such hardships were becoming steadily rarer among the current cohort of retirees, thanks to the spread of occupational pensions during the years of their working lives, and

– even more crucially – the maintenance of a decent social safety net for them. It is now worth fully three times more than the woeful £61 a week the young unemployed are expected to scrape by on.[12] These disparities map straight across to poverty: pick an older person at random nowadays and they are actually somewhat *less* likely to be below the breadline than a person picked at chance from across the population as a whole.[13] The same age imbalance applies with the more extreme deprivation which is most likely to tip over into destitution: it is working-age adults and children who are now the hardest hit.[14]

Past reformers like Charles Booth might be thrilled at the way the conditions of the elderly have been ameliorated since the 1900s, but they would be equally appalled by the flipside – and just how far we have recently allowed other groups to sink. Child poverty, which had soared in the 1980s before being tamed around the turn of the century after Tony Blair and Gordon Brown had vowed to eradicate it, was again racing back to past peaks in the years before the pandemic.[15] What those numbers mean is made vivid by the testimony of Blackpool single mother Lowri, concerning her battle to scrimp together the fuel to get her thirteen-year-old daughter to school and the food to get her through the summer holiday.

Disabled people have always faced special struggles, but thanks to cross-party reforms from the 1970s, destitution was rarely an automatic fate. Until recently. Now, thanks to a battery of restrictions, retrenchment and freezes, a colleague and I recently found that single disabled people were roughly four times more likely than the non-disabled to be falling behind with their bills, to face a six-fold excess risk of growing cold and a nine-fold increase in the chance of going hungry.[16]

If numbers like that don't stir you to rage, what assuredly will is the testimony of 'Sandra', whom we will meet in High Wycombe, an extreme asthmatic whose bones have been hollowed out by the heavy steroids she needs to keep air moving through her lungs. Benefit cuts forced her to move into unsuitable lodgings for three years where she had to sleep on the floor. That experience culminated in an asthma attack which briefly made her heart stop, necessitating a spell in intensive care. But having recovered and got the housing situation sorted, she now finds rising energy prices force her to switch off the air conditioning that soothes her breathing on hot summer days. Any thought that hers might be an exceptional case was banished when Contact, a charity for families with disabled children, published a large survey of parents recruited through its networks, which found that over a third reported having to cut back on their use of disability-related equipment (such as adjustable beds, wheelchair chargers and indeed breathing aids) because of electricity costs.[17]

Given the overall drift of Britain's demographics, it is no surprise that the 'new poverty' is also a lot more diverse than

the old. But after so much ink has been spilled on the supposedly singular plight of the 'white working class', it is worth
registering that *all* the main ethnic minority groups in this
country have consistently suffered from higher rates of poverty than the white majority. For some, like British Indians, the
gap is these days small, but for others – like Bangladeshis and
Black Caribbeans – the excess risk is still double or more.[18]

And indeed, many of the people you'll meet in these pages
– from Yvonne at the Tottenham food bank to Ian on his
Deliveroo bike – are from minority groups. Some, like Analetta, a Roma woman in Govanhill, suffer in particular ways
as their specific needs in terms of language and lifestyle go
unmet. Meanwhile, the 'no recourse to public funds' rule applied to many migrants weaponises destitution, condemning
the likes of 'Abena' and 'Stella' – both of whom we will meet
in London – as well as their British-born children to live in
squalid conditions and eat inadequately, even while other restrictions often preclude them from bettering their own lot
through lawful work. The term 'institutional racism' is often
considered contentious, but it is hard to imagine a public
policy that could do more to lock in the poverty race gap.

The final twist between the poverty of past generations and
the new poverty highlighted in *Broke* concerns work itself.
There is a particular irony here, given the way the austerity
assault on the welfare state was sold as necessary to safeguard
the toiling taxpayer from layabout spongers. The truth is
that during the 2010s, rhetorical binaries between 'grafters'

and 'grifters' became ever-less plausible. Year on year, the government's own data revealed that a remorselessly rising proportion of those officially classed as poor lived in working homes.[19]

The extremes of exhaustion, economic insecurity and even physical danger associated with delivering food in the gig economy are laid bare by the testimony of Ian, Bora and Ismail. Their seven-day, 12 p.m. to 12 a.m. rhythm of 'cycling, collecting, delivering' is bad enough even without factoring in the long hours many gig workers spend refreshing an app between jobs, time on call which has frequently gone unpaid. As it has pushed the atomisation of the labour force to new extremes, the gig economy has grown big enough to rank as important in its own right. Moreover, it sets the direction of travel for ruthless employers elsewhere. Amid rising rents and frequently unreliable shifts and pay, an army of 'grafters' – carers, couriers, hairdressers and more – require state top-ups to keep their heads above water, and even then frequently find life a serious struggle.

SOMETHING INSIDE

I'll come back at the end of the book and conclude with some thoughts on how we might fix this crisis of hardship. But as you read the intervening pages, look out for the glimmers of hope among the tales of grime and squalor. For, every bit as remarkable as the privations we put so many of our fellow human beings through in 2023 is the extraordinary resilience of spirit that people can so often summon to find a way through them. In the chapters that follow, you will meet many steadfast individuals, with something inside that enables them to 'keep on keeping on' and sometimes keep smiling too.

Perhaps even more important for finding a way forward than anything inside the heads of the individual Britons at the sharp end of this crisis is what's going on between them. We uncover abundant evidence of the powerful solidarity that can be forged in adversity. Through the firm friendship Mary strikes up with the fellow homeless woman, originally from the Congo, whom she met on the streets of Leeds, and through the church congregation that scraped together the solicitor's fees for her visa application, we are reminded anew of the huge difference that simple kindness and human connection can make.

More than that, though, we find inspiring examples of people making a common cause to disrupt and challenge circumstances that would otherwise be hopeless. In the determination with which downtrodden tenant Lizzie and her friends stand up to landlords and the fighting spirit that overworked Ian develops through his union, we will witness just how much can change when people stand together.

So let us turn now to the voices that can tell us what it feels like to reach a destitute pass and also exactly what it is that is trapping so many people in poverty just now. For, in their words, we might also find useful clues about how we can start to put things right.

'Full of fight': Lizzie (second from right) and her housemates in Brockley

CHAPTER 1

UPROOTED: NO PLACE LIKE HOME

JEM BARTHOLOMEW

Spring was unfolding and Tracy Benson's garden was blooming. Roses, clematis and daisy flowers were bursting out their buds. Her concrete-floored garden was no more than two paces across, but Tracy had affixed clever wiring onto the back stone wall, maximising space. This was an exciting spring: after six years putting down roots, white jasmine had chosen to flower at last.

Meanwhile, three metres away in the living room, Tracy got to work. She kicked up dust clearing books from shelves. She tore lamps down from their perches. She buried photos of friends and family in cardboard boxes. As she worked, hours ticked by on a clock above her, alongside a quote in calligraphy she'd stuck on the wall: 'Time is precious, waste it wisely.'

The days were slipping away before her eviction. Tracy, a fifty-year-old care worker, felt numb dismantling the life she shared with her 27-year-old son, Dan. Their two-bed house in Bideford in Devon had been home for eight years and become a sanctuary. But they'd been served with a 'no-fault' Section 21 eviction notice – meaning landlords can reclaim their property with just two months' notice for no reason during a rolling tenancy. This is a cornerstone of 1980s Thatcherite reforms, which tips the power balance so far against tenants that Conservative governments have admitted a need to abolish it since Theresa May was Prime Minister. But even after that promise was made, no-fault evictions have remained, for years, stuck in a lawmaking purgatory.

Tracy, who has brown hair, an infectious grin and a quick sense of humour, was working nights in a residential care home. She was in a great mood driving to see friends in Southampton when her estate agent called to say an eviction notice would soon fall through her letterbox. She didn't understand. Tracy had always considered herself a good tenant. She spoke to the neighbours, who rented a property from the same landlord, but they weren't being removed. Then she remembered the previous winter. Tracy had suffered with such alarming, thick and extensive black mould – when I visited her, it appeared to wallpaper a corner of her bedroom – that she had raised the issue with the council's environmental health team. By the side of the motorway, her mood soured as she wondered: was this a revenge eviction?

The letter would go on to push Tracy out of her home and into a much bigger story, one that reaches way beyond the particularities of the current Section 21 process and into every property in the country. Within six weeks, Tracy, Dan, their dog Romeo and cat Archie were made homeless. There were simply no local properties in their budget.

Their eviction in spring 2022, becoming one of 280,000 households in England made or threatened with homelessness in 2021/22, signals a profound sickness with the British housing system.[1] Over the past year, I have interviewed dozens of tenants facing evictions across the UK, as well as researchers on housing policy. The picture that emerges is grotesque: cancer patients evicted while in chemotherapy; locks illegally changed on a woman with a nine-month-old baby; homes so damp-ridden the ceiling beams have rotted clean off. News reporting on housing – fixating on market gains or price rises – overwhelmingly misses the human costs of this dysfunctional system. This chapter zeroes in on three women's experiences with housing and homelessness.

The bigger picture that emerges is of several overlapping housing crises playing out across Britain: precarity, unliveable conditions, no fixed abode. The most common, experienced by most private renters, is a general sense of precarity. Although the problems go far wider than Section 21, there is no doubt it has long both epitomised and aggravated the situation in England. 'It's hard for tenants to enforce their own rights when they can be made homeless for no reason,'

Anny Cullum, strategic development and policy officer at the tenants' union ACORN, told me. As Tracy discovered, repairs went unsolved and trying to ground her family was impossible.

The lack of rights fosters a reluctance to speak up, which in turn entrenches dangerous and dehumanising living conditions. 'People are putting up with rats, mice, mould, properties without hot water, broken appliances, windows that are nailed shut,' Kim McKee, the housing studies programme director at the University of Stirling, told me. Roughly 1.1 million private rental sector homes – 23 per cent – were found 'non-decent' in the 2019 English Housing Survey.[2] 'You feel like if you complain too much about something not being fixed, they're going to just kick you out,' Tracy said. Of course, this used to go by another name: squalor.

The grim conclusion of the housing crisis matrix is families thrown into homelessness. On the eve of the pandemic, in 2019's last three months, 19 per cent of statutory homelessness in England was caused by the end of a tenancy.[3] As Tracy's moving-out date edged closer after she received the eviction letter, this was a constant worry. She'd been homeless eight years before. 'It's little things, really,' she told me, 'like, how am I gonna carry on working if I've got no home?'

How did Britain get here? The answer is incredibly complex but also quite simple. Over the past forty years, a profound shift has taken place in the way people live. In the UK, there are three main types of dwelling: owning your own place, social housing and private renting.[4] In 1988, the year of the Housing Act that contained Section 21, just 9 per cent of households (about 1.7 million) lived in the private rental sector in England. Today, that's jumped to over 20 per cent (about 4.4 million households), according to the House of Commons Library.[5] Once intended as an option for a transient or temporary slice of the population, like young people and students, private renting has leapfrogged social housing. But the sector is staggering under its own ballooning mass.

Two radical acts of legislation propelled this change. First, in 1980, Margaret Thatcher's government enacted the Right to Buy, offering council housing tenants the chance to purchase their property at a sizeable discount on market price, of up to 50 per cent.[6] Social housing dwindled from about 31 per cent of households in England in 1980 to 17 per cent in 2021.[7] Second, in 1988, Thatcher liberalised the private sector: she introduced no-fault evictions and scrapped all rent controls. The motivation for these policies – which Labour did not repeal after 1997 – was to spread wealth, encourage 'investment' in private rentals and democratise home ownership.

But there were unforeseen consequences. Instead of expanding, home ownership in England has fallen from a peak of 71 per cent in 2003 to about 65 per cent in 2019/20; home-buying fell dramatically among the young.[8] Banks began to see buy-to-let mortgages as a safer bet than lending to first-time buyers, a trend compounded by the risk-averse attitude prevailing after the 2008 financial crash. 'The right to buy became the right to buy to let,' Vickie Cooper, a social policy specialist at the Open University, told me. Many of the same properties which were once maintained and let out cheap by local authorities were now being snapped up and leased out for lavish rents. Thatcher's reforms kickstarted a self-sustaining system, as landlords could draw down equity from their existing homes to mortgage new ones. 'It's profit without produce,' Cooper added.

All of this has produced a dysfunctional housing market that isn't serving people. Especially for low-income households, the market is, as Julie Rugg, senior research fellow at the University of York's Centre for Housing Policy, told me, 'broken'.[9]

When I visited Tracy's house in May 2022 before her eviction, empty picture hooks stood upright in formation on the exposed walls. She had no idea what would happen. After uprooting the plant in preparation for the move, Tracy's jasmine flowers had begun to wilt.

A SORT OF DISAPPEARANCE

Following the eviction notice, Tracy entered a frantic period of property searching. She signed up to alerts on her phone from all the major sites. Waking up, late in the morning after night shifts at the care home, she'd be scrolling Zoopla, Rightmove, OpenRent and OnTheMarket before her head left the pillow. But searching began to fill her with a strange terror: everything seemed wildly above the £540 a month she'd been paying. 'I'm scared to actually go onto these property sites now,' she said. 'It's exhausting.' Still, she never let her sense of humour dip. She told me how the town was dominated by Airbnbs over homes for locals. 'At night in the winter, there's probably about three lights on,' she said.

Tracy soothed her deteriorating mental health by gardening. Alongside her back garden, she maintained a plot at the town allotment. She grew artichokes, beans, asparagus and tomatoes and could spend hours weeding, digging, planting. She irked retired regulars with her adventurous style, trialling new and sustainable growing methods, like scattering wild flowers. Tracy had her way of doing things, she joked while showing me the allotment, whereas 'they like things to be cut within an inch of their life'.

The plot had a deeper meaning, too. Tracy is a domestic abuse survivor. Around nine years ago, she moved to Devon with a man, away from family in Southampton. He was abusive – manipulating her emotionally, controlling her finances and distancing her from loved ones. She managed to flee with Dan, then still a teenager, and they were housed by the council – first in a bed and breakfast for a strange three weeks, then in a hostel for a torturous seven months. Even after the council had helped her find the current rental place, it had taken Tracy a long time to feel at home. Growing things in the soil gave her this: roots in the ground.

But facing eviction, she couldn't see the point. 'I've kind of given up with it,' she told me. Flowers wilted, weeds sprang up. (Tracy even got a parallel notice from the allotment committee asking her to take action – or risk eviction.) In this way, Tracy was experiencing a sort of disappearance of the future that many private renters endure. In contrast to other European countries like France and Germany, where tenure of a rental property slants towards security, the UK – and, after Scottish, Welsh and Northern Irish reforms, England most particularly – fosters precarity.[10] Walls remain bare, boxes go unpacked, lives exist in a limbo space – never quite settling into a community.

The family's woeful previous experience in the homeless system cast a long shadow. Tracy, scared of losing valuable references for future tenancies, didn't have the appetite to challenge the eviction notice to leave, so it wasn't progressing through the courts. Dan, after finishing his shifts at Tesco, would retreat into the virtual world of gaming. Tracy's ten-year-old cocker spaniel Romeo developed the habit of flopping his head into Tracy's lap every time she was distressed or emotional. The eviction order brought up all the trauma of living in temporary accommodation immediately after escaping her abuser. Researchers have established a strong link between violence against women and homelessness, yet policy routinely fails to account for this gendered dynamic.[11]

Tracy's worry pressed in. At night she feared ending up among the beige walls and clinical plastic furniture of the hostel again. She would never seriously contemplate suicide with her son and her pets relying on her, Tracy told me in her living room, where cardboard boxes lay scattered by the sofa. 'But it gets harder to bat away those thoughts,' she said, as Romeo peered up at her through adoring eyes.

Even if Tracy had wanted to fight the order, the law would have severely limited the scope. If the landlord has filed it correctly, the only aspect of no-fault evictions that can be contested in England is the move-out date. After receiving a notice to quit, many people choose to simply leave a property on the proposed eviction date. After all, even when a case does go to court, the judge has no discretion to refuse the eviction – by law, they must side with the landlord. (This is a separate process than for so-called Section 8 evictions, for things like antisocial behaviour, which are slower and contestable.) The Bureau of Investigative Journalism even found, after analysing 555 no-fault evictions in 2021, that on average the court hearings were over within ten minutes.[12]

Public policy during the austerity years soured the situation further. Whitehall strove to save on housing subsidies after the financial crash of 2008 – effectively individualising society's problem onto the backs of the poor. In 2013, the benefit cap kicked in, a limit on a household's total benefit payments, which is inevitably most likely to be breached by large families in high-rent areas.[13] If exceeded, the deduction directly eats into rent support. There were various more specific curbs and freezes, including the notorious 'bedroom tax' and a shift down in what the benefits system would cover, from typical (fiftieth percentile) local rent to bottom-end (thirtieth percentile). Then in 2016, the link with rents was effectively entirely suspended: Housing Benefit was frozen for four years, despite private rents in England rising three times faster than earnings since 2010.[14] The upshot was a mounting crisis of household debt and – despite the strong jobs growth of the 2010s – a stubborn stream of evictions by county court bailiffs. Immediately before the pandemic hit, the courts in England and Wales were granting landlords 80,000 possessions annually, with 23,000 of their claims leading to eviction by county court bailiffs. That's ninety households being turfed out each working day, with several times as many losing the right to their home.[15]

The scale of the uprooting meant that even the likes of Theresa May – pressured by a nascent tenancy movement – eventually admitted the system was broken. In April 2019, three years almost to the day before Tracy's no-fault eviction notice arrived, May said, 'Everyone renting in the private sector has the right to feel secure in their home, settled in their community and able to plan for the future with confidence.' She added: 'Millions of responsible tenants could still be uprooted by their landlord with little notice, and often little justification. This is wrong.'[16]

But the proposed ban on no-fault evictions was soon lost in the fog of May's toppling, replacement by Boris Johnson and the pandemic. Then Johnson rescued it, but he too was toppled; Liz Truss briefed there would be no ban, then re-committed to it, before being forced out herself. At the start of 2023, Prime Minister Rishi Sunak's government appears committed to the reform but with no strict timetable. In the meantime – despite a Covid hiatus on evictions from March to August 2020 and relaxed rules until May 2021 – renters continued to endure the stress of facing eviction. Landlords began possession actions against tenants in court nearly 235,000 times in England and Wales between April 2019, when May announced the reform, and the end of 2022, the most recent government data at the time of writing. Counting evictions that didn't see the courtroom, the full figure is likely much higher.[17]

Under the reform proposals published in June 2022, land-lords will still be able to evict tenants, but they must argue their grounds – like non-payment of rent or antisocial be-haviour – before a judge. The government plans to strength-en landlords' ability to get tenants out for rent arrears and antisocial behaviour and create new grounds for landlords wishing to sell up or move family into a property.[18] What some researchers say this misses, however, is that for private renters being evicted, the most common reason cited is be-cause 'the landlord wanted to sell the property', the English Housing Survey found, covering 65 per cent of cases.[19] But the loudest alarm bell for critics is ringing over rent hikes. Under any planned reform, if landlords retain a free hand to jack up rents to unaffordable levels, they could use this as a lever to get tenants out. The government has promised there will be a check to ensure rent rises are fair, but everything will depend on the criteria and force of the mechanism.

Banning the particular no-fault eviction used on Tracy will be no magic tonic, as a visit to Scotland reveals. The Holyrood government jettisoned this particular procedure in 2017, but focus groups there have identified continuing confusion about the 'rights and responsibilities' of tenants and landlords as one major reason why the system continues to disappoint.[20] More fundamentally, landlords still have many ways in which to get tenants out, says Darren Baxter, a senior policy adviser on housing at the Joseph Rowntree Foundation.[21] In Scotland, unaffordable rent hikes, or claiming you need to live in the property, have become 'evictions by the backdoor'.

THE HOMELESS HOUSE

There is an old croft home near Stornoway, on Scotland's Isle of Lewis, with views that frame the craggy hills of Harris. Each spring, lambs graze with their mothers in the surrounding fields. Ten minutes' walk from the house, waves caress the land in a secluded water inlet; late-summer sunsets burn away in the west. Inside there are three bedrooms and, climbing steadily up the kitchen doorframe, a series of zebra stripes in pencil, where Jo Lapsley measured her children's height.

A few days before Tracy was told to vacate her home, Jo, a 44-year-old former social worker with diabetes who is unemployed due to chronic fatigue, and her two daughters, ten-year-old Winnie and nine-year-old Sylvia, were evicted. 'We thought it would be our forever home,' Jo said, looking reverently over my shoulder with her hazel eyes. Then she looked down. 'But, yeah, I guess that's always the thing about renting – you're at the mercy of another person.'

In Scotland, despite the end of no-fault evictions, a property can still be reclaimed by a landlord for their own habitation (or through the courts in the case of rent arrears and anti-social behaviour). Jo's landlord, she was told, was planning to build a new property and needed to occupy the house amid construction. A letter fell onto the doormat. It was a notice to leave. She checked the details; they were all correct. To her, the landlord lived in a different world. Housing is an absolute necessity, she thought; how can you make a family homeless just because you want to build a new property?

As with Tracy, 500 miles south in Devon, an exhaustive search produced no affordable homes. That's when Jo's daughters began to ask questions that embarrassed her.

'This isn't fair!' Winnie and Sylvia said. 'Why are there no houses?'

'Why do we not own a house like friends at school?'

'Are we going to have nowhere to live?'

Jo felt ashamed not to have good answers for her children's

curiosity. She felt she'd failed to protect them against a cruel system.

On 1 April 2022 – moving day – Jo was grateful it wasn't raining. A friend collected the girls after school while Jo packed up their childhoods into a moving van. Their possessions would sit in storage for as long as they were homeless. Taking apart the beds, she thought, 'When will we get our things back?' She was almost ready to set off for the temporary house the council was providing for homeless support. The saddest task she left until last: taking a small eraser, she scrubbed away the pencil marks decorating the kitchen doorframe.

That Friday afternoon, Jo opened the door to her drab new emergency dwelling, stepping over the threshold and into the homeless system. South of the border in England, almost 100,000 homeless households are in a similar position, living in temporary accommodation,[22] and the number of these families in England alone has soared by 65 per cent since 2011. Human Rights Watch flagged concerns about the system in a January 2022 report, saying, 'The right to adequate housing remains denied for an increasing number of people, many of whom are families with children, living in unsuitable temporary accommodation.'[23] Not only that, Shelter estimates a true tally would be much higher. While about 2,400 people actually sleep rough each night, according to the charity's analysis of government data, the total number of homeless people is at least 271,000, of whom the vast majority – nearly 250,000 – are stuck in temporary accommodation.[24] When I contacted Jo's landlord, multiple times, about why she and her children were told to leave, I got no reply.

Councils have a statutory duty to house unintentionally homeless people. But after the mass sell-off of council housing, today this very often means families must stay in 'bed and breakfasts', a housing system euphemism for dwellings without cooking facilities, or noisy hostels. Due to this shortage, there are even instances of landlords extracting their own properties from the private rental market. 'Unscrupulous landlords are seeing that as an opportunity to make a lot of money by taking property out of the regular sector,' Dan Wilson Craw, deputy director at Generation Rent, told me. Some individual properties, one might expect, must have made the full transition from subsidised council homes to profiteering buy-to-lets and then on to the extortionate emergency facilities modern Britain requires.

That afternoon, Jo looked around the family's temporary living room – dated '90s-style wallpaper, two beaten-up armchairs with cracked dark leather – feeling depressed and pathetic. 'It won't be long, it won't be long,' she thought, as if trying to steady herself with an incantation. 'It won't be long.'

Usually loud and talkative, on their first day in temporary accommodation, Winnie and Sylvia were uncharacteristically quiet. Jo noticed theirs was the street's only grey-walled house hidden almost entirely behind a bush. For the thirteen weeks they lived there, she said, not a single neighbour said hello. After all, they were just the latest occupants of the Homeless House.

The stigma took a toll. Over the coming days, the girls started fighting more. They had no memories of living anywhere else but their croft house by the sea. Prompted by her embarrassment and shame at being unable to answer her children's questions, by early June, Jo was forced to expand her property search to the mainland. She'd had to make peace with the fact that the girls' schooling would be disrupted; her dream of raising children amid the freedom of the island, where people didn't lock their doors and everything was a bike ride away, was over. Jo began searching for properties in Falkirk, where her parents lived.

A number of detested practices cling like barnacles to the search for a new rental property, underscoring the expensiveness and invasiveness of poverty. Jo was bombarded by a series of fees: mail redirection (£100), moving van rental (£1,200), petrol expenses (£80), cleaning and gardening costs (£130) and so on. She was also hit by a wave of petty surveillance. Without work and receiving Personal Independence Payments (PIP) for disabilities, Jo was asked multiple times to submit her entire banking transaction history for what would become unsuccessful home applications. Distrustful landlords ask homeless people for 'credit checks, guarantors, deposits, six months' rent in advance, references for five years', Saskia Neibig, senior policy and parliamentary affairs officer at Crisis, told me. The upshot is that even if people's finances reach a moment of stability, they can still find themselves excluded from renting decent homes.

When Jo came to view houses, she and I met and drank coffee under the Falkirk Wheel, a hulking 115-foot contraption that spins 180 degrees to connect boats from one canal to another. She wore a Blondie T-shirt and black cardigan. Jo was feeling increasingly desperate. Affordable housing was missing everywhere she looked and the family wasn't high on the local authority's council housing list. She felt trapped. 'Those who don't own the means of production are the cogs in the wheels,' she said.

As a former social worker, Jo's mind was sharpened to the way that cruel systems – not individual failings – condemn people to destitution. But, like many families who are forced into homelessness, when I met Jo, the experience was causing her to doubt herself. 'I feel like I've failed as a mother, bringing them into the homeless system,' she said. A boat arrived at the mouth of the canal and the steel contraption beside us began to spin. 'Maybe I've made bad choices?' Jo was turning the effects of a dehumanising structural problem inward, scratching around for what she might have done wrong. The private rental system seemed to copy the Falkirk Wheel's actions outside our window – constant rotation, moving, churn, instability.

OVER THE THRESHOLD

Listening to Jo come to doubt herself, I couldn't help but choose to step over a threshold journalists are often told not to cross: I reassured her. She'd done nothing wrong, I said; she was the victim of a brutal order. The system was failing people like her, Winnie and Sylvia. The truth was that Jo's story was pulling me back to parts of myself, and my family story, that motivate my reporting on poverty and destitution.

Before I was able to walk, I was made homeless. My parents, in 1995, had just suffered the death of a child, my sister Bethany. Then they were evicted; the landlord needed the property back. We were housed by the Taunton Deane local authority in a bed and breakfast above a pub called the Bear Inn. It was no place to raise a child, even for a few months. We endured freezing showers, no kitchen for cooking, drunken noise and the disappearance of privacy. Once, around 11 p.m., a drinker stumbled unannounced into our squat little room – searching for the toilet as I slept in my crib. My mum felt her dignity deflate to its lowest point, like an inflatable paddling pool cut with a knife.

Amid dire circumstances like this come small gestures of heroism. Many mornings, my dad hitch-hiked eleven miles to the local authority office, pressing for help. A council house nearby was empty. 'You know what I want,' my dad recalls telling them. A few months later, we moved in. And in the meantime, others discovered our situation. Neighbours let us use their kitchen to cook food – acts of compassion that, like cave drippings, helped calcify our dignity. The pressure of the situation, however, helped destroy my parents' relationship. Shortly after finally moving into the council house I would spend my childhood in, it was just me and my mum.

Yet we were lucky. A quarter-century later, the UK's temporary accommodation problem is much worse. Now, in order for a family experiencing homelessness to be offered a council property, they must top the matrix of misfortune. Britain has moved leagues away from the high-quality housebuilding dreams envisaged by Nye Bevan, Minister for Health in the bold 1945 government, which placed housing as part of the health brief. The ambition was to provide decent houses not just for the bottom of society but for *all*. Bevan imagined building social housing communities where 'the doctor, the grocer, the butcher and the farm labourer all lived in the same street'. Such a vision flowed from experience, after a national war effort that mobilised all citizens and after the Nazi aerial campaign bombed 1.1 million homes, making one in six Londoners homeless. The Conservative governments of the 1950s, too, understood that post-war housebuilding was an act of repayment and built both private and council houses. In the post-war era, Britain constructed the most new towns of any European country outside the Soviet Union.[25] Since the 1970s, by contrast, as housing has served half of society as a wealth-enhancing scheme, those in the other half have increasingly been forced to understand it as an individual problem of their own.

Over the past decade, however, the green shoots of a movement for change have come into being. A drive for tenants' rights has sprung up, exerted pressure and begun to change things – like ivy wrapping around a stately home and slowly destabilising its foundations. At first, 'a lot of people thought they were unlucky to have a bad landlord', Anny Cullum of the ACORN tenants' union says. In recent years, 'people have started realising, OK, this isn't just me falling on bad luck, this is a structural problem'.

FROM ANGER TO AWAKENING

In the autumn of 2019, Lizzie Skeaping was travelling home from work when she was handed a red leaflet. It was from the London Renters Union (LRU), an organisation aiming to tilt the scales back in favour of tenants. Lizzie, who has flowing brown hair and was thirty-one at the time, thought it was interesting but didn't act on it, returning to the home she shared with five other adults in Brockley, south-east London.

When Lizzie moved into the stock-brick home in 2017, she wasn't particularly political or engaged in activism. She described herself as a soft-left pragmatist then. She occupied her time with work as a history teacher, playing football and

socialising over a few drinks with friends. Lizzie's house pools
all their spending on food and runs a cooking rota; her signa-
ture dish is homemade pesto. Her kitchen, I saw when I visited, is decorated with charming Polaroids and a whiteboard
with little smiling portraits of all her housemates, past and
present, in black pen.

Lizzie's situation signals the way many people are increasingly living in the UK: locked out of home ownership deep
into adult life. There were 1.3 million families in England with
children renting privately in 2020/21, more than doubling
from 0.57 million in 2003/04. Ageing Britons, too, face the
prospect of renting past retirement: the number of over-55s
renting privately has more than doubled from 366,000 to
867,000 households over the same period.[26] Without a change
of trajectory, private renting will be the future.

This wouldn't necessarily be a problem if the private sector
was equipped to deal with the growing numbers. But the consequence of the social housing sell-off and buy-to-let boom
since the 1980s, Kim McKee of Stirling University says, is that
we have become a nation of small landlords. Half of all tenancies are run by private landlords with four or fewer properties,
the 2021 English Private Landlord Survey found.[27] The result?
Many landlords can't afford the repairs necessary to create
liveable homes. 'Being a landlord shouldn't be a hobby,' says
McKee, who is urging for a professionalisation of the sector.[28]

Before Lizzie's landlord tried to raise the household's
monthly rent by £500, at the start of 2020, she had raised a

shopping list of faults with the agency, according to emails shared with me. Kitchen surfaces were rotting, carpets were fag-burned, mould and damp protruded from walls after being painted over. Lizzie felt angry and powerless that the landlord was so intent on hiking the rent after providing such a shoddy home. They reached a sort of impasse: a few minimal repairs were carried out, but not enough to solve the underlying issues, and the rent went up by a smaller amount of £250, to £3,250 a month.

For Lizzie, the frustrations of paying more rent for expanding rot and mould accelerated an awakening out of her mild politics into something more engaged. The pandemic proved to be her call to action. Reading the news, she was overwhelmed by the scale of need – as many people's incomes dried up overnight but their rent kept being due. Arrears in the private sector had soared: 7 per cent of all renters there were behind in the second quarter of 2021, up from 3 per cent in the same period for 2019/20.[29] Lizzie dug out the LRU flier and got involved.

At 8 a.m. one blue-skied day in August 2021, Lizzie, feeling slightly nervous, travelled towards Elephant and Castle to attend an eviction resistance demonstration. A man called Caspar was being turfed out and bailiffs were expected that day. The LRU was planning to block the eviction. She found about fifteen people, in fluorescent pink jackets, barring access to the doorway. 'Thank you so much for being here,' Lizzie recalls Caspar telling her, handing her a chipped mug of tea. The action was a success: someone had tipped off the bailiffs, who decided it wasn't worth the trip, buying Caspar crucial time to find another place. Lizzie forgot what she'd been nervous about. 'There was a joyful aspect to it,' she said. 'We felt collective power in that moment.'

A DOOR FLINGING OPEN

A key function of tenants' unions like the LRU and ACORN is equipping the average tenant with the tools to fight in the trenches of Britain's private rental sector. They run training sessions on asserting tenants' rights. One evening in early June 2022, I joined a dozen people in a community centre in south Manchester for a workshop on how to resist eviction. These actions involve, usually, a large number of locals peacefully but physically blocking access to bailiffs, who are not permitted to use violence, while the tenants sit inside. That night in Manchester, people filtered in and took their seats; a large red banner demanding 'Landlord Licensing Now' draped the wall.

'Preparing for an eviction resistance is like preparing to go on a hike,' Louisa Olympios, an officer for ACORN Manchester, addressed the crowd. 'Pack your waterproofs, food, water, all of that, because you never know how long it's going to last. Pretend you're going to the Peak District.' Before an action, she explained, local support is drummed up and roles are distributed. It's best to assign someone non-threatening to liaise with bailiffs, who are 'always seeking to escalate', whereas the media spokesperson needs the gift of the gab. On the day, keep chanting to a minimum; babies and dogs are recommended, to exude a non-threatening vibe. At least one coordinator is affixed to each exit and someone documents the unfolding action via live stream. 'The landlord is relying on the tenant to give up. When we show up, we actually have more power,' Olympios said. 'We make the bailiffs question why they make someone homeless.'

ACORN's goal, Cullum later told me, 'is to cause a headache' for those pushing for an eviction, be they landlords, banks or local authorities. When the organisation's UK arm was launched, in Bristol in 2014, Cullum was unsure it would be a success. This is the paradox of unionising tenants, compared to a more traditional union: the potential members are by their very nature separated in different homes, rather than together in a workplace. But when Cullum began canvassing, people started to notice how much they shared.

The opponents they face are formidable. Tenant activists point out that MPs on both benches – including Boris Johnson and former Housing Secretary Sajid Javid – are landlords. In fact, Prime Ministers have stacked their Cabinets with landlords: nine MPs across Truss's and Sunak's Cabinets earn over £10,000 a year from rental income, according to the January 2023 parliamentary register of MPs' financial interests.[30]

And in recent years, the rentier class have been consolidating their power. In 2020, the two biggest landlord lobby groups merged to form the National Residential Landlord Association (NRLA), representing over 100,000 landlords. The NRLA does not oppose the abolition of no-fault evictions but wants a significant beefing up of other repossession powers. 'If you follow any other mechanism,' such as Section 8 evictions, chief executive Ben Beadle told me during NRLA's launch, 'it takes for ever and is very costly.'

Tenant groups like ACORN and the LRU have won a seat at the table. In this way, Cullum, who began as an on-the-streets organiser and now bumps elbows with landlord lobbyists in Westminster, has had a personal trajectory that mimics that of her organisation. Tenant mobilisation has also constructed a new political subjectivity. 'Ten years ago, private renters were not seen as a political group governments or parties had to consider,' Cullum says, which might be why policy was allowed to slide against their interests for so long. But now, 'that group of people have a voice and a collective identity'.

Lizzie's new activism tapped into something deep in her subconscious. It was like a door flinging open. She grew up in a private rental, then rarer than today. It was a financially stressed household in Marlborough, her mum a theatre director and her dad a piano tuner, often struggling to make their own rent. As boisterous children, Lizzie and her brother would sometimes play football in the house. But she recalls observing a complete change of character in her mum – who was usually fearless and carefree – when the landlord was visiting.

'Do you want us to be thrown out?' Lizzie remembers her mum demanding of the children. Before the landlord arrived, her mum would dust the surfaces, comb Lizzie's hair and dig out her finest blue dress. When the landlord entered, she became deferential. 'We were playing a part, it was a play: you got the set ready, you prepared your characters,' she said. This insecurity lingered deep in Lizzie's psyche into adulthood. 'The spectre of the landlord has been a feature of my life since I was a child.'

But Lizzie's new knowledge, gleaned from LRU training, equipped her with the skills to exorcise this ghost haunting her. So when a letter dropped on her doormat informing the house they were being evicted, Lizzie knew what she must do next. 'She was full of fight,' Lizzie's housemate Chloe told me.

HOPE FOR CHANGE

While Lizzie was preparing to fight her no-fault eviction notice, Tracy's jasmine plant was dying. Tracy and Dan, now homeless, were being housed by the council in holiday let apartments. At least it wasn't the clinical plastic furniture of the hostel. But their life had become a tale of constant moving: often a new property every few weeks, sometimes a holiday home and sometimes a Travelodge, where Tracy felt claustrophobic as they were forced to share a room. Although Tracy found the holiday home manager friendly enough, they faced no security of tenure: if a new guest needed their room, they were shuffled around again, suitcases in tow, to somewhere new. The number of moves was approaching ten, including one switch a week before Christmas. (Across the road, Tracy had noticed a gleaming block of flats built a few years earlier. It appeared empty.) But the worst part was the no-pets rule. Archie and Romeo were staying with friends in Southampton. Tracy desperately wanted their own place again, so she could be reunited with Romeo in particular, who was missing her deeply too.

Tracy still performed her morning ritual of checking all the property sites. But there simply wasn't a property in her price bracket for her and Dan to move into. When I messaged Tracy's landlord through the estate agent, Bond Oxborough Phillips, hoping to get the landlord's perspective on why the family had been evicted to homelessness, they declined to comment. Meanwhile, the burden of the eviction meant Tracy was finding it hard to cope working night shifts at the care home. It felt too much, so she switched jobs, finding a role as a Tesco delivery driver. Her GP had increased her dose of antidepressants to cope with the stress – she couldn't understand how the system had got this bad. 'This is something that's been going on for so long with countless different politicians,' Tracy said, 'and it's about time we started to see something happening, something moving, something being done to rectify the problem.'

So what would effective solutions look like? What policies might prevent Tracy and Dan being trapped in limbo; stop Jo being forced to move hundreds of miles to land a house in her budget; end the instability that hangs over Lizzie's home?

The Renters' Reform Coalition, a partnership of twenty leading organisations including Crisis, Shelter and Citizens Advice, is campaigning for a whole package of measures that could together start to build a just housing system. They demand lengthening notice periods, blocking eviction loopholes, strengthening tenant rights to challenge rent hikes, compiling landlords into a register for renters to monitor. Some demand rent stabilisation – pegging the amount that rent can be increased during a tenancy to inflation – or rent control across whole areas.

As it stands, the UK's approach to housing is front to back for the most vulnerable people of all. Currently, people experiencing homelessness can be considered 'not ready' to live in a permanent home and are instead shuttled up a staircase of hostels and temporary shelters while addiction and mental health issues are addressed. Bring them inside, 'Housing First' campaigners argue, and complex problems can be solved more easily once someone is housed.

The social security system, too, needs urgent reform if we want to make a reality of the right to shelter. Even back in 2017, before the past few years of rising rents and frequently frozen benefits, the Institute for Fiscal Studies was calculating that around 90 per cent of low-income households faced a gap between Housing Benefit and rent.[31] By 2022, the government's own data was consistently recording that the majority of those receiving benefits to help with private rent were facing a shortfall between that rent and the Local Housing Allowance, and moreover that the average extent of such shortfalls was large, at just under £150 every month.[32]

Jo, busy searching for a new home, couldn't find anything suitable below £750 a month rent, compared to Housing Benefit of £500. It meant she was forced to look beyond the community they loved. She and I stood outside a grey pebble-dashed property on an estate in Falkirk, some 250 miles' journey from the thatched cottage they'd been evicted from weeks beforehand. 'It's only two bedrooms, but they're double bedrooms, so the kids could share,' she said. Jo tried to imagine building a life there, but it wasn't easy.

But some argue that better benefits would merely patch things up. Bolder changes need considering too, including some things we have tried before. The UK had rent control and stricter rules on evictions before 1988. A little further back, the state built a lot more houses, including those for rent. Crisis wants to see a mass housebuilding campaign of 90,000 rentals a year for fifteen years. Some want a return to the post-war consensus: social housing for the people, not for the 'residuum' who fall on hard times. Other parts of Europe are thinking more radically. In 2021, residents in

Berlin voted to nationalise nearly a quarter of a million apartments, aiming to snatch control from big landlords and lower rents.[33] Rumblings from both the Conservative government and the Labour opposition suggest solutions like these are political carrion for now. But looking further ahead, the tenants' movement is building hope for such sweeping change.

A PLACE AND A FEELING

Lizzie was determined to fight her eviction. On the Friday they'd been served with a notice to leave, a new housemate, Chloe Windsor, was moving in. They'd planned a welcoming night of games at a nearby pub. 'It was supposed to be a new beginning,' Lizzie said. Instead, 'it felt like the beginning of the end'.

But then Lizzie checked the details of the letter. They were incorrect. She noticed the names on the eviction notice were those of old tenants, people who had moved out years ago. Two days later she was on the phone to the LRU, which advised her the Section 21 was invalid; and if the landlord was seeking a court date, it was an eight-week wait. They now had a bargaining chip to try to stay in their home.

Lizzie was nervous when calling the estate agent. But when she listened to what they were telling her – that the landlord was making a 'simple business decision' to kick them out, as she remembers it, so he could charge higher rent – the anxiety slipped away and she let rip. 'I am a *person*, not a tenant,' she recalls telling him over the phone, fuming about the brutality of the rental system. She pointed out they had transferred about £270,000 in rent since the initial tenancy began. 'This feels so cruel, what you're doing is so cold,' she thought.

A week later, Lizzie said, the estate agent called back. OK, he said, you can stay, as long as you agree to the £3,500 a month rent. Faced with the prospect of losing the house they'd made their home, they gritted their teeth and signed for one more year. It was part success – they'd fought the eviction and were staying! – but then part defeat: the rent was hiked and housemates already began making plans for moving on when the year was out. As for the incoming housemate Chloe, who had trudged back to her parents' house while waiting to move in, she ended up homeless for a couple of months herself due to the eviction notice and its upheaval – stuck at her parents' at the age of thirty-four. Chloe was left stressed and upset; at one point she felt self-conscious after crying in front of a new colleague at work. Moreover, the lack of a registered fixed address meant she was refused a vote in the council elections, denying her a say, among other things, on local housing policy.

Lizzie was devastated that their little living community seemed over, with her housemates preparing to splinter off. Soon enough the portraits on the whiteboard would have to be rubbed off. 'Home is a place, but it's also a feeling, and it's an idea,' she said. 'Can we lift that up and put it into a new space?'

Homes and communities are welded through time, through settlement in place.[34] We can only build strong relationships – with people, with buildings – when we share a future with them. We can't forge bonds if the future has disappeared or is stalked by threatening spectres of displacement.[35] That fear gets under our skin, hollowing us out and degrading our self-belief. Only with a fairer housing system can we hope to build a life in a natural way – at home.

On 30 June, Jo, Winnie and Sylvia were relieved to close the door on homeless accommodation for good. The trip to Falkirk had been a success – an offer was accepted. They drove onto the open road with apprehension to build a new life.

The family was excited about the new two-bedroom property, which I'd viewed with them a few weeks beforehand. On the way, Jo sought to manage expectations, just in case. 'It is on a busy road, and it's near the police station, which might be noisy,' she said.

'At least it's a home,' Sylvia replied.

As we walked around, they began to imagine themselves living there. The children were busy discussing how exactly to divide up the shared bedroom. Jo stood at the kitchen sink, which had a view of the small back garden, and imagined seeing the girls playing as she washed dishes. The minds of the family, once again, could return to putting down roots after months stranded in the homelessness system. The garden had three concrete slabs embedded in the grass; as we prepared to leave, Winnie hopscotched from stone to stone.

Parenting vs the 'price of protein': Lowri in Blackpool, with pictures from her daughter's younger days

CHAPTER 2

THE HUNGRY TWENTIES

SAMIRA SHACKLE

The first time Yvonne* went to the food hub, in late 2020, she took one look at the queue and turned back. She just couldn't go inside. Yvonne was sixty-three, a former social worker. She had worked all her life – always the person to take on the extra shifts – and brought up four children on her own. As well as working all hours to earn, she kept the household running: cooking, cleaning, looking after the kids. Friends and family used to joke that she never stopped.

The idea of falling back on charity was anathema. But in the end, she had no option. Things got harder and harder. Her cupboards were bare and she had no reserves of cash. Attempting to suppress her hunger, she drank glass after glass of tap water. 'I have to cut down on it,' she told me. 'Sometimes

---

* Some names have been changed.

55

I drink so much my stomach cramps up – that's me trying to make my stomach feel full.'

Yvonne came to the UK from Jamaica in 1969 when she was ten, part of the Windrush generation. Before times got so tough, she would sometimes cook traditional Caribbean food – salt fish, yam, plantain. Her daughter had severe food allergies growing up, and these were some of the few foods she could tolerate. Yvonne had never been a big fan of processed carbs so used to skip the rice and peas for herself, preferring to make wholesome pots of steamed vegetables – sliced leek and sweet potato. In the summer, she would barbecue fish or marinated spare ribs. When she had time, she liked to bake.

But in 2009, after forty years in this country, Yvonne developed a degenerative spine condition that meant standing up and walking could cause intense jolts of pain. None of what she used to do was possible any more: her body gave up. She continued working as long as she could after the diagnosis, but ultimately she had to leave her job and found herself reliant on Universal Credit. At first, the money just about covered her costs, but as prices rose things went from bad to worse.

And so, here she was, with her cupboards bare, reluctant to ask one of her four adult children for help – or even let them know that she was struggling – in case they jeopardised their own finances to help her out. Aged between thirty-five and forty-four, they had their own money worries, and so she told them everything was fine. Yvonne worried so much about them that even as she stood in a grocery shop holding a £2 block of cheese and wondering if she could really justify buying it, she continued to pay a monthly life insurance policy so that if she died, her children would not be landed with the cost of her burial.

But there was no way around it: it still cost money to buy the food she needed to stay alive. That was why, despite how painful it was to walk there, Yvonne made her way to the food hub, which operated from a community hall close to her council flat in Tottenham, north-east London. She badly needed the food, but that first time, shame prickled up, white-hot. She turned around, went home and ate porridge for the rest of the week.

Out of options, though, she returned the following week, and this time she went in. Volunteers stood behind trestle tables stocked with groceries. They were kind, encouraging Yvonne to take meat, fresh vegetables, whatever was on offer. But she was still reluctant. 'I kept on saying, "No, it's all right." And I came out with just a couple of things in the bag because I was too embarrassed.'

After that, she went to the food hub every fortnight. It was always hit or miss; it depended what people had donated or what the supermarkets had left. Yvonne preferred fresh food – lettuce, tomatoes, fresh vegetables. Sometimes there was meat or fish, but it was always close to the sell-by date and she didn't have a freezer, so she only took what she could realistically eat in the next few days. She didn't want to take food that someone else might make better use of. Other people arrived several hours early to queue up outside, which Yvonne struggled to do given her back problems, so sometimes by the time she got into the room the supplies were dwindling.

The intensity of her shame began to die down as she visited regularly, but Yvonne said, 'I still felt a way about going.' She didn't want her friends to know, and so she stopped socialising much. 'I don't want the question: "How are you coping?"' she told me. It was hard not sharing the mental load, the grinding anxiety of not knowing how long her food would last, but she comforted herself that even if she felt alone, she was not. 'I keep telling myself: "I'm not the only one. There are others out there that might be just like me, who don't want no one to know." I can't beat myself up.'

FACING THE FACTS

Yvonne was right. The hub she uses is one small part of a wider patchwork of emergency food provision which has grown exponentially across the UK over the past decade to answer exploding need. It is effectively a charitable substitute for the formal welfare state which has been squeezed by austerity policies. With the state ceasing to provide a financial 'safety net' at a truly safe level, in every borough of the UK, volunteers are staffing emergency food services. In

Tottenham and neighbouring Wood Green alone, there are currently twenty-two services providing free food to people who cannot afford to buy groceries.

Some of these are formal food banks run by organisations such as the Trussell Trust, which require a referral (issued by frontline workers such as GPs, social workers or the Citizens Advice Bureau) and provide a three-day food parcel to those in immediate need. Trussell is the UK's biggest food bank franchise and its growth speaks volumes: in 2003, it ran just two food banks. By 2009, despite the financial crisis then engulfing Britain, there were still only thirty. Today, there are more than 1,400. According to the Independent Food Aid Network, there are also at least 1,100 independent food banks.

And formal food banks are only the start of the makeshift responses that have sprung up to answer a relentlessly growing need. Food hubs, like the one Yvonne visited, provide more casual and ongoing support. Anyone can turn up – no referral needed, no questions asked – and fill their bags with free groceries every week. The stock comes mostly from donations or surplus supermarket produce which can't be sold because it's close to its sell-by date.

The 2021 'State of Hunger' report, commissioned by the Trussell Trust, combined the charity's own data with that from the Independent Food Aid Network to estimate that immediately before the pandemic, around 700,000 UK households – around 2.5 per cent of the total – had used a food bank.[1] If that number points to a big problem with hunger, statistics show that the situation is only worsening. Trussell's own operational data, which counts parcels rather than people, shows that by the financial year 2021/22, the number of packages issued was up 14 per cent over the two years since 2019/20 and up 81 per cent over the five since 2016/17.[2] In the intervening years, of course, the coronavirus crisis had caused numbers to dramatically spike. But the very latest figures – covering April through to September 2022 – recorded growth in the number of food parcels issued to a point that even exceeded the heights registered in the first emergency wave of the pandemic.[3]

Food bank use is only one measure of hunger: not everyone struggling to afford to eat ends up actually using an emergency food provision service. In May 2022, analysis of a large YouGov dataset by the Food Foundation think tank found that more than 2 million adults in the UK had gone without food for a whole day in the previous month, and that increasing numbers regularly skipped a meal. By that autumn, the next wave of the same study suggested those going hungry for a whole day had grown to 3 million or more.[4]

For some, there will be clinical consequences, which can be gauged using NHS Digital statistics. They record that, although still low, primary hospital admissions for malnutrition were, as of 2020/21, up by 74 per cent over the austerity years, since 2009/10, and by 106 per cent since the financial crisis of 2007/08. Secondary diagnoses of malnutrition in hospital, following admissions that were originally for other conditions, are up even more sharply: they have more than doubled (up by 168 per cent) under austerity, and more than tripled (up 274 per cent) since the banking crash.[5] Malnutrition is not the same thing as hunger, but medics confirm the close connection that common sense would expect: 'We know that health resilience in lower socioeconomic groups is lower, and a lot of that is due to food: either not having enough or not having healthy food,' says Yasotha Browne, a locum GP and spokesperson for the Doctors' Association UK.

BANKING ON HUNGER

On a hot day in late June 2022, I sat in the Trussell Trust-accredited food bank that operates from Tottenham Town Hall, a red-brick building with baroque stone detail which sits on a busy main road, not far from Yvonne's home. It is run twice a week by a local church called Freedom's Ark, which also operates a less formal food hub from the same venue three times a week – this is stocked by an organisation called the Felix Project, which collects and distributes supermarket surplus.

A group of around six volunteers gathered in a green-carpeted room with large windows that opened onto the high street. They divided up jobs: some packed the parcels, mostly made up of long-life food like dried pasta, tinned vegetables and powdered soups; others checked referral vouchers to see how many people are in the household, which affects the volume of food handed out; while others were on the door managing the queue.

'We're out of chocolate today, but we do have Jaffa Cakes,' Kirsty Johnson, a food bank employee who stocks the warehouse, told the volunteers. 'We've got some shaving foam in for the men, and there's instant mash if people want it.' Before opening, the volunteer coordinator advised people to download the Google Translate app. As the doors opened, the app was put to use almost immediately when a Turkish woman arrived with her two young daughters; through Google Translate, she explained that her husband had left her for another woman and she was suddenly alone with the kids. She had no income and, like many immigrants (see Chapter 7), no recourse to public funds. Volunteers checked her voucher and put together a package of food for her – bread, UHT milk, pasta, cornflakes, tinned carrots and peas.

Behind her in the queue was Jay, a well-turned-out 27-year-old with an amiable expression. He told me he'd lost his job as an agency bus driver a couple of months earlier. 'I've been looking for work and I tried to hold off coming as long as possible, but it just got...' he tailed off, his hand tightly gripping his bag of food. 'Maybe next month I'll find something.'

To use the food bank, people must have a referral voucher. In most areas, this is capped so that only three vouchers can be issued for an individual in a six-month period. The limit exists to avoid dependency: food banks are intended to be for emergencies. The Trussell Trust's stated aim is for people to no longer need its service. In the mosaic-tiled town hall lobby outside the room where people received their supplies, a table was set up with leaflets about other services: support with filling out benefits forms or with housing. 'We try to ensure we're doing more than just giving people food,' Pastor Tonye Philemon, who heads up the food bank, told me. 'We want to help resolve those underlying issues.'

Nonetheless, when so many people depend on the service, setting limits is a tricky balancing act: here in Tottenham, where many people are struggling, the cap is not three but six times in six months. The reality is that in Britain today, food insecurity is often a long-term condition rather than a passing crisis. Volunteers at the Tottenham food bank always make sure to tell people about the food hub, which anyone can attend once a week without a referral.

There are currently 4,000 people registered to use the hub, with around 1,300 coming in every week. When I sat in on one of these informal food hub sessions, there was a sense of pot luck. A different set of volunteers sorted through boxes of John Lewis panettone, a Christmassy cake incongruous on this sweltering June day, as well as 1,000 bottles of kefir, a fermented milk drink, which they handed out by the crate. The trestle tables in the room were piled high with fresh vegetables, ready meals from Amazon Fresh, sandwiches and pre-cut salads from Morrisons, plus a selection of meat.

Each table was manned by a volunteer who handed out the food, trying to ration it so that the last person in the queue would get as much as the first arrival. All the food has to go that day, so whatever remains is either taken by volunteers or left outside the town hall for passers-by to pick up. By the time the food hub opened at 5 p.m., around seventy people were queuing on the street outside. Some had been there for two hours. And, staff told me, this was a quiet day; sometimes several hundred people turn up. The doors opened and people started to come through: a woman with a small child dressed in bright African print, two older ladies with white hair and bulky shopping trolleys, a working man in a high-vis jacket and paint-stained trousers with a backpack. They walked over the mosaic floor of the town hall lobby in batches of five or six, as crates were wheeled back and forth to restock the tables.

Every day, this work is happening all around the country.

THERE BUT FOR THE GRACE OF GOD…

Back in 2016, Sophie,* who lives just outside Manchester, started volunteering at her local Trussell Trust food bank, keen to get some experience and rebuild her confidence as her children got older; now in her forties, she hadn't worked since becoming a single mum at eighteen. The first thing she noticed was that there was no particular type of person using

* Some names have been changed.

the food bank. There were people who came in after work, or families who would turn up only during the school holidays.

Some of them had circumstances not so different to her own. Both her children were autistic, which meant she had to get by on Carer's Allowance and other benefits. But she'd never considered herself poor. She simply prided herself on looking out for bargains, spotting reduced stickers at the supermarket. But working at the food bank made her realise how easy it was to slip through the cracks and suddenly find yourself unable to feed your family.

While there is no single demographic that uses a food bank, they have at least one thing in common. 'The main problem is that people don't have enough money: the benefits aren't enough or their salaries aren't enough,' says Kirsty from the Tottenham food bank. Issues with the benefits system are built in. Since 2010, various 'reforms' have broken the link between the money families are given and the rent they must pay, the overall cost of living they face and – through the two-child limit for family support – the number of mouths they have to feed.

'We're now seeing the progressive impact of the benefits freeze,' says Glen Bramley, professor of urban studies at Heriot-Watt University and one of the authors of the 'State of Hunger' report. 'Some of the benefits in Britain for working-age people are extremely mean by international standards, or indeed compared with how they were in the past.' He points out that for under-25s, the standard means-tested benefit allowance of

£265.31 a month is below the commonly used threshold for destitution: 'They are destitute by design.'

'Sanctions come up a lot,' says Kirsty, referring to the punitive reductions in benefits that are made when claimants slip up, for example by being late for a Jobcentre interview. 'People don't have a margin for error – they live and die in those margins. If you suddenly realise you're not getting that money next week that you thought you were going to get, you just don't have enough to survive.'

The effects of austerity, from 2010, were compounded after 2013, when the old benefits system was gradually replaced with Universal Credit, an amalgamated payment. It was supposed to be simpler, but some devastating shortcomings were built in, one of which is that it withholds the first payment for five weeks. In 2019, Sophie experienced this first hand. By this time, she was volunteering more regularly at the food bank – sometimes dealing directly with clients, sometimes stacking shelves in the warehouse. In late November that year, she recalls, she was switched over to Universal Credit and informed that she'd have to wait five weeks for the first payment. This meant it wouldn't come through until January.

While she'd always made her finances work, things were tight and she had no savings, no backup for the rainy day that had suddenly arrived. In desperation, she got her own first food bank referral. It was embarrassing having to use the service that she was helping to run; most of the other volunteers were comfortably off with professional jobs, and Sophie was self-conscious about the fact that they'd now realise she was in a very different position. When she told the food bank manager, she cried. But he was kind to her about it – as were all her colleagues – telling her to fill up her bag with whatever she wanted. Sophie felt guilty as she did so. 'For a client, you go down the list and hand things out. I was able to choose the cereal I wanted, the jam I wanted. And so even though I was in this position where I was getting help, it didn't sit comfortably.' She received three separate food bank vouchers that winter. Things stabilised for Sophie once her Universal Credit was established, and she has since tried to use her own experience of getting vouchers to reassure clients who she could see were feeling ashamed when coming to use the food bank. 'I've been there and I know what it feels like,' she says. 'I don't think that will go away.'

SMASHED INTO THE FLOOR

Lowri is a single mum who lives with her thirteen-year-old daughter just outside Blackpool. Her financial troubles started in 2017, when her husband left her. The couple had founded an events and audiovisual company together. A few years earlier, Lowri's mother had died, leaving her some money, which she had put into the business. But soon after the divorce, Lowri's ex convinced her to surrender control over the company before closing it down, leaving her without work. It happened a week before Christmas. 'I was left with no job, no income, no money for food, not able to pay the mortgage, literally zero coming in, unable to buy Christmas gifts for our daughter,' she remembered. Her inheritance had also disappeared with the company it had been invested in. At the age of forty-seven, she had to sign on for benefits.

A few months later, a mental health nurse visited Lowri at home. She was struggling to cope after the sudden implosion of her life. The nurse sat down with her and went through her finances. Her situation was dire: the Universal Credit payments were barely enough to cover her costs, and she had less than £10 left in the bank. The nurse referred her to a food bank. 'My first response was: "No way. I come from a family and a community that raises money for charity; we don't take from charity,"' Lowri said. As it dawned on her that she couldn't access the funds to do a basic supermarket shop, she felt a sharp sense of shame and failure. 'It's just utter desperation to have to use a food bank after working all your life,' she told me. 'It's like being smashed into the floor.'

Later that week, Lowri went to the food bank at her local church. There were tables set up with groceries to take home, as well as a hot meal in a slow cooker for people to eat there. When she entered, she burst into tears. Volunteers sat her down and brought her a meal, a cup of tea and a biscuit. After she had calmed down, Lowri got up and picked up what she needed: toiletries, cleaning products for the house, tinned food, bread and fresh vegetables.

The food bank got her out of an emergency situation, and on other occasions she used the informal community food hub too. But things slowly began to pick up for her, and she did not become a regular user; she started to work again, doing freelance jobs in the events sector. She got by, though it was not enough to start saving or build up any kind of financial buffer. Then the pandemic hit, and Lowri instantly lost all her work. Because she had set herself up as a limited company, she was excluded from Covid support grants for the self-employed and once again found herself struggling to survive on Universal Credit.

She threw her energy into campaigning for people excluded from these grants and for people in the events sector. She posted on Facebook about the issue without being entirely candid that she was writing from personal experience – or even telling her immediate friendship circle just how badly she was struggling. Eventually, Lowri wrote a post plainly stating that she was struggling to afford food. A few days later, a friend arrived at her doorstep in tears, with bags of shopping, telling her she'd had no idea.

Throughout the pandemic, Lowri did online supermarket shops for her elderly father – who is based in Wales – using his debit card. He told her to add on some food for herself and her daughter, so that's what she did, making sure that her cupboard was stocked with basics – pasta, rice, tins of tomatoes and baked beans. After the pandemic eased, Lowri continued to do a regular shop with her dad's card as she struggled to rebuild her career, although given that he is retired and prices kept going up, she worried about how long he'd be able to afford it.

This is an example of what academics working on destitution and hunger refer to as 'assets', which, as Professor Bramley explains, might mean 'things like having food in the larder or freezer, having tins or having family who can support you before you go to a food bank'. But even with some help from her dad, things are extremely tight for Lowri, and the anxiety gnaws away at her. 'It's the stuff that goes with the dried food to make decent meals which costs the money,' she says, especially 'the price of protein'. To try to make it work, she cooks more vegetarian food or uses cheap frozen fish. It is a constant worry, with no margin for error – an unexpected need to provide packed lunch for a school day out could throw off the whole week's finances.

When I spoke to Lowri in mid-July, she'd just been for a compulsory meeting at the Jobcentre to discuss her search for work. 'You have to justify your existence if you're self-employed,' she said. She had to drive to get there and was acutely aware that she had only 78p in the bank and twenty-seven miles left of fuel. She had to drive her daughter to school the following day. The woman saw how desperate she was and offered to advance her Universal Credit by £800. Lowri immediately said yes: it meant that she could pay the mounting bills and buy petrol. But it placed her in debt to the Department for Work and Pensions (DWP), meaning that

£67 would be deducted monthly for the next year. Such repayments can take a huge toll: the 2021 'State of Hunger' report found that the DWP itself was the biggest single creditor for people using food banks.

For Lowri at that moment, however, this was a problem for later. 'I can't even think of tomorrow,' she told me. 'Each day I go – right, today we've got food, we've got the roof over our heads, we've got fuel in the car, that's a bonus. I can't think of anything else.'

When it comes to children and food poverty, public discussion usually focuses on the impact that hunger has on learning. 'It massively affects concentration,' London-based teacher Emma Bowers told me. 'Children often come in not having had breakfast, or maybe just having had a chocolate bar. They might be hyperactive, aggressive or withdrawn. Sometimes a child is sent out for bad behaviour, and you ask them what they've eaten that day and they say "nothing". At times, she has kept 'slow-release energy breakfast bars in the classroom for those situations', which 'would make a huge difference to concentration'.

Although hunger clearly causes issues in the classroom, term-time can still be a relief for families who qualify for free school meals. When I spoke with Lowri, the summer holidays were coming and she was dreading the extra costs of feeding her daughter every meal. On top of this, she worried about not being able to afford outings. Even a trip to the famous local beach in Blackpool meant £5 on ice creams, an unmanageable cost. So when the £800 advance came into her account, Lowri took her thirteen-year-old daughter to a food shop and told her, 'Build up the cupboard whilst this money is there, because once it's gone, it's gone. You've got six weeks to think about.' Her daughter picked out some Brunch bars – four for £1 – and some Oreo cookies, multipacks of crisps and Tango sweets she'd tried at a friend's house. It wasn't much, but it was something.

BACK TO BASICS

If austerity pushed hundreds of thousands of households into eating less often or less well, the more recent rapid rise in the price of food and other living costs threatened to engulf many entirely. The Food Foundation's May 2022 survey found that around 7.3 million people – around one in every seven – were food insecure, a staggering increase of 57 per cent over a period of just three months. By the autumn, the number was 9.7 million.[6]

Up in Manchester, Sophie was certainly feeling the difference. Her children were grown up; the eldest was in her late twenties and living independently, and her youngest had recently started university. This sharply reduced the benefits she was entitled to. Alongside this, a recent bureaucratic error had meant that her Universal Credit had been overpaid. She flagged it immediately with the DWP, but it took several months of back and forth to correct. When action was finally taken, not only was the total amount payable lower but she was indebted to the DWP. Between this and the cut to her overall allowance, her total monthly payments fell from just over £900 to just under £200. After endless anxious calls to the DWP, the debt was written off because she had not been at fault, but her monthly payments were still much diminished. She started to look for paid work but feared sinking into what she calls 'the circle of problems', where any wages would cut her benefits further.

Between her sudden drop in monthly payments and the broader economic situation, Sophie was increasingly anxious about keeping her cupboards stocked. She was not the only one feeling the pinch. In September 2022, the Office for National Statistics (ONS) reported that 'rising food prices made the largest upward contribution' to both the main inflation rates.[7] Prompted by the campaigning cook Jack Monroe, who had highlighted the sharply increasing price of basic groceries on supermarket shelves, the ONS produced experimental statistics which suggested the cost of the lowest-price groceries had risen by 17 per cent in the year from September 2021, with some kitchen staples, like vegetable oil, rising by over 40 per cent.[8]

Sophie still had rice, pasta and tinned vegetables in the cupboard and meals in the freezer. For years, she'd been in the habit of saving scraps whenever she cooked to make stock and freeze it, never letting anything go to waste. If she saw something useful reduced in the supermarket, she always

bought it and froze it for a rainy day. 'My cupboards aren't col-
ourful,' she told me: they were full of supermarket own-brand
basics in plain packaging – and the freezer was awash with
orange 'reduced' stickers which slid off in the ice. 'The last six
months, the stuff in the cupboards, especially tins that have
been there as backup – they're disappearing quickly,' she says.
'I love going out and buying fresh fruit and veg, but actually
there's tins of carrots and peas in the cupboard. And now I'm
at the point where they might actually get used, because those
extra pennies aren't there to pop out and spend a fiver.'

As the price of basics soared, she found it difficult to ignore
the fact that costs were going up while quantities of products
were going down. Rebecca McManamon, a spokesperson for
the British Dietetic Association (BDA), told me that between
March and August 2022, the cost of some foods increased by
80 per cent: 'That is a really huge difference when you've got
a cost-of-living crisis.'

Too many times, Sophie found herself standing in a supermarket queue only to realise that the product she thought was
on offer was mislabelled or on the wrong shelf. Mortifyingly,
she'd have to put it back – the cost of each item in her basket
was calculated down to the penny. It caused her so much
anxiety that she switched, where possible, to doing her shop
online so that she could track costs privately, at home. 'It just
breaks you down,' she said. 'It makes you feel like you're not
doing as good a job as you could do. You're thinking: I feel
like I deserve better.' Sophie's heart sank when she made a

sandwich for her youngest, who said it didn't taste of anything. 'I know it's because I bought the cheapest meat and the cheapest bread in the shop,' she said. 'You lose quality, and then you start to think, well, is that all I'm worth?'

IF YOU'RE SLEEPING, YOU WON'T FEEL HUNGRY

Sophie knew better than most that she was not alone in any of this. If there was no single type of person using the food bank when she started volunteering in 2016, by 2022 the demographic was even more varied. When she spoke to people coming into the food bank, she always told them, 'Look, we're volunteers and we're here to help. I've had vouchers, I know how it feels and there's no stigma.' But she couldn't silence a niggling voice at the back of her mind that said, 'You didn't feel great when you were getting vouchers.' On other days, Sophie worked in the warehouse, where the shelves were increasingly bare. At the same time as food bank usage was going up, the volume of donations began to reduce drastically, as people who might have added food bank goods onto their weekly shop also felt the pinch. This painfully demonstrates why charity is not an adequate substitute for a functional welfare state. As 2022 drew to a close, a coalition of food organisations put together a letter signed by over 3,000 volunteers which warned the government that many banks were at 'breaking point' and

having to ration inadequate stocks to deal with rampant demand.[9] That November, the Trussell Trust said that need was
outstripping supply for the first time.[10] The patchwork of charitable food provision is beginning to fray, and the implications
are terrifying.

People across society are suffering from the combination
of soaring energy bills, rising inflation and benefits that have
lagged badly behind. But those suffering most of all are the
people who have been struggling for a long time, those who
do not have 'assets' such as a freezer full of food or a parent to
ask for help. Back in Tottenham, things were sharply worsening for Yvonne as summer drew to a close and her living costs
crept up. She tried applying for jobs, thinking that despite her
health conditions she could do something office-based – but
when she mentioned that she was sixty-three, or that her back
problems meant she needed regular breaks, she wouldn't hear
back. It felt like the world was closing in on her as the energy
bills got higher and higher.

She tried contacting the local authority. But they didn't
help with the energy bills, which she realised she'd have to try
to manage alone. She unplugged the TV and the washing machine. It was summer, she told herself, so she could wash her
clothes in the bath and hang them out to dry in the garden.
She didn't need the TV anyway – she could listen to the radio
on her phone. The news bulletins did nothing to reduce her
tension: 'I just kept on hearing, "this is gonna go up, this is
gonna go up".' She kept the lights off. The most painful thing

was unplugging her sewing machine. In the years since she'd stopped working, sewing had kept her sane and given her purpose – using offcuts of fabric to stitch clothes, curtains, throws and cushions. Now the hum of the machine meant pounds on the energy bill which she couldn't afford.

The only thing the council had done, when she asked for help with her energy bills, was refer her to a food bank, as opposed to the food hub she'd already been using. She went along with the voucher but found the experience demoralising. The package of long-life food depressed her – it would never have occurred to her to eat powdered soup or Spam – and nor had she ever been much of a bread eater. The packages felt like food selected for someone else, and it seemed wasteful to take it when someone else might appreciate it. She didn't return.

Instead, Yvonne continued to go to the food hub fortnightly. Standing in the queue and waiting was too difficult to manage every single week. Even worse was her increasing anxiety about cooking. Each time she switched on the cooker, that was money on her gas and electric bill. Even in June 2022, once energy costs and other unavoidable bills had been deducted from her Universal Credit payment, she was left with just £5 for the month. She sat down on her own, in her darkened living room, and wept. 'I'm just thinking, what do I do now? How do I cope?' she said. At the hub, she began to take only foods that she could eat without cooking. In a good week, she might get some fresh fruit – bananas, apples – or

salad and tinned sardines or mackerel. But it was unpredictable. Sometimes the only options were cornflakes, tinned fruit
or baked beans. Whenever there were cereal bars available,
she tried to stock up, because they were not only filling but
required no cooking or warming at all. 'Somehow I've got to
pay my bills, and I've got to survive,' she told me. This was the
middle of summer, when the evenings were light and the days
were hot. The thought of the winter looming ahead filled her
with dread.

Yvonne is not alone in this. At the Tottenham food bank,
staff told me that even in summer, they'd noticed that people
attending the hub were making different choices based on
their energy bills. People were refusing to take potatoes, because fifteen minutes on the hob or thirty minutes in the oven
was too expensive. 'People are looking more for things that
can be cooked quickly and easily so they're using less gas and
electricity,' Kirsty Johnson, the warehouse manager, told me.
'They're taking quick things like noodles or microwave rice
that take a minute in the microwave, as opposed to a bag of
rice that takes ten minutes on the hob.' Ready meals – always
a popular option for food bank users in temporary accommodation without proper cooking facilities – are increasingly
popular across the board.

Rebecca McManamon points out that a reliance on these
kinds of convenience foods is one contributing factor to
malnutrition, something the BDA now estimates 3 million
adults in the UK are at risk of. If someone already has a low

body weight, it can take just five days to start experiencing symptoms of malnutrition. 'People feel low, people can feel fatigued, feel like things are an effort and that can then be a vicious cycle within itself,' said McManamon. The effects don't stop with mental health. GP Yasotha Browne explains, 'The most obvious impact of malnutrition is that your immunity is weakened, so you're more prone to infections, not bouncing back or recovering as quickly. It's a big stress on your system.'

For Yvonne, food had once been a source not of anxiety but of pleasure – not just eating it but preparing it, planning it. She lived in a ground-floor flat with a garden, and she had an old barbecue that she used to use in the summers. She wondered if she could get hold of a bag of coal so that she could cook outside without using gas or electricity. (She enquired at the food hub if that was something they could help her with, but staff were stumped.) But more often these days, she didn't want to bother. One evening the thought of opening a tin was too depressing. She had a banana and went to bed, telling herself, 'If you're sleeping, you won't feel hungry.'

Each day, Yvonne woke up and told herself that she had to focus on today because no one is guaranteed a tomorrow. She repeated affirmations to herself. 'I tell myself: you will survive. You are strong. You are a survivor. You are beautiful.' Sometimes it helped; sometimes she laughed at herself. It was a relief to feel some lightness, so she carried on murmuring these affirmations to herself, along with her daily prayers. Carrying on was the only thing there was left to do.

'We'll grudge pushing that button' for the heating: Liam and Rochelle in Dingwall

CHAPTER 3

COLD COMFORT: THE NEW STRUGGLE FOR HEAT

CAL FLYN

Lindsay lives in a council house in Kirkwall, the largest town in Orkney. Orkney is a starkly beautiful archipelago off the north coast of Scotland, though Lindsay's street is not, perhaps, one of its most picturesque corners. Hers is a dainty one-bedroomed house dating from the 1970s, conjoined with its twin: two boltholes amid chains of blocky, pebble-dashed terraces in the town's Papdale neighbourhood.

Now in her mid-fifties, Lindsay has lived in the little house for seventeen years. She's tended the garden, hung her pictures on the walls. But she has no great love for the place. It's cold and damp. Very cold. Very damp. Cold enough that she can't sleep. Damp enough that the clothes in her wardrobe turn green with mould. And it seems like nothing she does ever helps.

There are radiators. They work, and she puts them on. But the house doesn't seem to get any warmer. As the cold weather began to bite this winter, she monitored the temperature inside her house and says she found it to be hovering between 10°C and 12°C – a chilly ambient temperature well below the recommended domestic temperature range of 18°C to 21°C and low enough to present an inflamed ongoing risk of hypothermia, strokes and heart attacks.

Lindsay has a halogen heater, too, and keeps it plugged in when she's at home. But the heat it emits simply seems to beam out, glance off and disappear. She bought special insulating curtains, net curtains to line them with, a dehumidifier, a draught excluder for the outside door. Despite all this, her house is still cold. When she climbs into bed, she finds the sheets clammy and uncomfortable. When she opens her drawers, a thick odour of mildew rises from her clothes. The relentlessness of it is getting under her skin. It is making her feel quite mad.

Curtains, excluders, dehumidifiers – this is all money she can't afford to spend. And every minute, as those heaters exude their vanishing warmth, the bills are ticking up, up, up. Currently, she says, it costs her between £10 and £15 a day to heat the little house – or to not heat it, which is what it really feels like she's doing.

Lindsay suffers from chronic pain, one symptom of the
fibromyalgia that affects her ability to work, and the cold
exacerbates her condition. Recently, she told me, it's all got
too much. She's in crisis. Watching her money run out as she
sleeps under a duvet that is wet to the touch – it feels like
more than anyone should have to cope with. She's not sure
that she can any more.

When money is tight, all winters are bad winters. But at the
turn of 2022–23, after energy costs soared, more Britons than
ever were facing hard choices and cold beds as they struggled
to get by while wages stagnated and prices skyrocketed. From
December 2021 to December 2022, domestic gas prices increased by 129 per cent and electricity by 65 per cent, according to data from the UK government.[1] With some fanfare, Liz
Truss's short-lived regime offered a 'guarantee' that the energy
price cap – which that autumn hit £2,500 for the average
household bill – would not rise any further for households
for at least another two years.[2] But Rishi Sunak's replacement
administration soon rowed back on that, announcing that
bills might after all be allowed to rise by £500 in April 2023,
with the whole scheme up for review in early 2024[3] – all of
which left the likes of Lindsay to get through one difficult
winter with little idea about what help they will or won't be
entitled to in the winters that follow.

And those living in rural Scotland are under singular-
ly intense pressure. Because the price cap and associated

guarantees apply to unit cost, not the total bill, bills will often end up far higher than £2,500 in households requiring higher consumption to maintain a decent temperature. As early as June 2022, data from the website Compare the Market was registering that average annual energy bills in both Orkney and Shetland were already breaching that threshold and respectively running at a touch less and a touch more than double the old cap for an average-using household (£1,277) that had been set in October 2021.[4] And for any homes where the principal energy source is anything other than mains gas or electricity, nothing is capped or guaranteed. Nearly 90 per cent of homes in Na h-Eileanan Siar (also known as the Outer Hebrides) and 100 per cent of homes in Orkney and Shetland are not connected to the mains gas grid, forcing residents to use more expensive and uncapped options like bottled gas or domestic heating oil.[5]

In autumn 2022, Energy Action Scotland published an analysis that showed that residents of some Scottish council areas – Na h-Eileanan Siar, Shetland and Argyll & Bute – have seen bills rise to more than £4,000 a year.[6] A huge outgoing when you consider that the median Scottish household income is £27,716.[7] Partly these higher bills are a function of the harsher climate – those raging gales that blow in off the sea, battering the rooftops, soaking the streets and bringing a bitter windchill for days at a time. But partly, too, they are linked to a poorer standard of housing; rural houses are less likely to be well insulated, and improvements to their energy efficiency are often far more expensive to implement.

ISLANDS APART

The Isle of Lewis in the Outer Hebrides is a far cry from St Kitts, the Caribbean island where Dieter spent much of his life. Still, he likes it. Every morning he puts on his coat and drives his electric wheelchair into the garden to drink his coffee in the cold Atlantic air. He likes to listen to the wind whipping over the wide open landscape, to taste the salt on the air.

Dieter, who is in his fifties, lives with his partner Catherine in a roughcast bungalow in a crofting township on the northwest coast of Lewis. They have a small pond and a vegetable patch. Starlings click and splutter from the bushes. Over a period of months, Dieter has forged a friendship with a local herring gull and brings it out an offering of cat food in a bowl every day. Together, the couple have purchased hundreds of native trees for their five-acre croft, which Catherine has planted – watching the 'slow maturing of nature', as Dieter puts it, is a form of therapy to him.

Nature is a great consolation to Dieter, who has suffered from a painful and debilitating back condition since he was a boy – one that pushed him into painkiller addiction as a younger man and now confines him to the chair. This house in Lewis represents a welcome still point after years of tumult. Born in Ghana to a British father and a German mother, Dieter is a British citizen. But he spent much of his early life in the tropics, the family moving to Montserrat and then to St Kitts. The latter proved to be no tropical paradise for Dieter; his mother was diagnosed with terminal cancer while he was still at school, and he cared for her during the decline. Eventually, St Kitts also brought him divorce, alcoholism, breakdown, homelessness – all of which prompted him to take a leap of faith, make a brand-new start in a strange new country: Scotland.

In 2007, he flew to the UK with little but the bag on his back and spent some years living in a council house in Stornoway, where he met Catherine, now sixty-seven. Several years ago, she inherited the house they now live in from her son, who died prematurely, and now the couple get by on a combination of Dieter's disability benefits (Personal Independence Payment and Employment and Support Allowance) and her pension – although for a time administrative glitches relating to the onset of her pension left the couple almost penniless. Like many of their neighbours, Dieter and Catherine often struggle to pay their energy bills; a recent edition of the Gaelic-language news programme *Eòrpa* reported on claims that 'at least 80 per cent' of the islanders of Na h-Eileanan Siar would be in fuel poverty in winter 2022–23.[8]

Around eight years ago, government schemes allowed Dieter and Catherine to fix the ageing roof and install an oil heating system. However, this latter improvement has now left them – and their fellow islanders – more vulnerable to ballooning fuel costs. As of early 2023, the only support that Whitehall has made available expressly for households using 'alternative fuels like heating oil' is a flat one-off payment of £200.[9] But Dieter and Catherine have seen their heating costs more than double. 'When we used to [fill the tank] in the winter, it would cost around £190,' he tells me. That would last them only around three months. 'Now it's gone up – to £390, then to £420. And let's not talk about electricity [which is on top]. We were paying £90 per month, now that's gone up to £185. An immense increase.'

Dieter's not quite sure how they are going to get through the next few months. They have already been cutting back as much as they can, wearing three or four layers in the house to keep warm. It's hard, he says, when the weather is so wild and their house is so exposed. Unable to move around and get his heart pumping, it's especially tough to warm himself up through physical exertion. 'It doesn't matter how many clothes you put on. Your body is still working in an abnormal situation.' The effect, he says, is of a dimmer switch having been turned down; every day feels like an effort.

The past few years have already been so difficult that he has sometimes felt suicidal. Often, he says, he has felt himself to be in mortal combat with the state and its services over his medical care and benefits. Dieter and Catherine are getting by, making do – but only just. It's one thing to dress up in your outdoor gear to sit out and watch the birds for a few moments each morning; another thing entirely to do it to spend an evening in your own front room.

HOMESICK

Lindsay's and Dieter's experiences underline what the statistics tell us: cold homes are associated with both mental and physical illness. Long-term exposure to the cold increases the risk of respiratory and circulatory illnesses, as well as exacerbating the symptoms of chronic conditions like arthritis, diabetes and chronic obstructive pulmonary disease. One 2019 study of British adults linked lower indoor temperatures to high blood pressure,[10] which may partly explain why more people die of heart disease and strokes during winter months.

Meanwhile, issues of damp and mould, common in poorly insulated and cold homes, are associated with asthma and respiratory infections, especially in children. On the winter solstice in 2020, two-year-old Awaab Ishak died from breathing difficulties caused by prolonged exposure to mould in his family's Rochdale flat.[11] His death was described as a 'defining moment' for the housing sector by the coroner, whose 2022 inquest inspired much soul-searching.

Dr Ana Raquel Nunes, an assistant professor of public health at Warwick University, has studied the impact of extreme temperatures on vulnerable populations. She told me:

> Physiologically, the body will try to compensate for the cold. What happens is that the blood becomes thicker and that can cause clots. The clots can then cause heart attacks or strokes.
>
> That might not happen on the same day, or even the day after, but in the future. That's why the cold is different from the heat – because the effects of heat are felt closer to the time of a heatwave. The effects of the cold are more prolonged. People might start seeing the effects a few days or weeks after cold weather and might not even associate the symptoms with the cold.
>
> Cold also affects the ability of the body to fight infection. That increases the probability of common colds, flu and other diseases.

Then there are more indirect results of the cold – falls in the elderly, for example, which are both more likely in icy weather and more dangerous, if a person must wait for help outside or in cold rooms. There are knock-on effects on almost all aspects of hospital care, and especially so at the turn of 2022–23. Long waits for ambulances, in A&E and in the queues for planned hospital treatments were causing concern across the UK's various health services. Actuaries began to spot connections between delays and other failings within the NHS and a frightening spike in the general death rate.[12]

But when it comes to the bite of the cold and its consequences, certain segments of society are more vulnerable than others. Some groups are far more likely than others to be stuck in chilly homes by dint of poverty. More than 12 per cent of black people in the UK live in cold homes, for example – double the proportion of white British people.[13] And the elderly, disabled people and the very young are then also particularly susceptible to the physical effects.

Unheated houses also have insidious effects on mental health. The fear of being unable to keep your family warm is a major source of anxiety. Those in fuel poverty often limit socialising – either because they stop inviting people to their homes or simply because they go to bed early to keep warm under the blankets. The constant discomfort of living in a cold house can also be very wearing over time, bringing with it a sense of exhaustion or overwhelm. Parents, in particular, feel the strain: a recent study of Irish families found that adults with children under nine were more likely to be depressed if they were unable to keep their houses warm.[14]

Worse, when people's homes become cold, the danger of more severe mental distress significantly increases – the risk doubles among those who have not previously suffered mental health problems and triples for those who have previously suffered even minor symptoms.[15] Researchers from the Universities of Essex and Adelaide concluded, in measured but damning language, that the 'magnitude of cold housing in a country that benefits from a mild climate indicates indifference towards, or acceptance of, a significant minority of people living in inadequate conditions'.

This all rings true to Miranda, a woman in her early thirties who lives with a dog and a cat in a row of old farmworkers' cottages amid broad, flat arable fields near the Dornoch Firth, in the north-east Highlands. She lives with complex health problems, including the bowel condition Crohn's disease and the speech and processing issues that are the long-term consequence of a brush with life-threatening bacterial meningitis. As a result, she says, she has been 'medically retired' for some time and must rely on disability benefits. This has left her in dire financial straits.

Miranda's old stone cottage is only 'a small two-bedroom', which though well built, is not good for retaining warmth. 'It costs £15 a day to heat. I can't afford that.' Modestly proportioned as her home is, in an attempt to limit her energy bill, she has shut off 'half the house' and uses only one radiator. The cold, and the aches and anxiety that come with it, is 'definitely having an effect on my head', she says. She finds it difficult to think clearly. Sometimes the pressure she has felt under has been suffocating. Her cold house is a constant source of discomfort and worry. Her depression, she says, is 'horrific'. She just cannot see how she's going to get through the next year.

'There are multiple studies showing links between fuel poverty and poor mental health outcomes,' confirms Dr Laurence Wainwright of the University of Oxford, who has researched the impact of extreme weather events on psychiatric health. 'For those with an underlying depressive disorder, energy poverty – especially the associated financial strain and energy bill anxiety – can exacerbate symptoms and in some instances act as a trigger into relapse of a depressive phase.'

He draws my attention to a 2008 paper evaluating an English and Welsh scheme that helped house-owners insulate their homes; it found that householders who had 'great difficulty' paying their fuel bills were four times more likely to suffer anxiety or depression.[16] Those at most risk, Dr Wainwright adds, are those who suffer from a depressive disorder but who have never received a diagnosis or treatment. Those with underlying psychiatric disorders are also more likely to be admitted to hospital or die during periods of extreme cold. 'For those with conditions like major depressive disorder or bipolar disorder, periods of unusually cold weather can under some circumstances exacerbate and worsen symptoms.' There are a number of factors at play, he says – including the ability of the patient to heat their home, medication, the severity of their illness and their access to a support network.

Miranda's neighbours, she says, are a lot of help. Hers is one of five households living cheek-by-jowl in a traditional L-shaped terrace. Others chop her firewood for her, and Miranda's sister lives close at hand too – in a house on the same farm, a couple of minutes' walk away. So she has some support. Plus, it's peaceful and pretty out in this sea of cropland – but, being seven miles from the nearest small town, Tain, petrol prices are a worry too. Costs, costs, costs. Help or not, there's a lot for her to fret about. After a while it gets to you.

BLEAK MIDWINTER

Miranda's problems are, unfortunately, increasingly common. Research by the Joseph Rowntree Foundation found that nearly a third of low-income households – more than 3 million of them – were already unable to adequately heat their homes in the first half of 2022,[17] before the impact of the energy price crisis was fully felt.

If the problems are distinctly intense in the Highlands and Islands of Scotland, its people are also turning to one distinctive solution, which until recently seemed to be passing into history. Recent reports point to residents in the Western Isles, Caithness and Orkney reverting to traditional methods, cutting and drying peat to use as fuel over winter; neat stacks of drying peat bricks line up along the roadsides all through Lewis and Harris. In January 2023, the *Press and Journal*, the newspaper of the Highlands, carried an interview with Uist crofter Anne MacLellan, who had 'got peat on the fire just now' as she talked, despite having 'never heated her home with peat' in the past.[18] She felt a 'massive conflict' in light of the grim environmental consequences of disturbing and burning this carbon sink, which her scientist daughter had underlined to her. But the quarter of Anne's wage that was disappearing in energy bills each month was simply too much to bear. In the struggle to keep warm, her cousin Mary Margaret Rose, also on Uist, was another recent convert to peat.

Those in urban areas have different options and take different tactics – spending more time on public transport and in other public spaces where they are not on the hook for keeping warm. All over the country, churches and community centres have opted to open their doors to those in need of a warm place to go. St Margaret's Church on South Ronaldsay, Orkney, for example, announced in August 2022 that it would be opening every weekday to offer locals 'somewhere to go and read, knit, chat, play cards'. 'We have a refurbished building with ground source heating, which means it has a nice, comfortable, ambient temperature of 18°C,' explained the minister, Rev. Marjory MacLean. 'We are happy to help anyone who needs it.'[19]

The Warm Welcome Campaign maintains online listings of similar 'warm banks' across the UK.[20] There are more than

4,000 such hubs now open to the public for free – including synagogues, Salvation Army halls, pubs and arts centres – their proliferation attesting not only to a remarkable commitment, concern and generosity of spirit across civil society but also to the extent of the crisis we now face. For although those unable to work – whether due to age, health or caring responsibilities – are facing the most pressing concern over their ability to heat their homes, even those in full-time employment are not exempt.

Liam is a joiner and part-time gamekeeper who lives with his partner Rochelle and her teenage daughter in Dingwall, a market town around thirty minutes' drive from Inverness. After finally managing to get together a deposit after years of saving, they bought a house – which when we spoke they were on the cusp of moving into – just as the cost-of-living crisis came to bite.

He gets a good wage, he says. And Rochelle works too, in an outdoors shop, albeit on a zero-hours contract. But even so – Liam runs the figures in his head as we talk – almost a quarter of his salary goes on energy, which works out at around £350 a month. Until recently, in their rented house, they were able to avoid turning the heating on a lot of the time by burning offcuts he brought home from work in a wood-burning stove. In the new house, they won't have that option, so heating costs will rise even more. 'We'll grudge pushing that button.'

The gamekeeping offers him a bit of extra income. He has to fit it in around work – in the evenings, or most often on a Saturday. But it comes with the added bonus of birds that can be brought home for the pot – another helpful economy, now that even the grocery bill feels intimidatingly high. Liam and Rochelle feel fortunate, relatively speaking. Recently, his family banded together, chipping in to help his grandmother with her heating bill. He was pleased they could do that; he knows not everyone can.

But the couple are not immune from the pressure. And it's visible all around them, etched into the faces of their Highland neighbours. 'There's no spirit,' Liam says. 'Everything has gone. It's bleak. Very bleak. No one wants to enjoy themselves – there's no going down the pub for a couple of pints, or having drinks with the girls. People think: that's three days' heating.'

He and Rochelle are made of stoic stuff. They've been through hell and back, he says – both are previously divorced, and lost family members in upsetting circumstances. Money worries are nothing new. They've got a lot to deal with, but who doesn't? They talk about it, get it off their chests, figure out a plan. It's all anyone can do.

Such is the picture in homes all across the UK: couples sitting down to crisis talks; single parents checking their balance, turning down the heat. The black dog at the door. For many people, it is all too much to bear; one of my interviewees spoke to me from a psychiatric unit, following a mental breakdown.

At the time of writing, wholesale gas prices have finally begun to drop but remain five times higher than the historical average. There are no guarantees they will fall further. Exactly how they will translate into household bills during future winters is anyone's guess. For those with a nervous hand on the thermostat, there is no relief in sight.

'Too scared to write it all down': Phoebe in Greater Manchester

CHAPTER 4

PAY LATER? OF DEBT AND DREAD

JENNIFER WILLIAMS

A few weeks before Christmas 2022, half a dozen Mancunian mothers are gathered in a room above their local leisure centre, discussing money and fear. Everyone here, a mixture of women in their twenties and thirties from a range of ethnic backgrounds, is living hand to mouth, nervous to confront the disconnect between their incomes and outgoings.

'I'm too scared to write it all down,' admits mum-of-two Phoebe Cross of her assorted debts, to nods of recognition from the semicircle of other young women. Phoebe is not in the semicircle itself but sitting at the front. As a community support worker at Visit from the Stork, she helps to convene these sessions in the deprived north Manchester neighbourhood of Harpurhey, in which women gather weekly to share their experiences, to vent and to listen to each other. But she is living hand to mouth as well.

'I have cold showers,' Phoebe says. It is 3°C outside. 'I tell myself it's for my mental health, but it's because I don't want to put the hot water tank on.' When Phoebe first contacts me in response to a social media post seeking experiences of household debt, the stories she tells seamlessly blend bleak anecdotes of clients battling energy arrears with a candid picture of her own struggles. Those cold showers are the result of trying to save on heating, keep on top of her payments and thereby avoid being saddled with one of the dreaded prepayment meters that plague her clients – devices which were installed in an estimated 600,000 households during 2022.[1]

Within a couple of months of our conversation, such meters briefly became headline national news, amid revelations about energy companies breaking into vulnerable customers' homes to install them.[2] The devices epitomise the whole cost-of-living crisis, functioning as both the response to and a perpetuator of poverty – and a phenomenon intricately bound up with debt. At least until they became a scandal in 2023, energy companies enjoyed terrific latitude to forcibly install them on anyone who fell behind on their energy bills. And if you started out with a traditional rather than a smart meter (which can be flipped remotely), Citizens Advice warned that you may 'be charged up to £150' for the privilege.[3] Worse, once stuck with a prepayment device, a family not only pays a higher tariff but also faces immediate deductions for existing arrears on whatever credit they can afford to top up. 'The utility debts for my casework clients are insane – they are all on prepayment meters,' Phoebe had told me a few days after our first chat in December 2022. 'Yesterday I spoke to one woman who said they take off 25p [in debt repayment] for every £1 she puts on the meter. People are just not able to get out of gas and electric debt because it's now just basically getting worse and worse. They're just digging deeper.'

Sure enough, one such woman is sitting in the Harpurhey support session the following week. 'I put £95 on, on Tuesday, and thirty-odd quid has gone out in debt,' says Caroline* of her energy meter. With shades of Phoebe, the indebted debt support convener, Caroline is a trained childcare worker who says it isn't worth her being in employment due to the cost of childcare. She has done the maths, she adds, and prostitution would be the only line of work that would cover her family's costs, a remark that generates no shock in the room.

In times gone by, when utilities became unaffordable, the story might have gone 'bill – arrears – final "red" bill – disconnection'. But these days disconnection is superfluous, because after the forced move to prepay you can simply run out. It is what charities refer to as 'self-disconnection', a trend raised as a concern by MPs just before Christmas 2022.[4] By that winter, it was happening remorselessly. Noticing an astonishing rise in the numbers turning to Citizens Advice who couldn't afford

---

* Some names have been changed.

to top up their meters – during 2022 it saw more such people than 'in the whole of the last ten years combined' – the organisation commissioned a large survey, which suggested that 'more than 3 million' Britons, 'or one person every ten seconds', had been 'disconnected at least once in the past year because they could not afford to top up'.[5] Closer to Harpurhey, an autumn 2022 survey by the Greater Manchester Combined Authority, carried out before the winter really began to bite, found that the proportion of respondents on prepayment meters in the region had risen by a third (from 17 to 23 per cent) in a single year.[6]

As a forced move, the switch to prepay was always meant to be controlled by legal process. But, as the *i* newspaper reported a couple of days before I visited the Harpurhey support group, this may not count for much. Journalist Dean Kirby spent weeks trying to pin down one of the court hearings during which such installations were signed off. When he did find one in Wigan, twenty miles from Harpurhey, it took just three minutes for magistrates to issue nearly 500 warrants.[7] A few weeks later, on the basis of a freedom of information request, he reported that magistrates across the country had refused just seventy-two out of more than half a million of the 'utility warrant applications' used to force entry into homes and businesses.[8] Not long after that we got the sudden explosion of interest in this previously entirely neglected topic, with noisy condemnation (though not mandatory action) from minister Grant Shapps, warnings from the regulator, a succession of promises to do better from the energy companies themselves and – perhaps most consequentially – an order from the senior presiding judge in England and Wales to magistrates to stop issuing the warrants for forcible entry.[9] But with so much in flux it is hard to know what rights indebted customers will truly have when the dust settles, especially since so many people are on smart meters which can be switched to prepay without any need to enter the home.

More to the point, there is the question of all those millions of often hard-up homes that already have prepay meters, devices that are aggravating an emergency in Harpurhey and beyond. Even in June 2022, months before the nights began to draw in, I interviewed a mother of three who illustrated the impossible dilemmas facing so many of the human beings on the wrong end of all these trends.[10] As she struggled to top up her prepay, Leah Shields, a 38-year-old former hairdresser in County Durham who is unable to work due to osteoporosis, was having to choose whether to charge her electric wheelchair or feed her kids. 'Some days I'm having to sit and think: well, we need the electricity because we have two small children,' she told me. 'When it comes to powering my power chair, I have to decide if it's worth charging it, or do I save the electricity for my kids, so it doesn't go off?' Leah made her choice, which she felt was no choice at all, and so ended up under what was, in effect, economic house arrest.

NORTHERN EXPOSURE

I had been put in touch with Leah by the Bread and Butter Thing, a 'food pantry' that operates centres across the north of England from Warrington to North Tyneside, including in half the boroughs in Greater Manchester. The charity regularly tracks closely how the cost-of-living crisis is hitting its clients, including through borrowing, of which utility debt is only the start. Among more than 6,000 people using the Bread and Butter Thing's services in autumn 2022, getting on for two thirds (62 per cent) had borrowed more than in the same month a year earlier. Overwhelming majorities reported finding their main household bills at least 'somewhat difficult', and a non-trivial 8 per cent reported that they were actually 'already behind' on their rent or mortgage, as did 15 per cent in respect of their energy bills.[11]

What makes the speed at which the charity's clients are sinking into debt so striking is the fact that, as its partnerships director Jane Partington stresses, these are generally *not* the people in immediate crisis. This isn't a food bank: to use a food pantry people have to have enough money to pay the small amount it charges for a bag of mixed groceries, comprising produce gathered from donations via supermarkets and other local businesses. Clients also need a kitchen, since much of the food is fresh or needs cooking, which rules out many destitute people. Those queuing up at the pantry are generally their family's 'feeders', Partington says; 80 per cent of them are women and they tend to have children or other caring responsibilities. 'They have some income. But it's really, really tight. And they are the people who are, in Theresa May's words, "just about managing" – or they were.' The numbers – and the reality – that Partington is seeing paint a darker picture than suggested by the nationwide data from the Office for National Statistics (ONS) covering a similar period, which found that just 23 per cent of people were borrowing more than at the same time the previous year.[12] 'The figures that get put out nationally', Partington says, 'don't reflect what we are seeing and the people that we deal with. What we're seeing is that every time a headline number comes out, we're going… "no".'

The link between scraping by and indebtedness isn't new, of course. But since the pandemic, the connection has been getting tighter. During lockdown, much of Middle England suddenly found itself saving on meals out and holidays, while many with more precarious lives experienced disrupted incomes. Crunching data from personal budgeting app the Money Dashboard during the first Covid wave, the Institute for Fiscal Studies discovered that poorer families had witnessed 'a £170 per month decline in their saving (or increase in their debt) relative to normal', whereas those in the middle-income bracket had saved more (or repaid debt) to a very similar extent.[13] The skewing of indebtedness towards the lower end did not end with lockdown – quite the reverse. As of new year 2023, the Resolution Foundation stated that the share of poorer workers reporting rising indebtedness (20 per cent) was nearly twice as high as among the wider population (11 per cent). Most frightening of all was the foundation's finding that this rising indebtedness is due not to some passing emergency, one-off outlays or other special circumstance but rather to 'rises in the price of essentials [that] are making some families' budgets unsustainable'.[14]

Cost-of-living pressures are, Partington says, widening the divergence between the Bread and Butter Thing's food pantry clientele and more prosperous families. The official inflation figure when we were speaking in autumn 2022 may have been running at 10 or 11 per cent, 'but if you ask the people we deal with, they're saying costs have gone up 30 per cent'. She says prices are – and long have been – rising faster 'if you disproportionately spend your money on fuel and food and if you have very limited access to good food locally'. Dr Nicola Headlam, formerly the head of the Theresa May government's Northern Powerhouse unit and now chief economist at Manchester-based Red Flag Alert, a consultancy that monitors business solvency trends, lends support to this claim. 'The basics and things that are cheaper are inflating faster and harder,' she says, noting that this trend long predates the current cost-of-living emergency: Asda's basic range of marmalade has gone up from 9p to 54p, or 500 per cent, in the past decade, she says. After the food campaigner Jack Monroe highlighted steep rises in many other basic groceries in 2022, the Office for National Statistics began producing an experimental price tracker for lowest-cost grocery items, which, as of September that year, were up by 17 per cent over twelve months.[15]

To the extent that essentials have been going up faster than general inflation, the cost of living will also vary geographically – pressing harder in places where basics loom largest in the budget. Analysis in summer 2022 by the Centre for Cities think tank found inflation running two percentage points higher in the northern towns of Burnley, Blackpool and Blackburn than in Cambridge or London, for precisely this reason – which means the squeeze is tighter in the post-industrial economies that formed the backdrop to Boris Johnson's 'levelling up' 2019 election slogan.[16]

The same disparities map straight across to debt. The think tank Demos recently mapped the blackspots by overlaying two indices – its own Good Credit Index, which measures local accessibility of credit, and the Financial Vulnerability Index produced by credit management company Lowell – to 'identify the places most prone to the toxic combination of a desperate need for affordable credit, and the absence of it'.[17] Again, Blackpool is right up there, ranking second in the 'credit desert' league, only Middlesbrough faring worse. All bar one of the top twenty – Newham, in London – are in the north or the Midlands, including the Greater Manchester boroughs of Oldham, Manchester, Rochdale and Salford. 'We are in the midst of a private debt crisis – one that preceded the Covid pandemic and has only been worsened by it,' concluded Demos, adding that 'a problem of this magnitude will only continue to grow if ignored'.

Certainly, when asked about the outlook for her clients in places like Harpurhey, debt support worker Phoebe Cross finds it hard to imagine it brightening any time soon. 'I cannot see how there is any way out for people without a serious overhaul of the benefits system, wages and energy rates,' she says. But these are improvements that she doesn't judge likely because 'the people with all the money do not care about the rest of us'.

THE FEAR FACTOR

To borrow from Franklin D. Roosevelt, one big thing to fear with this drift towards indebtedness is fear itself. Of the nearly two thirds of Bread and Butter Thing users who said they were borrowing more in September 2022 than the year before, almost all (97 per cent) also said that the rise in living costs had affected their mental health.[18] Survey responses included phrases such as 'I can't see an end to it'. The issue is not always or even usually, as Jane Partington is at pains to stress, an immediate descent into crisis – just as often 'it's worry'. She says of her paying pantry clients, 'These are not the people who live their lives constantly in debt, without thought.' Instead, it's the idea that they could now lose control and end up there that terrifies them: 'That's the story. That's what's getting to people.'

As a charity worker herself, Phoebe is among these pantry clients. When I meet her again a few days after the Harpurhey drop-in, this time at a support group in Salford, I ask her more about the bills that she is herself too scared to write down. It soon transpires that there is a burgeoning industry that is more than happy to think energetically about the problems she would rather put out of mind.

Phoebe explains that she has paid for some of the costs of Christmas through 'buy now, pay later' (BNPL) credit, an innovation in online lending that has taken off globally since 2019, facilitated by the rapid shift towards internet shopping in what has – until very recently – been an environment of exceptionally easy money. New lenders have sprung up at the checkouts of online brands, offering to split payments for products into several instalments at 0 per cent credit: free, short-term borrowing, funded by the lender taking a cut from the retailer. Its great appeal to shoppers – and its great danger – is that it is exceptionally easy to use.

The original – and best-known – purveyor of BNPL loans, prominently advertised by retailers like H&M, is Klarna, a Swedish fintech giant. (There is no interest or charge as such, but should you miss payments, its terms and conditions explain, that fact may be passed on to credit reference agencies, affecting your ability to borrow in future, and an 'external debt collection agency' may be engaged to chase the money.)[19] Dr Headlam compares the loans and the companies peddling them to a friend egging you on to buy that dress. 'They're with you in the changing room talking you into the thing you can't afford,' she says. 'Debt is very emotional and it feels very female, like catalogues.' But the loans are in no way restricted to fashion: Klarna announced, for example, that it was part-nering with Deliveroo in autumn 2022. You can now use it to buy anything from luxury makeup brands to a vindaloo. Just one click, and shoppers are in debt.

Klarna does, however, do a soft credit check, and Phoebe doesn't have a good enough rating for that. But there are others. Many others. 'I have PayPal Credit, PayPal "Pay in 3" and Clearpay,' Phoebe says. It is hard to keep track of the amounts owed on PayPal, she admits, although other lenders are easier to manage. Then there is another one called Tymit, which – when we speak in December – she is holding in re-serve to potentially cover Christmas food.

> It's like an online bank, but it's almost like instant credit. I did it with my friend last weekend because she was like, 'I can't afford Christmas,' so I said, 'See if you can get Tymit.' She'd never had a credit card or a loan or anything. She was instant-ly given £1,500. You can pay it off 0 per cent over three months or the fee goes up.

She appreciates the irony that she is advising on debt while also weighing up such options to make ends meet herself – although, equally, this ensures that she is well placed to understand the situations of her clients. Immediately after we had left the Harpurhey session just days earlier, someone had also told her about another lender – Zilch. 'I had £760 available to spend immediately. And I've got really bad credit.'

Just how new and worrying is all this? Klarna's founder and CEO Sebastian Siemiatkowski has reasonably argued that 0 per cent credit is a vastly better option than credit cards, which are also accepted by Deliveroo and everyone else. But amid concerns about the way this kind of lending is being carried out, the Financial Conduct Authority is gradually moving towards tightening up regulation of the sector. And Martin Lewis, the prominent consumer finance campaigner, criticised the Klarna–Deliveroo link-up, warning that BNPL might seem 'innocuous' but was ultimately still debt which was yet to be regulated. 'Borrowing should only be if NEEDED, for planned one off budgeted purchase, not a cheeky Nandos,' he tweeted.

But if some are concerned about BNPL being offered for discretionary spending, others worry – and increasingly so – about its use for essential purchases. Sue Anderson, of the national debt advice service StepChange, warns just how deeply such loans are now working their way into day-to-day life. She points to research, both by her own charity and by consumer magazine *Which?*, 'that does tend to support the idea that people who are struggling financially seem to be more likely to use BNPL'. She adds, 'And so that rings a warning bell, because instead of just being used for discretionary purchases,' like the fashion treat it was typically advertised for at first, 'now we're seeing it beginning to be marketed and promoted against cost-of-living essentials, even groceries, this sort of thing.' This doesn't sound encouraging. In the US, economists have for some time highlighted the role of credit as a prop supporting an economy with too many inadequate incomes – a prop that eventually collapsed in the financial crisis.[20]

Indeed, StepChange's annual survey showed that 40 per cent of those Britons planning to borrow for Christmas 2022 were – like Phoebe – intending to use BNPL loans, up sharply from 27 per cent the previous year.[21] Problem cases are emerging 'in line with' the overall 'growth in the market, and that does worry us', Anderson says. StepChange first noticed clients presenting with BNPL debt 'a couple of years ago' and it began to 'rack up' from there. A separate survey released by the financial education charity Centre for Financial Capability in early 2023 confirmed a recent surge in demand for BNPL products – and also a rise in people being charged late fees.[22] These aren't the only ways in which people can end up paying for lending touted as 'free'. When people can't keep up the payments, they might move the debt into other interest-charging forms, such as credit cards, which recent Bank of England data has suggested are being relied upon increasingly heavily.[23]

Those who come forward to StepChange with BNPL debts, Anderson reports, 'might be presenting with a fair number of them that may or may not be with the same providers', and they then struggle to keep a grip on what is owed to whom when. Phoebe's experience is consistent with all of this. 'It's hard to keep track of what's going out,' she says, since some lenders might take payments on a fortnightly basis, and others on a different schedule that 'might not be in line with your income'.

But it's no longer only those, like Phoebe, at the sharp end who are now getting frightened about how this is all going to end. As interest rates have started to rise internationally at the very same time as squeezed family budgets are increasing the risk of consumer default, questions have begun to loom over the BNPL market's business model. During a summer 2022 funding round, Klarna's valuation dropped from $46 billion the previous year to under $7 billion.[24] If a reckoning is already under way, that could well be because in the end, as Claer Barrett, consumer editor at the *Financial Times*, sums things up, 'Borrowing money isn't a solution for not having enough money.'

INTO THE SHADOWS...

Whatever the issues with 'buy now, pay later', there are far more insidious – and illegal – types of lending out there.

Loan sharking has been on the rise not just during this latest cost-of-living emergency but throughout the underlying one that has seen wages stagnate since the financial crash of 2008, according to the 'Swimming with Sharks' report, published by the Centre for Social Justice (CSJ) in February 2022.[25] The study, underpinned by Opinium polling, put the number of loan shark victims across England at more than a million – more than three times as many as had been suggested by government-sponsored estimates from back in 2010.[26] And, like BNPL credit, illegal borrowing is increasingly being used to buy essentials. Except this credit is in no sense free.

'We're seeing people saying they're borrowing for food and fuel – and that's new for us,' says Cath Williams, liaise manager at the Birmingham-based England Illegal Money Lending Team, which leads on loan shark investigations and prosecutions and carries out regular surveys of victims. 'Before, it was much more one-offs, so things like school uniforms, white goods, the car that's broken down. What we're seeing much more this year is food and fuel, food and fuel, food and fuel.'

The north-west, and Manchester in particular, has the highest number of prosecuted loan shark cases in the country, though Cath says that is in large part due to the proactive nature of Greater Manchester Police, who consistently pass on intelligence. These days the lenders are rarely Phil Mitchell types coming round with a baseball bat, she says. They have been moving online, a trend that was turbocharged by the lockdowns of 2020 onwards, using Instagram, Snapchat, WhatsApp, Facebook Marketplace and Reddit boards to target their victims, often using public 'outing' or humiliation as the equivalent of a punishment beating. The potential personal effects can be devastating where, for example, a social media message tells someone's partner about a debt they had previously kept hidden.

The CSJ highlights particular concerns raised by the Wales Illegal Money Lending Unit about social media channels, echoing Cath's observation. 'Borrowers often request loans for basic necessities, such as food, electricity, and gas, and requests are frequently associated with an explanation of the financial hardship that victims are facing,' summarises the CSJ, recommending that the government legislate to hold social media companies responsible for illegal lenders operating on their platforms. 'One lender in Doncaster ... used Snapchat to threaten victims by showing his location as near their house. One victim was sent a picture of a house and vehicle by the lender in an attempt to intimidate them. The lender believed them to belong to the victim's mother.'[27] But it's not all about broadcasting information online. Loan sharks also use 'family and friend' networks to target their victims, says Cath, subtly working out when people might be vulnerable to an offer of cash.

Just outside Greater Manchester, in Cheshire, Kelly* fell

---

* Some names have been changed.

into the clutches of a loan shark in exactly this way, not due to extravagance or any particular emergency but simply because a relative of a friend overheard her talking about the kids wanting snacks. 'There was food in the house, in the fridge and the freezer,' she recalls, but the kids would pester for more 'biscuits, crisps and sausage rolls' when money was pretty tight. 'And it just basically came around like that, because [the loan shark] knew.'

Initially, the woman just lent her £30 because she had forgotten to pay her Sky bill. Kelly then got a text saying 'there was always money there, I could borrow it, any time I wanted' but at a minimum of £100. So she did. 'But when it came to paying that back, I had to borrow again because I was left short. I did borrow off her over a number of times, but it was never large amounts, it was always £100 or just over.'

Between 2019 and November 2021, Kelly borrowed £2,500 in small loans. The loan shark always made sure her debt was prioritised, implying that the people behind her were dangerous, so Kelly fell behind on her rent, TV licence, water, 'everything' – even council tax, for which non-payment can spell jail. She would lie to other creditors, telling them she was a bit short because one of her kids had had to go on a trip. The woman knew what day Kelly was paid and what day she got her benefits. 'She used to take the majority of my Child Benefit, £1,600 off my Universal Credit and then when I was working, she was taking £900 off my wages,' says Kelly.

By the time a friend persuaded her to tell her social land-lord, who in turn contacted Cath's team, Kelly owed £26,000 – more than ten times what she had cumulatively borrowed over a mere couple of years. These sorts of loans aren't usual-ly discussed in terms of annual interest rates; the borrowing gets rolled over too often and too rapidly for a twelve-month frame of reference to make much sense. Instead, lenders might be offered terms of 'double bubble', where you borrow £100 and have to pay back £200 after some brief spell. Kelly's case highlights the explosive exponential logic at work. A lot would depend on the precise profile of the borrowing, but – for illustration – imagine that she had borrowed the whole lot a full year before the borrowing stopped; it would be equiv-alent to an interest rate of somewhere north of 900 per cent. This during a period of borrowing when the official base rate at the Bank of England was mostly at its historic low of 0.1 per cent. And beyond Kelly's financial ruin, the effect was to render her a prisoner in her own home, fearful of going out in case she ran into those she owed.

Phoebe Cross's colleague Nicola Leonard has worked with vulnerable women in Manchester and Salford for years. She tells a story of a mother of six in Little Hulton, Salford, that illustrates why it can be so hard to help people in such situ-ations. She recalls that when any of the services that might ordinarily want to look at the woman's finances, perhaps with a view to helping her get them in order, approached her, she simply couldn't produce her bank statements, because of what they would show. Namely, that

> every month £600 comes out straight to the loan shark at the door. At no point does she want me to negotiate with him [the shark] because it's her lifeline. But this cretin knocks on her door all times of the day. She hasn't got a record of what she's giving him. He threatens her children. It's almost like Stockholm syndrome; she feels that she needs this person. And it takes months for [such women] to be open enough with you to tell [you about] that situation.

Again, fear and shame are the key themes. The CSJ refers to Britain as a 'nation of money secrets'. The 'emergent cost-of-living crisis casts a looming shadow of financial anxiety', it says, recommending subsidised savings schemes and expanded and 'revolutionised' mutual credit unions, offering low-cost loans to people who truly need them. Without action, the right-leaning think tank warned just before the first big rise in the energy price cap in spring 2022, 'the combination of pressures on household budgets, low financial resilience and increasingly limited credit options is liable to create a perfect storm in which people are driven towards exploitation'.[28] Those fears are echoed by every charity spoken to for this chapter – indeed, they were already coming to pass.

Christmas is traditionally the period when people bury their heads in the sand, possibly coming up for air in the new year, when the bills appear. But as 2022 drew to a close, Rachel Howley, director of Greater Manchester's Citizens Advice, was already worried. Since the previous summer, she had already seen the number of people seeking help with energy disconnections 'go through the roof'. Some problems are familiar. Council tax arrears remain the most common source of debt problems, and that bill was due to go up again in spring 2023, after the government gave local authorities, long on their knees financially, permission to hike it by 5 per cent.

But Howley is also seeing the profile of people coming for help change. 'I think what we're seeing is just people who've never been in this situation before,' she says.

> People who you might think are on decent wages, middle incomes, who have just never missed mortgage payments or not been able to pay their credit cards. So it's getting support to people who are new to debt. But on the flip side, we're also seeing a big increase in people who are kind of repeat clients, who are coming back to us.

In other words, debt is not only deeper but wider as well.

Nationally, only 1 per cent of people told the ONS in December 2022 that they were behind with their mortgage payments, while 7 per cent were behind on their rent.[29] The mortgage arrears have not quite started coming through yet, agreed Howley, speaking the same month, but added that before long – as the big squeeze is intensified as rising borrowing rates begin to trickle through – 'we are expecting people to start defaulting'. And she echoes several Citizens Advice workers and volunteers I have spoken to in other areas, who say they are running out of ways to help people, a situation she finds 'heartbreaking'. Even back in the summer of 2022, before things got as bad as they would in the winter, a debt adviser in North Shields told me he was 'used to having the answers' but that trying to help people whose income simply did not match their basic needs was like 'trying to empty out a boat that's got a hole in it'. Summing up the nationwide situation in 2022, Citizens Advice said it had 'never seen a higher proportion of people in a negative budget' – in other words, they had more going out than coming in.

Back in Harpurhey, only one of the women at Phoebe and Nicola's support group writes down her incomings and outgoings. She explains why she has to do so: her partner is self-employed, so the household income is changeable. Even so, she says, doing so 'makes me feel sick. I get paid on Monday and it's gone on Friday.' Everyone else in the room prefers not to know.

'These mums live day to day in the headlights, like scared rabbits,' says Nicola. 'They have no time to sit and reflect on trauma – they have no time to sit back and look at what's affected them in their lives, because they're living hand to mouth, day to day.' It's why the group sessions are so important, says Phoebe. 'There is a need for people to talk,' she says. 'But me and Nic are those people as well.'

'Sixteen tablets in the morning, four at night': Kevin from Glasgow

CHAPTER 5

A WINDOW ON FRAILTY:
FROM DEPRIVATION
TO DISEASE

DANI GARAVELLI

'I'm a survivor,' says David, as he sways to the strains of a Scottish air drifting on the summer breeze. 'I've been surviving all my life.' The self-declared pagan is sitting in the Growchapel Community Allotment Gardens on their first open day. His bucket hat chimes with the festival vibes of the impromptu ceilidh band, but the tired eyes peering out from under it betray a vulnerability at odds with the bravado.

The allotment gardens have sprouted like cress from a patch of derelict land in Drumchapel, one of Glasgow's sprawling estates. If you want to see how deprivation translates into disease and lives cut short, Drumchapel is an ideal place to go: a community where, in the twenty-first century, death typically strikes men well short of the 'threescore years and ten' benchmark of the Old Testament. One of four large peripheral estates built in the post-war years to house those displaced during the slum clearances, it was supposed to be a haven; but it lacked amenities, transport and community cohesion. One of Glasgow's best-loved sons, Billy Connolly, called it a 'desert wi' windaes'. Today, it offers a particularly frightening window on the very real challenge of surviving in so much of poorer Britain and Scotland.

Nonetheless, the allotment truly is a small green haven, sandwiched between two streets of low-rise houses, and flanked at either end by multi-storeys. Like many of those who come here, David, fifty-three, suffers from anxiety, which is intricately and increasingly bound up with his economic and physical condition. For decades, he developed strategies to deal with that anxiety, working nights as a security guard to avoid having to socialise, and heading out into the hills at weekends. 'When an alarm went off, I'd be sent to check for burglars or a fire,' he says. 'It could be dangerous, but it kept me busy.' In 2017, however, those strategies were ripped from him. One day he fell and broke his hip; arthritis took hold and he became housebound. He was still on the waiting list for a hip replacement when Covid struck.

David's mother died years ago from cancer at the age of fifty-seven, his father soon after 'of a broken heart'. He lives alone and spent most of lockdown playing his favourite computer game. 'I didn't have to shield, but I couldn't go to the supermarket and stand in a queue and then get myself home again,' he says. 'I was so isolated I forgot how to interact with people.' Though he finally got his new hip last year, David has never seen a physiotherapist. His left leg is an inch and a half shorter than his right and he is in constant pain. To make matters worse, on his last day in hospital after his hip operation, he collapsed with a seizure and was diagnosed with epilepsy. 'I used to be super-fit, which makes the loss of mobility harder to bear,' he says. 'Today, it was an ordeal just to walk the half-mile from the shopping centre to the garden.'

All his working life, David prided himself on staying 'off-grid'. 'I never claimed anything and I wasn't on any government list,' he says. Now he receives benefits and has to report to the Jobcentre under threat of sanction. With the price of food rising, he often goes hungry. 'I only eat one meal a day, and at least one day a week that meal will be cereal,' he says.

Going to the allotment helps keep despair at bay. The plot he uses belongs to so-called community links practitioners at Drumchapel Health Centre, all-purpose fixers who lighten GPs' loads by tackling the social issues affecting their patients' health. They run a weekly group here. For David, it's not the same as being out on the hills, but it lifts his mood. 'I like getting my hands dirty,' he says. The plot has yielded potatoes and a box of herbs. Earlier that day, someone spotted the first strawberries: red, but not yet ripe.

It's 3 p.m. The musicians – two fiddlers and an accordionist

– are packing up their instruments. 'Let's go and join the others,' I say. 'I think they are planning to replant the sunflowers.'

'Yes, let's,' he replies. 'We could all do with sunflowers in our lives.'

NO CITY FOR OLD MEN

In 2022, the experts at the Glasgow Centre for Population Health (GCPH) accompanied a chunky new report interrogating some worrying trends in Scottish and wider UK life expectancy with a short animation summing up the big picture.[1] Since the 1800s, it said, the figures had gone up and up, stalling only briefly, in times of crisis, such as the two world wars and the Spanish flu pandemic of 1918–20. But in 2012, longevity plateaued in the UK, while continuing to extend in many other countries.

The flatlining chart was depressing enough; but it masked an even bleaker reality. A close analysis of the seeming stasis revealed life expectancy in the most affluent areas was continuing to rise, albeit at a slower rate than before, while in the most deprived areas it was actually falling outright. In the poorer communities, people are being 'swept up', the GCPH warned, 'by a rising tide of poverty. They're dragged under by decreased income, poor housing, poor nutrition, poor health and social isolation.' And all of this had recently translated into far higher Covid infection and death rates in communities where people could not afford to shield.

Nowhere are the maladies that the Glasgow centre highlights more visible than within Glasgow itself. A post-industrial city, whose once-thrumming shipyards long ago fell into decline, it is pockmarked with areas of multiple deprivation where money is short, multiple overlaying illnesses – or comorbidities – are rife and the future is bleak. The same could be said of other post-industrial cities, of course. But Glasgow has excess levels of mortality and poor health *even after* its economic problems are taken into account. In other words, its population is less healthy than the populations of Liverpool or Manchester, which also suffered the loss of their heavy industries.

This so-called Glasgow effect is visible in almost every set of health statistics, not least life expectancy. According to the National Records of Scotland, across Glasgow as a whole, between 2018 and 2020, the figures stood at 78.3 years for women and 73.1 years for men: that is, respectively, four and a half and six years less than the UK national average.[2] As for *healthy* life expectancy – defined as the number of years in which people feel themselves to be living in good health – for men in Glasgow city, the Office for National Statistics (ONS) reported it to stand at 54.6 years in the run-up to the pandemic. This was not only eight years below the UK average (62.9) but also significantly lower than the figures for Manchester

(58.6) and Liverpool (59.5). Across the whole of the British mainland, the only local authority to fare marginally worse on this particular metric was the washed-up coastal economy of Blackpool.[3]

The relative position of Glaswegian women was not much better, with their healthy-life expectancy of 57.6 years against a UK average of 63.3[4] – and for Scottish women as a whole, this measure, which has merely stagnated in the rest of the UK, has recently been in freefall.[5] Even within the context of an increasingly sickly Scotland in which it looms so large, Glasgow still stubbornly stands out. Across the city, one in four men will die before his sixty-fifth birthday.

You need to drill deeper again, and explore the disparities *within* the city, to find the most chilling variations of all. In 2021, a GCPH report, 'Health in a Changing City', found that in 2017–19, the men in the most deprived 10 per cent of Glasgow zones could expect to die 15.4 years earlier than those in its wealthiest communities, a gap that had widened from 12.4 years in 2000–02.[6] For women, the same gap rose from 8.6 to 11.6 years over the same period.[7] Getting still more specific, and looking at named individual neighbourhoods, the report revealed a 17.6-year gap between the highest male life expectancy in Pollokshields West (83.0 years) and the lowest in Greater Govan (65.4 years).[8]

As for Drumchapel, it ranks third from the bottom on this morbid league table of male deaths, with lives only two years longer than in Govan.[9] Amid its tower blocks and modern tenements, conditions have often been little better than in the old slums the original residents left behind. With houses built not of brick but of porous Wilson block, damp spreads. 'We had the highest level of child asthma on earth,' David, who moved to Drumchapel in the 1980s, told me. 'I remember the dysentery outbreak in the early '90s, too, with sewage flowing down the street.'

What throws Drumchapel's disadvantage into sharper relief is its proximity to prosperous Bearsden. Just a few hundred feet separate the two; yet moving from one to the other is like swapping Kansas for Oz. A walk along Drumchapel's main shopping street is a grim pilgrimage past betting shops, pharmacies, a solicitor's office, a vaping shop, a One O One convenience store (with off-licence), a Jobcentre and a range of takeaways selling pizzas, chips and kebabs. Middle-aged men in jackets and caps, their faces hardened by poverty, smoke in the rain outside the Butty Bar. Young men in tracksuits smoke in the rain outside Greggs.

At the tree-studded junction of Roman Road and Drymen Road in Bearsden, by contrast, I count no fewer than seven cafes and restaurants, all with pretty names like Grace & Favour. They nestle in beside a florist's, a craft butcher's, a Paul Smith clothes shop and an estate agent advertising at least one property close to £1 million. Even Bearsden's takeaways are luxurious. The Scallop's Tale sells moules marinière at £16.95; Dining In With Mother India, king prawn curry for £24.99 per kg.

Way back in 1995, when Glasgow's deindustrialisation was already well advanced, in the wake of a BBC documentary, the then shadow Secretary for Social Security Donald Dewar, whose constituency included Drumchapel, told the House of Commons:

Most Members of Parliament recognise the link between deprivation and health … Between 1981 and 1991, male mortality between the ages of fifteen and forty-six rose by 9 per cent in Drumchapel; in Bearsden, it fell by 14 per cent … Young men in Drumchapel are twice as likely to die as those living in an affluent and leafy suburb. They are 75 per cent more at risk during major surgery. This may not be a pleasant subject, but it is a fact that for a person living in a poor area such as Drumchapel who requires a bowel operation, the chances of developing complications and dying are 50 per cent higher than those of a person living in the neighbouring affluent area.

All true, but a generation on we might have hoped to have made some progress in closing this chasm. Instead, the statistics suggest, we are doing precisely the reverse.

PLUGGING THE DEEP END

Before meeting David at the allotment, I spend a morning shadowing Lorna Robertson, one of those links practitioners at Drumchapel Health Centre, a few hours that demonstrate all too clearly the myriad ways poverty has of getting under the skin. All the GP surgeries at the health centre are 'Deep End' practices – the term used for the 100 practices serving the most deprived areas in Scotland, whose expertise is pooled in the hope of tackling health inequalities through the Deep End Project at Glasgow University. Eighty-six of those 100 practices are in Glasgow.

One of the biggest challenges of such practices is the 'inverse care law': the principle that there is an inverse relationship between the availability of healthcare and the populations that most require it. Patients who attend Deep End practices tend to be suffering from a combination of conditions: diabetes, chronic obstructive pulmonary disease (COPD – that is, lung disease, which doctors overwhelmingly blame on smoking), asthma, high blood pressure, heart problems, strokes, along with depression and addiction.

These conditions, their immediate causes and the capacity to manage them can all be affected by past trauma, including childhood sexual abuse, which a significant proportion of patients will have suffered, and homelessness or the urgent need to find money for food or the gas or electricity meter. These are not problems that can be easily dealt with in a ten-minute GP appointment, but they still have a deleterious effect on people's well-being and prognosis.

Links practitioners were created out of a desire to address this shortcoming in the system. Today, there are more than seventy of them based in Deep End practices in Glasgow, helping patients access benefits, dealing with housing associations and connecting with third-sector organisations that run the likes of bereavement counselling or recovery cafes. On the morning I spend with Robertson, she sees Christine,[*] a 45-year-old wheelchair-user born with cerebral palsy, and Michael,[*] who suffers from long-term mental health issues.

Christine had always coped well with her condition, living independently with little outside support, but a recent cancer diagnosis knocked her for six. She is struggling to perform tasks she once took for granted and is distressed about the loss of her hair. Robertson contacts the social work department to chase up a homecare referral and scours the internet for a pre-tied bandana which Christine will be able to pull on and off with ease. Transport is also an issue for patients like Christine. 'The health system is designed by – and geared towards – people with cars,' Robertson says. 'Those without cars may be taking three buses to get to an appointment in the Queen Elizabeth University Hospital one day and another three to get to an appointment at Gartnavel [Hospital] the next. That adds to the financial pressure and the stress.' And, of course, where the result of this lack of access is missed appointments, it can easily translate into treatments being missed, with dangerous consequences.

Michael is on a months-long waiting list for the Moira

---

[*] Some names have been changed.

Anderson Foundation, which counsels survivors of child-hood sexual abuse. He talks frenetically and fidgets on his chair as he tells Robertson how the card for his electricity meter hasn't been working and he has been unable to heat his flat. Attempts to top it up at the local shop have been unsuc-cessful. Robertson sorts it out with a single phone call.

The links practitioner says a significant proportion of the sixty people she currently works with have COPD and/or di-abetes. 'We are also seeing younger and younger people with cancer.' In her five years in that role, Robertson says her case-load has grown: a result of welfare 'reforms', the pandemic and now the cost-of-living crisis. Everyone is scared of what will happen as energy prices soar. 'There is already so much pressure on support services,' Robertson says. 'I often see Drumchapel Foodbank on social media, looking for more donations just so they can keep going until the end of the week. We try to plug the holes, but the water keeps coming.'

DYING OF LIVING

A life of poverty is a life spent firefighting. If you are well off, you are more likely to invest in your own well-being. You are more likely to eat good food, get fresh air and go to the gym. You will probably remember to make an appointment for cer-vical smears and breast screenings; and then you'll remember to attend those appointments. But everyone's financial and emotional resources are finite. If you're always living on the edge, it can take so much energy to navigate your way from one crisis to the next, you have nothing left for self-care.

'One way of understanding this is to look at the idea of "treatment burden",' says Andrea Williamson, a Deep End GP and a clinician at Glasgow's Hunter Street Homeless Services. 'Say you have type 2 diabetes and you have to think about what you are eating and when you are eating it; you have to think about how to lose weight, work out an exercise regime – well, all of that takes money and effort.'

It's difficult to stick to a healthy diet if you are struggling on benefits and the price of fruit and vegetables is going up. Or if you're using a food bank and everything comes in tins and packets. Just as it's difficult to keep exercising if you have no safe open spaces nearby – or, indeed, no free time to use them. 'One of the horrific things about modern Britain is in-work poverty,' Williamson says. 'You might be taking on extra hours, you might be on a zero-hours contract. How can you stick to an exercise regime if you have no idea if you're going to be working tomorrow, or if you're going to be earning money this week?'

Williamson also runs a clinic for women in alcohol and drug recovery, where attendance is erratic. 'Sometimes, life just overwhelms them,' she says. 'Sometimes, their mental well-being is so poor, it's impossible for them to turn up to appointments or even answer the phone.' But not turning up for appointments can be deadly. Recently, the GP led a study which examined the records of more than 500,000 general practice patients in Scotland. 'We found that those who had missed two or more GP appointments in the preceding three years and had mental health and substance issues were eight times more likely to die than those who hadn't,' she says. The figures were less stark for those missing appointments for physical conditions alone, but there were still excess deaths.

'We used to think that if people didn't turn up, it meant they didn't really need medical help,' Williamson goes on. 'Our research blows that out of the water. These are people with unmet healthcare needs. We need to work out what we can do better.'

Williamson's Deep End colleague Dr Ula Chetty works in a part of Glasgow where the life expectancy for men is sixty-six. It is a neighbourhood once populated by metalworkers but which became plagued by heroin when the local factories closed.

That legacy of deprivation remains, more recently compounded by benefit sanctions that have pushed some people into destitution. Others seem to have simply lost the fight it takes to survive. Chetty tells me about two patients whose ill health has been compounded by poverty. She has changed some of the details to protect their identities. 'One middle-aged woman was diagnosed with bowel cancer but refused treatment because she had a significant fear of needles,' she says.

> She decided she would rather die than have treatment. It's been heartbreaking to witness. She has very little money, survives on microwave meals and is reluctant to put the heating on. She has lost weight and her cancer has progressed to the point where it can no longer be cured.

Recently, Chetty has been helping the woman access additional benefits available to those whose condition is terminal. 'She'll get a bit of extra money and the Jobcentre will stop nagging her about whether she is fit to work,' the GP says. It's a stark irony at the heart of the system. Only now she is about to die will this woman have enough to live on. Only now it's too late is she to be granted dignity.

Chetty tells me about another patient, in his fifties, with many overlapping conditions. 'His young brother had died unexpectedly and he struggled to cope with the grief,' she says.

> He went through rehab and stayed off heroin, but he had so much wrong with him: inflammatory bowel disease, fibromyalgia, depression, anxiety, asthma, heart disease. Then he became forgetful. At first I thought it might be his anxiety, but it worsened and he was diagnosed with early onset dementia.

Our links worker managed to get him a more suitable flat and shopping vouchers and he was delighted with that.

'How is he now?' I ask.

'He was found dead one morning,' Chetty replies. 'It took about a year for the post-mortem results to come back. They said his death was caused by street drugs in combination with his poor heart, poor lungs and prescription medications.'

FOOD COMES SECOND

In the US, the rise of such 'deaths of despair' – that is, lives directly lost to suicide, drug overdoses and alcoholism – in less-educated white communities was at points during the 2010s so marked as to drag down average life expectancy across the nation as a whole.[10] Here in the UK, at least in the nationwide picture, we are not there yet. But none of the trends is especially encouraging. Recorded suicides were creeping up in the immediate run-up to the pandemic, before edging back down in the singular circumstances of lockdown.[11] Alcohol deaths in both Scotland and England increased after the virus arrived.[12]

It is rocketing drug deaths, however, that truly set Scotland apart, leaving it with the highest per capita rate in western Europe. (Drug deaths in England have also risen sharply since 2012, up by around 80 per cent, but from a far lower base.)[13] The record Scottish drugs toll in 2020 of 1,339 was 5 per cent up on the previous record – set in 2019. The Scottish government's declaration of a national emergency has made little impact: the 2021 figure was almost unchanged, at 1,330. Look at graphs of these deaths over the past decade and the gap between rich and poor opens up like a menacing jaw: those living in the most-deprived fifth of areas across Scotland are now fully fifteen times more likely to leave the world this way than those in the least-deprived fifth. And Glasgow is the second-worst hit city – only Dundee fares worse.[14]

In Drumchapel, our links practitioner Lorna Robertson is crystal clear: 'People are dying prematurely of physical conditions but also of overdoses and suicides.' And every Deep End GP I speak to lost patients to substance abuse during lockdown. There were many relapses as Community Addiction Teams stopped making visits, recovery cafes closed their doors and Alcoholics Anonymous meetings moved to Zoom. Nowhere was this plainer than in the blackest of all Glasgow's health blackspots: Govan.

Dr John Montgomery tells me how a partner in his Govan practice knocked on a patient's door after he failed to pick up his methadone prescription. 'The man was clearly suffering from gross alcohol misuse, but he still had capacity and declined all offers of help,' Montgomery says. 'Sure enough, days later he was dead.'

A few streets away, at GalGael – a charity which runs woodwork courses for men with physical and mental health difficulties – I find Francis Corkhill chopping timber. Many of those who, like Francis, have completed GalGael courses stay on as volunteers. Inside, rows of workbenches stand to attention on a floor carpeted with wood shavings. Scattered around are fruits of the men's labours: bowls and boxes so smooth you yearn to run your fingers along them.

Corkhill wipes his hands on his overalls and comes to talk to me. He is so diffident it is hard to picture him in his gobby glory days, when – as he explains – he used to flog computer games down the Barras, Glasgow's famous market.

He says his physical health is good for someone of his age, fifty-seven. But as he talks, he lets slip a litany of ailments. His high blood pressure. His anaemia. And, not least, his yearning for escape. A former heroin addict, he did not relapse during the pandemic; but he did start drinking. Just a couple of glasses of wine a night, he says, at first. Then a bottle. Then maybe two.

'I was on my own during lockdown,' he says. 'I felt quite isolated. I got into a routine of drinking while watching Netflix. It was more enjoyable with a drink. I think alcohol is very difficult. It is a social drug, so you don't see yourself as having a problem.' And does he have a problem? He hesitates. 'It's not physically addictive for me. I don't shake if I stop. But yes, I think I may have a problem. I know I drink too fucking much.'

The drinking worsens Corkhill's anaemia. 'I don't eat properly,' he says. 'I do cook sometimes. I make pasta and throw in some broccoli and potatoes. But right now, it's about not having enough money. Because I am still buying the wine. One bottle a night. That's £35 a week. The food tends to come second.'

SAME DIFFERENCE

A visit to Govanhill, the city's most diverse district, always induces a rush of just-arrived-on-holiday excitement. An area of high immigration – there are said to be more than forty nationalities squeezed into a square mile – its streets titillate all the senses. Eyes goggle at the brightly coloured vegetables laid out as if on a market stall. Nostrils tingle at the aroma of tacos and dosas drifting from cafe doors. Ears twitch like radio antennae trying to tune into a myriad of competing languages.

Not yet rendered bland by gentrification, Govanhill is a pleasure to spend time in. Moreover, the neighbourhood, at least as defined in the GCPH Glasgow Indicators Project, is not an especially unhealthy place by city standards. On the league table of male life expectancies, it is in line with the city-wide mean of 73.1 years,[15] and its women actually live slightly longer than is typical across the city as a whole. And yet averages can conceal a lot. In the handful of streets most

Glaswegians would recognise as Govanhill, there is no mistaking the deprivation. For a long time, slum landlords held sway here. There are still pockets of squalor, and litter piles up in closes. In some tenement blocks, bedbugs are endemic.

Govanhill is both stigmatised and highly politicised. Its large Roma population is a lightning rod for racists who mutter about 'gangs of men hanging around on street corners'. Located in former First Minister Nicola Sturgeon's constituency, it was often weaponised against her. Her critics said she was always talking about her government's commitment to ending child poverty, yet – at 69 per cent[16] – this patch of land in her own backyard had the worst child poverty rate in the UK. Every so often the police investigate, and dismiss, rumours of systematic child sexual exploitation.

This cocktail of poverty and ethnic tension has implications for those trying to improve the lives of the people who live there. Frankie Rose is a links worker at a practice in the Govanhill Health Centre. She says her job relies on building up trust, especially with the Roma patients, many of whom have multiple health issues but are wary of authority.

'A lot of Roma women wouldn't come to the surgery during Covid because they thought they were going to be vaccinated against their will,' Rose says. 'They are also suspicious of procedures such as smear tests. The anxiety is understandable. They have experienced so much persecution, they expect to find it here. For them, the threat seems real.' There are other cultural barriers, too. 'Literacy and numeracy tend to be low,' Rose says. 'Their health beliefs are very different to ours, and they will trust those in their own community over doctors.'

There is also a double language barrier. Rose often communicates with patients through an interpreter. But very few interpreters speak Romani, so the conversation will be carried out in the language of their country of origin – mostly Czech, Slovak or Romanian, which is their second language. Since Covid, this has been done via telephone, which can be quite stilted.

Even when good relationships are built, they tend to be transitory. 'It can be frustrating,' Rose says. 'You work to create a degree of stability, and then the patient goes to their home country for the summer. Their benefits are stopped, their tenancies abandoned, they fall off the GP register and when they return, all these things need to be reinstated.'

Govanhill's Roma and South Asian families tend to live multi-generationally, but larger properties are expensive and difficult to come by, so overcrowding is rife. 'The worst I've come across was eleven in a two-bedroomed flat,' Rose says. 'At the moment I am seeing a family with nine people in two rooms, one of which is meant to be a living room. That family has a baby with complex needs. But having so many people breaches the terms of their tenancy, so they could end up homeless.'

Living like this can make you ill. 'These big old tenement

flats may already be damp,' Rose says. 'If you add to that nine people breathing, cooking, doing laundry – that creates a lot of moisture. Many homes have black mould, so you get a lot of respiratory tract infections. Add to that the stress of having no privacy.' One woman Rose sees gets chronic migraines; her kids are constantly fighting.

When Analetta enters the room, she looks askance at the tiny chair set out for her. Rose jumps up and swaps it with her own, and Analetta grimaces as she lowers her large frame into it. She looks to be in her fifties but is actually thirty-five.

Analetta has chronic back pain. Neither she nor her husband is fit to work. They live in a housing association property in Govanhill with very little furniture. There is no carpet; no table to eat at. But what Analetta wants is a better sofa – one she can sit in with a degree of comfort.

Rose phones a charity specialising in adapted furniture to see if it can provide a sofa, but she is told it cannot help unless Analetta is on Personal Independence Payment, a benefit she has been rejected for. She is submitting a new claim, but it won't be heard for another four months. Rose puts in calls to other charities which say they'll see what they can do. 'There is so much demand,' she says. 'People ask: "If she has a sofa, why does she need another one?" But you can see she is in pain.' Analetta also struggles to wash properly and in accordance with her culture in the cramped bathroom. She shows Rose a picture of a bidet on her phone. 'She is supposed to wash after using the toilet and it's physically difficult for her to do that while standing over the bath,' Rose says, 'but the housing association isn't going to pay for a bidet. I have referred her to Occupational Therapy, who can supply a bath board or a walk-in shower or personal care, but the waiting list is six to twelve months.'

Next, they talk about money. Analetta and her husband are in rent arrears. She and Rose go through some figures together: £40 for gas; £25 for electricity; £30 for internet and line rental. There's less coming in than going out (and this is well before the huge energy price hikes in the second half of 2022). Rose refers her to a financial inclusion officer and hands her another food bank voucher.

Eventually, Analetta hauls herself from the chair, her face blank, and I realise that – for all the cultural differences – her existence is not dissimilar from the others I have met. '[Many of the people here] are constantly in emergency mode,' Rose says. 'They are worrying about keeping their tenancy, loaning money to extended family, going to the Jobcentre, figuring out when to go to the food bank. They don't have the bandwidth to look ahead.'

SCRAMBLE AGAINST THE SYMPTOMS

We have become so inured to health inequalities, they can seem inevitable. But it didn't – and doesn't – have to be like this. Regions in many other countries have gone through a similar process of deindustrialisation with fewer aftershocks. Already by 2011, the GCPH was highlighting unflattering comparisons between its own hinterland and the Ruhr. That region had once been the heart of German steel and mining production but lost a majority of its industrial jobs between 1970 and 2005. And yet life expectancy had 'been consistently higher' in the Ruhr than in West Central Scotland (WCS). Moreover, lives were shorter in 'the *majority* of WCS local authority areas' (my italics) than in Gelsenkirchen, the Ruhr district with the very lowest recorded life expectancy.[17]

When the GCPH analysed the peculiarities of the 'Glasgow effect', it concluded it was rooted in the country's approach to urban planning in the mid- to late-twentieth century: its creation of the four peripheral estates and its decision to 'skim off the cream' – skilled workers – by decanting them to its five New Towns. The city's heavy focus on council estates became problematic when the Thatcher era ushered in a long squeeze on investment in social housing. This was more true in Glasgow than, say, Liverpool, where the council committed to an ambitious regeneration strategy.

'There was also a greater diversification of industry elsewhere,' says Gerry McCartney, a professor of well-being economy at Glasgow University who has worked with the GCPH on major recent research which attempts to move from offering analysis to offering solutions.[18]

In Scotland, we had companies such as IBM and Caterpillar who were here for a while and then dramatically downsized or moved on. So we ended up with low-paid service industries rather than higher-tech home-grown industries. This created layers of vulnerability which have fuelled drug use, alcohol abuse, suicide and violence.

Entrenched though it is, McCartney and his colleagues insist the situation is fixable. 'Between the 1920s and 1970s, life expectancy increased and health inequalities narrowed dramatically,' McCartney says. 'We know what worked then and we know what is working now in social democratic states. We need to invest in the welfare state, the NHS, council houses and industry. We need to give trade unions greater power and reduce income inequalities.' The report McCartney has been working on makes forty recommendations which include increasing benefits and tax credits in line with inflation every year (together with a one-off increase to compensate for the loss of real income incurred since 2010) and the introduction of more progressive income tax bands and rates to narrow income inequalities across society.

It all sounds logical and yet… unlikely. Two days before she arrived in Downing Street in 2022, Liz Truss complained on the BBC that the 'economic debate for the past twenty years has been dominated by discussions about distribution',[19] before stampeding into tax cuts which favoured the rich. Market anxieties about their affordability soon forced the abandonment of most of the cuts, shattering Truss's authority and unleashing chaos in the Conservative administration but also ushering in yet another drumbeat of demands for 'economies' in welfare and public services from Whitehall. Nor has the Scottish government displayed any great appetite for taxing the rich: while the Institute for Fiscal Studies judges that Holyrood has used its powers to make Scotland's tax and benefits systems more progressive than those elsewhere in the UK,[20] the SNP has steadfastly refused to reform the regressive council tax.

While politicians drag their heels on the fundamentals, clinicians go on doing what they can to improve their patients' lives against terrible odds. But they, too, can come a cropper on the finances. The Govan Social and Health Integration Project (SHIP) was a four-year initiative whose features included employing two social workers and holding multidisciplinary team meetings to identify those patients most at risk. According to Dr Montgomery, who chaired the project, it was working wonders across the four practices in Govan Health Centre before funding was withdrawn. 'Everyone would have their IT systems open, so they could very quickly share information, come up with a management plan and implement it,' he recalls. 'What we were doing was highlighting the most vulnerable: children, the elderly, those in need of palliative care.' The practices also hired two newly qualified GPs, which allowed the existing, more experienced GPs to have longer appointments with the most complex patients. Auditing the effect across the four practices and comparing them with others, Montgomery witnessed a 12 per cent decline in demand for GPs. And yet a bid to extend the project failed.

Since it stopped, demand has shot back up and then some. Just before the pandemic, as the funding was ending, the number of consultations at Montgomery's practice was 1,100 a month; it now stands at 2,000 a month. Of course, there have been many other things going on, not least the virus itself, but the sinking of SHIP hasn't helped. 'When we had SHIP, I was pretty confident I knew all the vulnerable at-risk children in my practice. I'm not now,' he says.

But other valuable Deep End initiatives have been adopted – and kept. The links workers are now seen as indispensable. The embedding of financial inclusion workers, like the one Analetta was referred to in Govanhill, is now being rolled out after a successful pilot in two practices in Glasgow's East End. In the pilot, 'they helped patients with financial difficulties access the benefits they were entitled to', Montgomery says. 'In the year it was running, those workers realised more financial gain for their patients than the surrounding twenty practices combined.'

WHERE THERE'S LIFE, THERE'S HOPE

Charities like GalGael and Simon Community Scotland, which runs access hubs and street teams supporting rough sleepers in Glasgow and Edinburgh, tirelessly demonstrate that there is no such thing as a hopeless case.

It is through homeless charity Simon Community Scotland that I meet Kevin Buchanan, a fifty-year-old man hewn from post-industrial blight. Born in Govan as the shipyards were closing, he had a challenging childhood. His father was in jail for much of it, leaving his mother to raise three children alone. By sixteen, Buchanan himself was in and out of young offenders' institutions, then adult prison. By nineteen, he was taking heroin. Over the next two decades, he had periods of stability – times when he was 'clean' and in employment. 'But when things got bad, I always went back on the drugs,' he says.

A few years ago, things got very bad indeed. One of his two sons took his own life at twenty-three. Buchanan still finds it difficult to talk about this. 'The police had taken him home after he threatened to jump in the Clyde,' he says, his voice breaking. 'He overdosed on his mother's medication, and my life just crumbled.' Buchanan ended up back in jail and then – on his release – in one of Glasgow's homeless hostels. Surrounded by other users, he started taking heroin again.

He has multiple health problems. A type 2 diabetic, he also suffers from arthritis, anxiety and depression. He rhymes off his medication. 'I'm on metformin [for diabetes], ramipril [for high blood pressure], atorvastatin [given for reasons connected to arthritis] and quetiapine [an antipsychotic] as well as the opioid replacement therapy buprenorphine.' The last is injected, but even so: 'I take sixteen tablets in the morning and four at night,' Buchanan says.

In his years in the hostel, he sometimes stopped taking his medication. His diabetes became so bad he started suffering seizures. He shows me his misshapen collar bone, which he broke when he 'hit the ground and started bouncing about'. His drug use escalated; he was topping up the heroin with street valium, and he stopped attending appointments. On no fewer than nine occasions, he overdosed and was repeatedly saved by the heroin antidote naloxone.

'What you have to understand is that [life as an addict] is hectic,' he says. 'Your first thought in the morning is getting your drugs and drink, and after that you still have to get your money for the next day. So if you have appointments here, there and everywhere – you're not going to make them.' During lockdown, Buchanan became increasingly isolated. He had lost touch with his mother and sister and most of the support services disappeared: no phone calls, no welfare visits, nothing.

Except for Cally Archibald. An outreach worker with homelessness charity Simon Community Scotland, Archibald met Buchanan one day when he was collecting food vouchers, after which she wouldn't leave him alone. 'She chased me round town, made sure I picked up my prescriptions and took me back to the community addiction team. If I'm honest, it was kind of annoying at first, but she helped me pull my life together.'

Now Buchanan has his own flat. He is back in touch with his mother and sister, who live nearby and sometimes cook him dinner. Four days a week, he volunteers at the access hub; on a Tuesday, he trains with the Scottish Drugs Forum. His health is still poor, but at least he is taking his medication. He tells me proudly he only has two more buprenorphine injections to get before he's 'clean' again. I check back in after a couple of months, and he is indeed completely off it.

'My flat is great,' he tells me in the Simon Community access hub.

I have done it up by myself, I spend time with my other son and my five-year-old grandson. Now I am not buying drugs, I have more money for food. I can spoil my grandson occasionally … bring chocolates in here for the girls. This is the best life's been for a while.

'The cost is just too much': 'Sandra' in High Wycombe on the electricity required for taking a shower – and for her disability equipment

CHAPTER 6

THE 'COST-OF-STAYING-ALIVE CRISIS': DISABILITY TODAY

FRANCES RYAN

In his front room in High Wycombe, Buckinghamshire, Mike is working out how many meals he has to skip this week to make sure his wife can afford to eat.

Having bipolar disorder, on top of multiple physical health problems, means Sandra, thirty-eight, has long been too sick to work and Mike – himself slowly recovering from agoraphobia – is needed at home as her full-time carer. A large turntable fills one side of the room – 'I was a DJ in another life,' Mike, forty, explains wistfully – with a basket stacked with pill packets and an NHS nebuliser on the shelves below.

Heavy steroids for severe asthma have damaged Sandra's bones and she struggles to walk to the bottom of the garden, let alone do a nine to five. Like many disabled families in

161

houses across Britain, including in its prosperous home counties, the couple have no choice but to rely solely on benefits – or to put it another way, the kind of income that leaves your kitchen cupboards empty.

The front room is filled with space film memorabilia, collected at a time when there was still a little money for hobbies; stormtroopers stand in a display case, topped with a life-size metallic red helmet and large model spacecraft. But these days, Mike can't escape more earthly concerns.

As well as caring for Sandra full-time, he helps her disabled son, Andy, in nearby supported living ('I deal with his meetings and all the things that come with a lad with quite severe behavioural issues') and has now also started caring for Sandra's nan, cooking her dinners, keeping her house clean and doing her shopping. 'It feels like a lot of caring for £69 [Carer's Allowance] a week,' he admits. To get through it all, and make everything add up, Mike typically has just one meal a day: 'whatever is yellow stickered at Morrisons'. Sandra's pain and breathing would only worsen if she became malnourished and so Mike prioritises her meals. Some of the few meals they can count on come from a local food pantry – a charitable scheme that sells donated food close to its sell-by date.

HIDDEN WORRIES

Mike and Sandra are not their real names; they speak to me

anonymously, for painful reasons that go back a few years. As the 2010 coalition government brought in a wave of 'welfare reforms' in the aftermath of the financial crash, disabled people like Mike and Sandra were recast as 'scroungers' by prominent politicians and the right-wing press. The then Chancellor George Osborne stoked a division between 'workers and shirkers', famously referring in a set-piece party conference speech to shift workers 'leaving home in the dark hours of the early morning' while glancing resentfully back 'at the closed blinds of their next door neighbour sleeping off a life on benefits'.[1] TV programmes, from Channel 4's *Benefits Street* to Channel 5's *Gypsies On Benefits & Proud*, played to this mood, normalising the myth that disabled benefits claimants were not people in need but fakers trying their luck. In this climate, suspicion over people's disabilities and illnesses became the new normal.

Charities warned at the time that this rhetoric fuelled an increase in abuse levelled at disabled people,[2] and Mike and Sandra were two of the many victims. After they were featured in their local paper in a story about the impact of benefit cuts, the couple received abusive comments online – keyboard warriors behind a screen declaring them 'scroungers' leeching off the state. Propped up in a chair with her ginger cat sat protectively on the arm rest, Sandra admits it has left her with an intense fear she'll be maliciously reported to the Department for Work and Pensions (DWP) and lose her benefits. 'It worries me every day.'

There are plenty of worries to go with it, not least mounting energy bills. Disability has always been expensive – whether that's care bills, specialist food, unavoidable taxi costs or extra heating. Just before the pandemic, the extra costs of being disabled were totted up to an estimated average of £583 a month.[3] The record rise in energy costs in 2022 only added to this weight. Sandra needs extra electricity for her health: a nebuliser, a mobility scooter, air conditioning, a walk-in shower and a soon-to-be-installed stairlift. Swapping part of her disability benefits gets Sandra a Motability car and with it, a shot of independence, but that's electric too; Mike driving Andy the one-hour round trip to college each day only adds to the electricity cost.

The couple were paying £50 a month for electricity, but when I speak to them the bill has already more than tripled, even before the steep further rises in later 2022. Told to find £170 a month, Mike says they've increased the direct debit to £70. 'It's all we can afford.'

Instead, the two of them are going without. The couple are going out less and less, because they can't pay the electric bill for the car. Sandra rarely uses her scooter now – they haven't got the money to charge it. Tattoos lacing her arms and her brown hair cropped short, she admits to me she has also started showering less. 'The cost is just too much.'

I speak to Sandra again the day after a June heatwave and she has been struggling to breathe. The air conditioning would normally ease her asthma in the heat, but with the rise in energy bills, it is too expensive to put on. Nowadays, she says, breathing 'is just a luxury we can't afford'.

Spend an hour with Mike and Sandra and phrases like 'the squeeze on living standards' and 'cost of living' that have dominated politics in recent years sound increasingly like dodgy euphemisms, a muted Westminster-built terminology that can't come close to describing what's actually happening in Britain today. As rising energy and food bills put the greatest pressure on Britons in many decades, the couple have found themselves without enough income to meet the most basic human needs: keeping warm, properly fed and with medical equipment running. For people like Mike and Sandra, this isn't a cost-of-living crisis; this is a cost-of-staying-alive crisis.

EXTREME BUT NORMAL

It would be easy to hear a story like theirs and dismiss it as a one-off – a sad but ultimately rare example of extreme situations. And yet the truth is, this is what is happening to millions of disabled people in Britain today: grinding penury is being normalised. The scale of hardship is astonishing. Well over 40 per cent of those below the official poverty line – that is, 6.1 million people in all – are either disabled or living with a disabled person.[4]

And the official tally counts disability benefits, such as Personal Independence Payments (PIP), as 'spare income', when in practice, such cash has to pay for the extra costs of disability (anything from care costs to wheelchair parts) and rarely fully covers them. Stripping these benefits out, the Joseph Rowntree Foundation (JRF) has shown that as of 2019/20 the risk of being in poverty for disabled working-age adults (38 per cent) is more than *twice as high* as the risk (17 per cent) for their non-disabled counterparts.[5]

Disabled people aren't just more likely to be below the breadline – they're more likely to be far below it. Analysing data from just before the pandemic, the JRF found that 15 per cent of those in disabled families were in 'deep poverty', compared to 9 per cent of those in families without a disabled family member. For single-adult disabled families, without the cushion of a partner's income, this 'deep poverty' figure rises to over 20 per cent. The impact of this is brutal: among this 'single disabled' group, nearly a fifth reported being severely food insecure (18.7 per cent), being unable to heat their home (18.5 per cent) or falling behind with basic household bills (18.5 per cent) due to lack of money.[6] Compared to those in homes where no one is disabled, that means they are four times as likely to be falling into arrears, six times as likely to be growing cold and nine times as likely to be going hungry.

---

* 'Deep poverty' is defined at 40 per cent rather the usual 60 per cent of the median income.

It's worth summing up what this really means: in one of the richest societies that has ever lived, a fifth of single disabled people are effectively destitute. And this was before the full energy shock that seems bound to worsen the figures. Survey after survey confirms this. The Office for National Statistics itself reported that as of September 2022, more than half (55 per cent) of disabled people were finding it difficult to afford their energy bills, while over a third (36 per cent) were struggling to pay their rent or mortgage, in both cases far more than the proportions for non-disabled people.[7] A large bespoke Savanta ComRes survey of working-age disabled people, carried out in February 2022, suggested that around 600,000 disabled people had just £10 or less per week left after taxes and housing to pay for food, heating and everything else.[8]

Meanwhile, an Abrdn Financial Fairness Trust and Bristol University cost-of-living tracker poll found that by mid-2022, huge proportions of households with a disability were cutting back on both the quantity of meals (31 per cent v. 12 per cent for non-disabled households) or the quality of food (43 per cent v. 25 per cent). Hot meals, in particular, are increasingly out of reach for those in disabled households – nearly half of those in them (48 per cent) were cutting back on use of the oven. So, too, were other ways of warming up. Virtually a third of the disabled group (32 per cent) were leaving parts of their home unheated. And little less than half (44 per cent) were – like Sandra – taking fewer baths and showers than before.[9]

Forget just turning the heating down a touch; this is sitting in a duffel coat in the front room to keep from freezing.

UNFIT FOR PURPOSE

In a civilised society, this is where the welfare state would step in – but in recent years, Britain has reduced its safety net to a set of gaping holes. Through a mixture of cuts, squeezes and Kafkaesque tests, it has refashioned a system created to help people in need into an instrument of punishment. Even those with severe disability or serious illness are frequently threatened with having their benefits cut if they don't comply with work-related 'requirements'. The UN's special rapporteur on extreme poverty and human rights, Professor Philip Alston, concluded in his damning report on the UK in 2019 that disabled people were 'some of the hardest hit by austerity measures'.[10] Research commissioned by the Equality and Human Rights Commission into the cumulative impact of post-2010 benefit and tax changes lays this bare: on average, households with at least one disabled adult and a disabled child lost over £6,500 a year, while the wealthy and healthy were protected.[11] Ministers have, in effect, picked out cancer patients and paraplegics to carry some of the heaviest burdens.

Back in 2019, I experienced 'welfare reform' first hand. Like a couple of million other disabled people, for two decades I had received Disability Living Allowance (DLA) to pay for the extra costs of disability. But when it was replaced by PIP, ministers decided that each of us had to be reassessed. This included people like me who had permanent and incurable disabilities, who now needed to 'prove' they were still disabled.

'Welfare reform' is an innocuous term, a positive spin that suggests sensible and helpful change. In reality, it means sitting in front of an often-unqualified assessor – sent by an outsourced private company – and answering their intrusive questions, on pain of losing your financial lifeline. The pages of medical evidence provided by your medical notes mean little here – just a stranger with a tick-box list asking, as one did to me, 'How do you put your bra on?' or, in the case of one 25-year-old woman I reported on, 'Can you tell me why you haven't killed yourself yet?'[12]

I was lucky. I didn't lose my benefits. I wasn't pushed into poverty. I can eat regular meals. But it says something about the current shape of the welfare state that disabled people feel 'lucky' if we are only treated a little badly.

For Mike and Sandra, it was with other welfare 'reforms' during these years that their real financial problems started. In 2017, like hundreds of thousands of other disabled people, Mike was reassessed for his out-of-work sickness benefit, Employment and Support Allowance (ESA), and promptly declared 'fit for work'. It is plain that thousands of these rejections are in error from the fact that the majority of the numerous decisions which have been appealed have gone on to be overturned.[13] Like many others, though, Mike didn't feel able to take on the DWP. Scared that the system dismissed mental health problems and aware that backlogs meant it could take a year to even get a hearing, he chose not to appeal.

Mike had slowly been making gains with his agoraphobia – on a good day, he could go to the supermarket without a panic attack – but holding down a job may as well have been a Herculean task. 'Being trapped behind a till or something would have been impossible for me.' He couldn't even use public transport to get there, he explains, tufts of dark beard shaping his face. 'A bit of support might have helped me in to work at that time, but they just decided I was fine and that was that.'

Back then, Sandra had limited disability benefits of her own and the two of them relied almost solely on Mike's social security to get by. With his benefits stopped, the couple had practically 'nothing' – just Sandra's low-rate PIP – to survive on for six months. 'Food banks were a godsend,' Mike says of that time, 'but it's never enough food to actually live on. We would have three pies and a few tins of veg for a week.'

Once again, Mike's experience – in this case, resorting to

charity to keep himself and his wife fed – is all too typical. The records of the country's largest network of food banks show that more than six in ten (62 per cent) of the working-age people referred to them in early 2020 had a disability. The Trussell Trust adds that this is more than three times the rate of food bank use in the general working population.[14] Throughout the Victorian era, before the advent of the welfare state, the 'sickly' and 'crippled' had to beg 'relief' organisations for help to survive. Nowadays, rather than the workhouse, we send disabled people to a food bank.

When the state stopped supporting him, Mike's mental health plummeted, along with their finances. Things he'd painstakingly learned to cope with became hard again: going out shopping, dealing with hospital appointments with Sandra or even opening letters. 'I hit rock bottom,' he says. 'I struggled to get out of my room and slept almost constantly. I barely ate. It took me months to get back to where I was before being found "fit for work".'

It was only a few years earlier that the 'bedroom tax' had forced the couple out of the three-bed home that Sandra had lived in for four years. Officially a charge for 'under-occupancy', this is yet another austerity cutback that disproportionately hit disabled people – and yet another case where Mike and Sandra's story is only too typical. In the past, I have interviewed dozens of disabled families who have relied on extra space for anything from oxygen cylinders and specialist beds to a room for carers to sleep in but who nonetheless had their benefits cut due to having a 'spare' bedroom.[15]

Saddled with this 'tax', Mike and Sandra soon got into rent arrears. In the end, the council cleared the debt, but it was not enough: the couple were forced to downsize to a one-bed house. When Sandra's eldest son, Sam, then thirteen, moved back home from his dad's less than a year later, the family found themselves crammed in with a teenage boy, medical equipment and one bed to sleep in. Eventually, the council moved them back up the social housing list for a two-bed house, but this required more upheaval – and a painful wait. For three years, Mike and Sandra slept on the living room floor. That'd be hard for anyone, but when you have breathing problems and chronic pain, it's torture.

These are the sort of deprivations we have been asking ever more disabled Britons to live with over the past decade. Much of non-disabled Britain is disturbed and shocked by the unprecedented hardships of the current squeeze. But for the likes of Mike and Sandra, the terrors of the latest 'cost-of-living crisis' are nothing new. They are more of the same.

Her pet lizard lounging in the tank behind the sofa, and now settled in the new home, Sandra tells me that the housing saga led to her health significantly deteriorating. At one point, she had an asthma attack that made her heart stop. 'I was in intensive care for a few days after that,' she says. 'Luckily,' she adds with a learned stoicism, 'there was no lasting damage to my brain.'

MOTHERING V. THE MATHS

Even when she's too ill to get out of bed, Becca knows her mum has popped over – when Becca eventually makes her way down to the kitchen, there's food in the fridge. The constant pain of fibromyalgia, compounded by exhaustion from myalgic encephalomyelitis (ME), leaves the 47-year-old largely bedbound. Speaking from her bed under a grey weighted blanket, Becca glances around her bedroom in Glasgow – her microcosmic world. A kettle sits on her bedside table, a way to get a warming drink without going downstairs to the kitchen. Opposite, a cat 'tree' looms down for her feline companions Dex and Afra – otherwise known as 'a vain attempt to get them to sleep there, instead of on and around me'. Green houseplants and a pile of books line the window ledge, while a small smart speaker sits by the bed, full of audiobooks. 'An escape from reality,' she says.

'Reality' has been tough for a while. Through her teens and twenties, Becca's health knocked out her plans like dominos: first, she had to drop out of studying psychology at university; then she had to leave her job as a cash-office clerk. One role she has held onto over the years is that of mum, though her health means her nineteen-year-old son cares for her more than she would like. Alongside college and his part-time job, he supports her as she walks, does whatever shopping there is money for and then cooks, too. 'I try to be as undemanding as possible,' she says. 'I want him to be doing normal things nineteen-year-olds do.'

Without her own wage coming in, Becca has only a string of benefits to get by – ESA, PIP, Housing Benefit and Council Tax Reduction – but do the maths and, even before the full horrors of the energy price spike, they leave her nearly £200 short a month. 'My benefits don't cover [utilities and debt repayments], let alone allow for me to purchase food. The budget for that goes towards not falling into arrears.'

Becca is far from alone in this: disabled parents UK-wide are struggling to provide their children with life's absolute basics. Along with all the findings about skimping on heated rooms, hot meals and warm showers, the Bristol University tracker survey looked specifically at parents and recorded that by mid-2022, 38 per cent of those in disabled households were reporting that the cost of living was negatively affecting their ability to 'give your children what they need', against just 22 per cent of parents in non-disabled households.[16]

Still, parents – and children – do all they can to take care of those they love. I first speak to Becca a few days before her own mum is due to have surgery for womb cancer, and she has been gently trying to calm her down. 'She's terrified,' Becca says. It is a stressful time for the family, but the day-to-day problems aren't going away. The food shop still needs doing. The electric bill still has to be paid. With that cost rising, Becca has switched off most of her appliances. She doesn't watch television. The oven is only used now and again. The thermostat is set strictly at 16°C max. 'Thank goodness for hot flushes,' she laughs. 'A wee heat.'

In the middle of a recent worry-filled night, Becca was googling what extra help might be out there 'for folk like me'. Her bills mounting, she'd realised that that week's supermarket shop money would have to be spent on utilities and rent. With no other way to buy food, Becca hoped a grant would at least help her 'stock the cupboards'. Had she found herself in a similar crisis a decade earlier, she would have been able to apply for an interest-free crisis loan from the DWP Social Fund. But this 'ultimate safety net' was shredded during the 2010s, to be replaced in England only with vague, time-limited and cut-price grants. South of the border, there is now a good chance she would have received nothing at all.[17]

In Scotland, Becca's late-night googling revealed she could at least apply for an emergency grant from her local authority. She had hoped for enough money to keep her head above water for a few weeks – perhaps pay for a month's energy and food. She was awarded £26.40. '[They] calculated [it] based on when I was next in receipt of a benefits payment,' she explains. 'Since I'd applied in the wee small hours of a Thursday or Friday morning, and I was due a PIP payment the following Tuesday, this was all that I was eligible to receive.'

As we talk, Becca wears a broken pair of glasses. The right lens has gone – a casualty of an accidental drop in the toilet a while back – and she can't afford to fix it. 'I'm either going to have to make friends with an optician or I'll have to make do with my left eye.' Being able to see straight is a luxury when you can't afford regular meals.

The cost of groceries in the UK was identified by the Office for National Statistics in 2022 as one of the biggest of all cost pressures on households, with food bills estimated to be rising at their fastest rate in fourteen years.[18] For a lot of comfortably off non-disabled Britons, the effects of this – like the energy price surge – are relatively new. But Becca – just like Mike, far away in High Wycombe – has long been forced to skip meals. 'I eat once a day, so there's enough for my son,' she explains. It is a brutal plan for someone with fatigue, but it is what mums do – even when their child is fully grown. Becca's own mum has been funding the 'bits and bobs' she leaves in her daughter's fridge with the Attendance Allowance she receives, intended to cover her extra costs during her cancer treatment. 'I hate that she does this,' Becca admits.

THE SPIRAL

Four hundred miles is not all that separates the stories of Mike and Becca. The many experiences they share – the skimping on food, the rationing of electricity – arise even though they have had quite different interactions with the benefits system. The real hardship of Mike and wife Sandra, like many other disabled people, kicked in when payments were cut or refused. But Becca shows the other reality: even if you get all the benefits you're entitled to, it's still nearly impossible to stay afloat. For all the press propaganda of disability benefit claimants living a life of Riley with wads of taxpayer cash and free £20,000 coupé cars, Becca illustrates the reality: for many people who are forced to rely on the social safety net long-term due to illness or disability, the benefits they receive are barely enough to cover basic living costs.[19]

The government can hardly deny this: its own research said so. NatCen research – commissioned by ministers – found that despite claiming the money they were entitled to, some disabled benefit recipients were 'still unable to meet essential living costs such as food and utility bills'. The then Welfare Secretary Thérèse Coffey went to extraordinary lengths to see to it that this analysis never saw the light of day. But in the end, a parliamentary committee ordered the researchers to publish it anyway.[20]

Becca doesn't need a study to confirm something she gets reminded of every month. 'When my benefits come in, I disperse the money to my direct debit accounts. The account they're paid into is empty within a few minutes.'

If the money coming in doesn't match the money going out, there's really only one solution: borrow it. To make up the difference from her benefits, Becca's had to max out her credit cards. She currently owes £2,800, but the interest is mounting. 'It's crippling,' she says. 'My interest payments are [at least] 30 per cent. One online store card is 49.9 per cent APR.' A consolidation loan last year gave her some breathing room, but her beloved cat, Jasmine, got cancer and things spiralled again. 'Her lungs filled with fluid and they had to euthanise her there and then. I had to put that bill and her cremation on my credit card. That was just under £400 in total. I couldn't bear not to have her ashes.'

Becca's indebtedness is nothing unusual: a Censuswide survey of disabled people and carers in June 2022 found most (54 per cent) of those polled reported being in the red.[21] Back in High Wycombe, Mike and Sandra are £10,000 in debt; years of desperation spread across two credit cards and two store accounts. The couple started relying on credit when Mike lost his benefits, before the pandemic compounded their problems. Sandra's severe asthma left her especially at risk from coronavirus and, like 3.7 million other people in England who were classed as 'clinically extremely vulnerable' and advised to shield, the two of them stayed inside for months to protect her.[22] Unable to get out to their discount food shop or the supermarket reduced aisle, they were forced to pay full price online. Often, they couldn't get a delivery slot as the whole country competed for one. Instead, they had to put takeaways on their credit cards.

'It's just become a snowball now,' Mike says. 'We can't get the debt down quick enough to get into a position where we can stop using credit cards.' He has a method of survival: pay for everything on credit cards, then do a balance transfer from multiple cards and settle whatever interest is imminently due.

Dressed in a T-shirt with a satirical *Daily Mail* logo with the headline 'Who buys this shit?', Mike tries to keep his sense of humour, but the strain of it is clear. 'Without all the credit card offers, the interest would be at least £300 a month,' he says. '[I'm] just kicking the can down the road – but I'm running out of road.'

PAST THE EDGES

In a decade of reporting on disabled people in hardship in the UK, including for my book *Crippled*, I've increasingly seen the sort of abject poverty that falls past the edges. The woman who had one bag of pasta in her cupboards to last three days but who couldn't get to the food bank because she was too ill to leave the house. The pensioner with arthritis and lung disease huddled up in a tent in his front room in the hope it would be warmer in a confined space.

Years of 'scrounger' narratives peddled by politicians and newspapers alike have taught many to see such scandals as very little to do with 'us': an extreme sort of poverty and isolation that is instead imagined to be the problem of people inherently different to you and me. This way of thinking draws simultaneously on prejudices towards disabled people and those in poverty. It exploits the assumption that a disabled person's life is guaranteed to be miserable and unfulfilled, to stoke the thought that none of this is worth worrying about. At the same time, it perpetuates the idea that disability is something that happens to other people and that if it ever did somehow befall us, 'we' – unlike those others – would somehow have the moral strength to protect ourselves from hardship.

That is a comforting fantasy. What I've witnessed time and time again is that it only takes one bit of bad health luck – a cancer diagnosis, a breakdown – to push previously secure people into financial crisis. Before you know it, life starts to unravel: having to leave work and go on benefits; getting into debt to pay the bills; falling into rent arrears; missing a mortgage payment and finding your house is in peril. As Becca puts it to me, 'I wish people understand that all it takes is a divorce, redundancy or illness to turn life upside down … I was always on top of my finances. Now, I can't afford to be alive.'

A month later, Becca emails me panicked: the DWP say she owes a 'benefit overpayment'. For years, Becca has received the Severe Disability Premium of ESA, an additional payment on some means-tested benefits that's designed to help with the extra costs of disability. What she didn't know was that it stops when any dependants turn eighteen, on the grounds that there is now another adult in the house. And at nineteen, Becca's live-in son becoming an adult meant her payments should have stopped last year. 'It didn't occur to me that I had to inform the ESA folk that my son had turned eighteen,' she writes. 'I sincerely believed that once the claims for Child Benefit and Child Tax Credit ended, the system would be automatically updated.'

Benefit bureaucracy can be impenetrable if you're healthy, but when you're ill, it's all the harder. ME cognitive dysfunction – sometimes called 'brain fog' – means Becca often can't remember something she's been told, let alone work out what she hasn't. 'I've failed to remember that I'd been running a bath, causing it to overflow and water damage in the kitchen. The last time it happened, I fried my washing machine,' she explains. 'I've also caused an oven fire. I forgot I was cooking.'

Becca promptly returned the form to the DWP, explaining how her condition led to these cognitive difficulties and that the overpayment was an honest mistake. A month later, Becca got a reply: she owed the government £1,615.20. For good measure, the department also fined her £50 because the 'excuse' of ill health was not deemed reasonable. 'If cognitive dysfunction isn't an acceptable reason, then what is?' she says. 'I feel like I've been punished because of my [health].' Becca could be deducted up to £29.60 per week from her benefits during a protracted pay-back period, the letter explained – a huge chunk of her income and a figure that could increase.

A statue of Ganesh presiding over her ottoman, Becca quietly tells me how the news had pushed her to the brink. 'I'm not ashamed to admit that it crossed my mind that there was little reason to want to be here.'

Becca is far from alone in her plight. As of February 2022, 2.1 million households – the equivalent of nearly half of all claimants on Universal Credit – had on average £62 docked from their benefits each month to repay benefit advances, overpayments and debts; the government effectively clawing back from such households hundreds of pounds of benefit payments a year.[23] In July 2022, a cross-party select committee of MPs urged ministers to halt the practice until rocketing inflation eases, warning it was tipping people into destitution.[24]

Only days after I speak to Becca, I hear from Mike: the DWP have quadrupled Sandra's overpayment penalty overnight. Just like Becca, Sandra had been told by the DWP that she owed thousands for benefits 'overpayment' – in Sandra's case, on her son's disability benefits from a decade ago. The couple had been paying back £20 a month but suddenly received a demand for £80. Within weeks, the DWP backed off – but it is more needless anxiety and a sign of just how frequent such threats are.

Back in Glasgow, after Becca talked again to the DWP, they agreed a reduced repayment plan of £5 per week, with a review in eighteen months. It is some reprieve, but it is yet more debt for the pile. In many ways, the repayment crisis looming over Becca sums up so much of what disabled people in Britain are facing: the system that's meant to help them through disability ends up compounding the harm.

CHOOSING A BETTER TOMORROW

Perhaps the most pervasive myth about poverty for disabled people is that it is all somehow inevitable. That it is 'simply written' that people like Mike, Sandra and Becca are bound to fall into hardship, and it will always have to be that way.

In truth, destitution for people with disabilities and chronic illnesses flows from man-made public policies, predominantly a social security system that neither assesses nor supports people appropriately. Or to put it another way: it is not disability that is denying so many disabled people in the UK the essentials right now; it is the fact that we choose to run a welfare state that leaves them systematically short.

This is not new but a problem that has got steadily worse during the austerity years. The 2022–23 general 'cost-of-living crisis' has simply exposed the underlying inadequacy of the social security system. Even when inflation comes down, the forces and policies that have sunk increasing portions of the disabled community into poverty will remain. Mike and Sandra will still be thousands of pounds in debt. Becca will still be eating one meal a day. These are not passing scandals but deep-seated problems in need of far-reaching solutions.

The good news is that the solutions are there, if we want them: reforming and making fairer disability benefit assessments; increasing benefit rates to meet the cost of living; building more social – and accessible – housing; properly funding and reforming social care, scrapping the impoverishing care charges increasingly placed on disabled people, while also taking the strain off unpaid family carers;[25] improving access to employment for those who could and want to work but currently too often face discrimination and inflexible conditions;[26] and funding squeezed local authorities to reinstate England's fast-disappearing emergency welfare funds and all the debt and benefit advice centres closed down by austerity.

Some would say we cannot afford to do all this, but really, we can't afford not to. Even a few years ago, before the cost-of-living crisis increased hardship, the myriad costs of poverty on society, such as the toll it takes on public services, was estimated at £78 billion.[27] Invest in social care, and a paraplegic teacher could be able to get to work and pay taxes. Fund social security that is sufficient to buy healthy food, and a malnourished multiple sclerosis patient will need less care from the NHS. The right thing to do is often the most cost-effective.

Few could look at the current state of Britain and think the old way of doing things is working. There has rarely been a more pressing time to acknowledge that it is possible to arrange society differently, or to reflect on the policies and prejudices that led us here. No one chooses to fall ill. But some politicians have chosen to make ill people's lives harder. This is remarkably bleak, but it is also rather hopeful. If poverty is a political choice, society also has the chance to choose something better.

'This is my life. You have to hold it tight': 'Mary' in Leeds on her bag

CHAPTER 7

DESTITUTE BY DESIGN: TRAPPED IN THE IMMIGRATION SYSTEM

DANIEL TRILLING

'I would sleep on the bus, or in doorways. I'd try not to sleep outdoors for long because I have asthma. When I slept outside, I couldn't breathe and I coughed a lot, especially when it was cold weather.'

Javed, in Leeds

'If I had a bit extra, I would stretch myself and maybe I'd buy a value box of chicken or something. I'd just treat [my kids]. I'd go, "Oh, I'm treating you today." And they'd go, "Yeeeeahh, we're having a treat today." They'd know they were going to have food with a bit of protein in it.'

Abena, in London

This chapter tells the stories of people like Javed and Abena, people who live in Britain but whom we collectively treat in a way designed to make them go anywhere else. Before we get to their individual accounts, we need a bit of context about the substantial – and growing – group of residents that policy seeks to make desperate. Who, exactly, is denied basic opportunities and even the compromised safety net that most others in the UK can still take for granted? And what is the system that locks them in penury?

The migration rules sort people into categories of deserving and undeserving. The logic is that the 'undeserving' need to be treated harshly, both to punish them and to encourage them to leave the country. The state achieves this either by restricting their access to benefits or by banning them from working – or sometimes through a combination of the two.

The system is very complex, having been constructed by successive governments, largely over the past three decades. The aim is sometimes explained as curtailing calls on the public purse and sometimes put in terms of deterring newcomers. A web of overlapping rules targets people of disparate backgrounds with many different reasons for wanting to settle here. But it's useful to think of them in four broad categories.

The first is made up of people who have the right to live in the UK but have the legal condition 'no recourse to public funds' (NRPF) attached to their visas. These restrictions ban them from most welfare benefits, as well as social housing and homelessness assistance. NRPF was dramatically expanded by the coalition government in 2012, as part of a wider set of reforms designed to make the immigration system more punitive, known collectively as the 'hostile environment'. People in well-paid, secure jobs may be able to cope with these stringent conditions, but for those who encounter hardship, the options for easing them are extremely limited.

The second group is of people who come to the UK to seek asylum. Since the turn of the century, asylum seekers have been banned from working in most instances, or from claiming welfare benefits. Instead, the Home Office offers subsistence payments to people waiting for their asylum claims to be considered. These are set at a much lower level than the regular benefits system – asylum support currently stands at £45 per week, or just £9.10 a week if you are living in Home Office-provided hotel accommodation.*

The third group is made up of EU nationals who came to the UK under pre-Brexit rules on freedom of movement. After Brexit, people who could prove they'd lived in the UK for five years or more were given 'settled status', which generally entitles them to benefits. Those who hadn't lived here for as long   or couldn't prove they had – were instead given 'pre-settled status', which carries fewer rights. As a result,

---

* Survivors of what the government calls 'modern slavery' – human trafficking or forced labour – are offered similar subsistence payments while their cases are being heard.

people with pre-settled status can end up being denied essential benefits at precisely the moments they need them most.

Finally, there are all those who don't have the legal right to live in the UK, either because they lost it or because they never had it in the first place. If your visa expires and you don't or can't renew it, if you are refused asylum and exhaust all your rights of appeal or if you entered the UK without permission, by default, you are banned from claiming benefits, working and more.*

As a result of all these restrictions, the immigration system now leaves very many people with either partial support or no support at all and at a higher risk of destitution. This is no longer a marginal issue but accounts for a substantial proportion of the deepest poverty seen on our streets and across our communities. The leading academic analysis, which surveys users of crisis services, estimated that by 2019, 28 per cent of destitute households were 'headed by a migrant'.[1] That is twice the total proportion, estimated at 14 per cent, of migrants in the population as a whole.[2]

The stories that follow are all of people who have been made destitute, or who have been trapped dipping in and out of destitution, or whose destitution has been compounded, by immigration restrictions. I contacted them through three migrants'

* The 'hostile environment' reforms introduced in 2012 also ban people without immigration status from many everyday activities such as opening a bank account, renting a home or obtaining a driving licence.

rights charities – Praxis, in east London; the Leeds Asylum Seekers' Support Network (LASSN); and GYROS, in Great Yarmouth – because I wanted to speak to people who felt supported enough that they could be open about their immigration histories. For the same reason, their names have been changed.

Although the system makes a distinction between the deserving and the undeserving, I would ask you to avoid playing that game when you read these stories. Instead, think about it this way: these are people who cook for us, clean for us, gut fish and pluck chickens for us and staff our shops. Or at least, they do when the system doesn't succeed in barring them from working at all. They have built lives here, or imagine the lives they might be allowed to build here. They have made the UK their home and have deep reasons for wanting to stay in that home. Their experiences are a part of our society, whether or not that is officially recognised.

MARY

'This is my life – my life savings have been in there for years,' says Mary, gesturing to a grey and red rucksack by her feet. 'My toothpaste, my toothbrush. Shield [deodorant], face towel, maybe my tights to wear once in a while. Tissues, Vaseline, medication, [sanitary] pads for women to have … those things – but sometimes you don't even have them.'

We are speaking in 2022, exactly twenty years since Mary arrived in the UK from her native Zimbabwe. Yet for the entirety of that time, she has had no right to work and has only very rarely had access to financial support from the state. For the past ten years, she has rarely lived anywhere for more than a few months at a time – and when all else has failed, as it frequently has, she has slept rough in Leeds, the city she has come to call a home of sorts. 'I can't remember how many places I've lived in,' she says. 'Dozens and dozens. You could even ask me my last address and I'd have forgotten.'

Mary came to the UK in search of asylum at the age of thirty, after fleeing political violence in Zimbabwe. 'I was being targeted. They threatened to kill me, they were coming at night trying to burn the house down and so forth. I ran. I had to run,' she says. 'I had no time to look for my paperwork.'

That absent paperwork, however, proved to be her undoing. After staying with friends in the UK for a few years – to 'work out what was happening', she says – Mary applied for asylum, only to be rejected for lack of evidence. As her claim worked its way through the appeals process, Mary was moved from one set of Home Office-provided accommodation to another, under the UK's dispersal policy for asylum seekers. By the early 2010s, however, her options had run out: Mary could not appeal her case any longer, so she was faced with a choice between returning to all the dangers she had fled in Zimbabwe or trying to live undocumented in the UK.

Since Mary had often been housed in Yorkshire, she gravitated towards Leeds. Some of the time, Mary says, she would try to stay with people she knew through the church she attends, but this was rarely a stable arrangement. While some friends were generous, she says, other people tried to exploit her, sexually or financially. 'Sometimes you live with a "friend" thinking, "I've got a partner."' At other times, 'you are the maid that does not get paid. People take advantage,' she says.

If you have been refused asylum and have exhausted all rights of appeal, then the state will usually only step in to rescue you from destitution if you agree to leave the country. The only other housing option for Mary has been to stay with hosts provided by LASSN – a network of volunteers in Leeds who loan out their spare rooms. But these were usually only short-term stays, sometimes offered on the day itself. As a result, she has become an expert at finding places to sleep rough in Leeds.

> I think I know most of Leeds now. I slept at bus stops. Or I'd go to sleep at St James's Hospital – it's always open, people go in and out, so the doors are always unlocked. You just go inside, you look for a small place and just hide yourself there.

Sometimes, she says, she'd even take journeys on cut-price coaches travelling between Leeds and other big cities. 'The

Megabus goes overnight. Sometimes I would take that bus, it will go to London, it will reach there in the morning. Maybe you get a ticket, maybe somebody gives you a ticket or you find a ticket on the floor, and you come back again in the evening.'

In 2018, during a four-month period of sleeping rough – the longest stretch she can remember – Mary made friends with another asylum seeker, a woman from Congo she met wandering Leeds city centre during the daytime.

> We'd meet by mistake, not like we were making an appointment. We'd just find each other, sitting there trying to work out: where am I going next? During the day at least you move around, but now you are tired, your legs are aching, so what do you do now?
>
> We'd go and sit down in cafes at the end of the day before they closed. Maybe she'd have £2 for us to drink a cup of tea. We'd chat, 'Hello, hello', and say, 'Where are you going?' Sometimes we'd part ways. Other times we'd say, 'Why don't we go to St James's together?' It was either this or get on the buses. On the buses you can sleep because there are not so many people.

'But remember,' – she points to the bag again – 'this is my life. You have to hold it tight.'

Last year, LASSN found Mary a spare room where she

could stay longer-term, but she will still have to leave if the family who owns the house needs the room back. Even if she can stay, Mary has no means to support herself and depends on donations from local charities for food and toiletries, along with the occasional voucher for new clothes.

The only way Mary can hope to resolve her immigration status is by applying for settlement on grounds of her twenty-year residency, a costly process that could take many more years to resolve. If her application is successful, she could be placed on the so-called ten-year route to settlement – a longer waiting period, introduced in 2012, under which she would have to apply for repeated visas over another decade before becoming eligible for permanent residence. For her fiftieth birthday this year, Mary says, her church congregation offered to club together and pay for a solicitor who could help her apply.

'It pains me to think I've wasted twenty years,' she says. 'And look, I'm still in the same limbo, I'm still going around. The government thinks that if I become destitute, why wouldn't I go back to Zimbabwe? But what about the things that made me leave? Do you think they [the people who threatened me] have forgotten?'

Instead, as difficult as it is, she remains. 'Sometimes I feel like I should have died. This is not how I should be living, because I'm begging. I am a beggar. I don't eat during the day because I don't have the money,' she says. 'I only have one meal a day. It's very hard, but I have to make a choice because if I eat a sandwich, it means I won't have supper. I can hear my tummy at night just twisting and rumbling. My brain is saying: what am I doing here?'

STELLA

When Stella's son started secondary school recently, she had one piece of advice for him: don't let your new friends see how we live. 'When my son was a bit younger,' she says, 'he would come home from school crying, saying his friends have their own room, so why doesn't he have his own room?'

For the past two years, Stella and her son have been sleeping in the front room of her brother's two-bed flat in south London.

One time, one friend's mum came to our house because I was doing a bit of cash-in-hand work, looking after her children. The children started telling friends at school – you know how children are – saying they saw our things in boxes in the sitting room. My son was bullied. When he started secondary school, I told him, 'It's better not to bring anyone home, you remember what happened to you the last time?'

If she were somebody else, there would be no reason why Stella and her son should have been forced into a choice between crashing on a relative's sofa and ending up on the street. In a good month, Stella can earn up to £1,500 from her job as a healthcare assistant – less than the London Living Wage, but still an income, and one that could be topped up with benefits. Until just a few days before we spoke, however, she had been banned from claiming Universal Credit or from applying to be housed by her local council.

To make matters worse, Stella says she is in so much debt that the money she does make disappears almost before she knows she's got it. 'If you look at my bank statements, every month you will see money is going to this person's account, that person's account – like, every month I'm paying three to four people,' she says. 'Any time I work, my account is always minus because I have to pay back all the money I have borrowed. And when I've done that, my son might want something and I'll find that I only have £5 left, or maybe only a little bit of food left.' She adds:

And you know children of his age, they want cereal, they want this and that – things that I can't even provide.

It causes stress and panic. I have to live and my son has to live. I don't want him to join a gang, for people to be enticing him with new Nikes and things like that.

Stella's situation – and many of those debts – are the direct result of the immigration system.

Now in her fifties, she explains she originally came to the

UK from Nigeria in 2004, to escape an abusive relationship. 'It got to the stage that friends in the UK told me: you will die one day if you don't run away from this man,' she says. 'I had a good job back home; I worked in a bank. But it's the relationship that made me run to this country.'

Stella arrived on a visitor's visa, but with no safe home in Nigeria to return to, she stayed when that ran out, with no way of regularising her status. For many years she lived in the shadows, surviving on cash-in-hand domestic work and cooking for social occasions among her network of friends and acquaintances. She met a new man, but he too started abusing her when she became pregnant. 'He started beating the hell out of me, saying he didn't want the pregnancy. Later I heard he was married [at the time], but you know, when you are in love, it's what they tell you that you follow,' she says.

It was only after Stella's son turned seven that she became potentially eligible for leave to remain, on human rights grounds. (After a child has clocked up seven years of residency, the system begins to take seriously that they might have an interest in staying here, which can sometimes give the parent the right to stay too.) In 2018, Stella borrowed thousands of pounds from friends to apply; Legal Aid, which covers solicitors' fees for people on low incomes, is no longer available for most immigration cases.

Stella's application succeeded, but she was given a series of punitive conditions. Like many who regularise their status on human rights grounds in recent times, she was placed on the ten-year route to settlement. The extended waiting time is a punishment twice over: it allows the government to keep you in a state of limbo for longer, but also to charge you more money – you have to apply to renew your visa every two and a half years, at a cost of thousands of pounds each time. The standard application costs £1,033, far higher – on the government's own figures – than the cost to the Home Office of processing the application.[3] On top of this, visa holders must usually pay the 'immigration health surcharge' – a charge for use of the NHS, imposed even on those who already pay for the NHS via their taxes – which currently stands at £624 per year. And to cap it all, Stella's visa came with the condition 'no recourse to public funds' attached.

She could, however, now lawfully work. Stella found employment as a cleaner – sometimes working two or three jobs at a time – while she and her son lived with her brother, contributing what she could to rent and bills. But the situation deteriorated when Covid arrived. 'Before, my brother and his wife shared a room and they gave us a bedroom,' Stella says.

But my brother has a kidney problem and goes to dialysis three times a week. He caught Covid in hospital, and it was serious. He stayed in the hospital for a month or two and when they dispatched him, the doctor said that nobody could share a room with him because he's vulnerable and his wife had to move into the other bedroom.

At the same time, during the first lockdown, Stella's main employer went bust. She was left unable to afford even the very basics. 'Thank God that at this time, my son's primary school introduced me to an organisation' – a local migrants' support charity. 'They started giving us food, they'd put it in a bag and knock at the door. We'd have some, and I'd share it with other people – I have a neighbour, she's a single mother with three kids and she doesn't have [immigration] papers, she's not on any benefits.' After the lockdowns lifted, Stella was able to resume work, eventually leaving cleaning for her healthcare job. 'Now I've told the organisation they can stop bringing things, so that my own can go to other people.'

But her situation remained precarious. London's private rental market is out of her reach – she even paid to rent a single room in a house-share, but the landlord then told her they won't accept children – so she has been forced to keep on living with her son in her brother's front room.

My salary is not enough for two bedrooms. If I had a girl I would say, 'Oh, we can live together, we can manage with one,' but I have a boy. We are different sexes. When I have to get dressed, he has to go out. That's the way we live.

In summer 2022, shortly before we spoke, Stella's visa was up for renewal. With the help of a caseworker at Praxis, she successfully applied to have her NRPF restrictions lifted, on the grounds that her son was at risk of destitution – one of the few exceptions the Home Office makes. For the first time in years, Stella says she has some hope that her living conditions might stabilise: she has applied for Universal Credit and is preparing an application for housing to her local council.

But she is worried about what might happen in future, if NRPF conditions are reimposed the next time she applies for renewal. 'I used to do two jobs, three jobs,' she says.

> I went from one place to another, I worked like hell, because I didn't have any support and I'm the kind of person that doesn't ask people for help. I don't want to inconvenience people – it's only when I'm pushed to the wall that I will ask for things. I was doing so much work that even the doctor pushed me to reduce it.

Stella fears that her age and her worsening health mean she would not be able to withstand a return to her old routine. 'The cleaning job was difficult for me: I am a diabetic patient, I have high blood pressure, I have sciatica pain,' she says. 'But now I can't even do two jobs any more. I stopped around December time. I looked at myself, people looked at me – they said I looked haggard, do you understand?' The next renewal date for her visa is only a year away. 'I've been panicking already, because I don't have any savings.'

ZHENYA

At the start of our conversation, Zhenya takes his passport out of his pocket, opens it at the photo page and pushes it across the table towards me. The taciturn sixty-year-old, a Russian with Lithuanian (and therefore EU) citizenship, looks uncomfortable speaking to me – in his eyes, probably, I'm an extension of the various agencies and charities he has been visiting to ask for help over the past few weeks. And he doesn't like asking for help.

'I have *problema*,' he says, in a mix of English and Russian, gesturing to his back and his leg. 'I'm angry and worried. I've worked here for twelve years and when I get sick, this happens.'

Zhenya is currently sleeping rough with a friend in some woods just outside Great Yarmouth, in Norfolk. 'It's a big tent, for four people, and two of us live in it,' he says, adding, 'It's not dangerous, I'm not afraid.' But when it rains, he says, making a gesture to show water soaking up from the ground, 'everything gets wet'.

Zhenya has lived and worked in the UK for twelve years, mainly in factories. First he tried London and Birmingham, then he moved up to Peterhead, near Aberdeen, to work in a fish processing plant. For the past five years, he has lived in Great Yarmouth. Agriculture in this part of the country – chiefly the poultry industry – has for many years relied on

European migrant workers. Until earlier this year, Zhenya was working on the production line at a chicken factory in nearby Thetford, via an agency contract.

Just over six months ago, however, Zhenya says he was forced to stop working by a long-term back problem that flared up and started causing intense pain. 'I walk fifty metres, twenty metres and I have to stop,' he says. 'It's *problema*, standing or walking, for me.' As Zhenya's job required standing on a production line for twelve-hour shifts, he was signed off sick by his GP.

In theory, there should have been support available to prevent Zhenya from falling into destitution. His contract entitled him to several months' sick pay – and after that, since he'd been living and working in the UK for so long, he should have been entitled to apply for benefits if he still couldn't work. But two things have combined to make him homeless.

First, he says, he couldn't afford to fully pay his rent and bills for the room in the flat he rented in Great Yarmouth town centre. 'When I stopped working, I got into big debt,' he says. 'I couldn't pay for the room and, erm—' he makes a throwing-away motion to indicate he was out on the street. During the day, a friend lets him visit his flat to wash and to make meals with the food parcels he receives from local charities.

Second, when Zhenya then went to his local Jobcentre to ask for support, he was told he wasn't entitled to any because he only had 'pre-settled' immigration status. In 2019, when the EU settlement scheme opened its doors, Zhenya didn't know enough English to make the application himself. Instead, he used the services of an 'advice shark' – it's illegal in the UK for people to offer immigration advice unless they are officially certified – who was charging members of Great Yarmouth's EU immigrant community to make applications on their behalf.

Over the past few years, the practice of advice sharking has become widespread as EU nationals grapple with an entirely new bureaucracy surrounding their lives. Some price gouge their clients, charging hundreds of pounds per application. In Zhenya's case, he says, he was only charged £15, but the shark made the wrong application, getting him the lesser 'pre-settled' status, even though he was eligible for settled status.

EU nationals with pre-settled status aren't automatically entitled to benefits, and in particular can be barred from them either while they are new in a job or after they have been out of work for a long time. After several months sleeping rough, during which time his sick pay ran out, Zhenya started to ask for help – but he has so far been rejected at every turn.

GYROS, a local immigration charity, contacted the borough council's housing office on Zhenya's behalf, but they were told that because he has pre-settled status and isn't currently working, the council couldn't house him. All he has been offered is temporary accommodation, but even that hasn't yet come through. Another local charity helped him apply for Universal Credit, but Zhenya was told that because he'd now been out of work for longer than six months, he wasn't entitled to it. Which may or may not be true: the complex rules do have exceptions for people who can't work on medical grounds. But staff at GYROS, as well as staff at several other migration charities I spoke to around the country, told me that because the EU settlement scheme is still relatively new, it's common for officials at local councils or the Department for Work and Pensions to mistakenly tell people with pre-settled status that they're not entitled to benefits even when they are.

It isn't only the state that is shutting off resources. One of Great Yarmouth's main food banks, which is having to ration supplies because of increased demand this year, recently told Zhenya that he had been coming to them for help for too long and should move on.

'I didn't know anything about all these rules here,' he says. 'I was surprised, because I have been living here for twelve years and other people immediately receive this Universal Credit and all these benefits, so why not me?'

Now, Zhenya's two options are to apply for settled status – a caseworker at GYROS has recently submitted the paperwork – or to find another job and earn for three months, which would qualify him for benefits.

'I want to work, but at the moment it's very difficult,' he says, pointing to his back again. Even though it was damaging his health, he has considered going back to the chicken factory. The trouble is that living in the woods, and being unable to charge his phone, makes it difficult to keep in touch about shift patterns. But he has to try. 'Three months' work, and after, I will apply for Universal Credit and be able to live normally,' he says.

JAVED

'Sometimes you don't get to shower for weeks,' says Javed, a 34-year-old with piercing grey-green eyes. 'You just walk around and look for somewhere to wash, or when it's raining you just, you know—' he turns his face skywards and laughs. One of the worst things about being homeless, he says, is the constant feeling of being dirty. 'You feel dirty, you think everything around you is dirty. It's so—' he looks for a word. 'Bad.'

Since 2017, Javed has been living in Leeds without a home of his own. He has sofa surfed between a handful of friends, although he never remains in one place for long because, he says, he worries about outstaying his welcome. He has also spent periods in temporary housing for destitute asylum seekers – at the moment he is a guest of LASSN's hosting project. But when nothing else is available, he takes to the streets. 'I would sleep on the bus, or in doorways. I'd try not to sleep outdoors for long because I have asthma. When I slept out-side, I couldn't breathe and I coughed a lot, especially when it was cold weather.'

Javed's story shows how insecure immigration status can end up compounding other problems in life. He came to the UK in 2011 from Peshawar, Pakistan, to study for a business and management diploma in Manchester. Buying, selling and marketing is his passion, and he had plans to launch his own internet marketplace, where he would sell goods from China to westerners. While Javed was studying, he also fell in love.

'I met a girl, and we got married. We planned to live to-gether and have children, but it didn't go that way,' he says. Having arrived in the UK on a temporary student visa, Javed hoped that he would be able to apply for permanent residency via his partner, a British citizen. After a few years, however, the relationship broke down. 'She got addicted to drugs and her behaviour changed. She became very abusive towards me and started stealing things from the house. So I decided to leave. But after that, my immigration case was stuck.'

After leaving his wife, Javed received a letter from the Home Office telling him that his application for a spousal visa had been refused, since he wasn't in a genuine relationship. With his student visa expired, and no right to live or work in the UK, Javed felt trapped: he couldn't go back to Pakistan, he says, because he is bisexual and during his time in the UK, he came to reject Islam, the religion he was raised in. His father 'cut me off because he doesn't agree with my lifestyle'.

In 2017, Javed moved from Manchester to Leeds – because, he says, his former partner was stalking him – to stay with a friend. His savings, given to him by his father when he first came to the UK, were running out and he had been juggling credit cards to stay afloat. He spent the last of his money on solicitors' fees to apply for asylum, on the grounds that he would be persecuted because of his sexuality and beliefs if he went back to Pakistan. Six months later, this application too was refused. 'When my asylum claim was in progress, I had some hope,' he says. 'When it was refused, it put me in a depression. My savings were finished, I owed money. I was completely in the dark and I didn't know how to manage things.'

Increasingly, Javed found himself wandering the streets of Leeds. When he wasn't able to eat with friends, he would scavenge for food in the city centre. 'Sometimes I'd eat leftovers – some days I'd have a few chips and drink water, that's it. Or I'd wait outside shops and ask someone to buy me a meal.' He learned the schedules and the distribution points of the network of Leeds charities that hand out free food, and he'd try to hide his poverty from friends and acquaintances by staying in the city centre, 'where there are lots of people and nobody who knows you around'.

The longer Javed stayed destitute, the worse his depression became. 'I really started thinking it wasn't worth living. When you don't have hope, you're just blind and dark,' he says. At the beginning of the pandemic, in spring 2020, Javed lost hope entirely. 'I jumped into the river Aire because I was so confused and depressed. I was really trying to, you know, take my own life. The cops came and they took me to the hospital and the psychiatrist.'

This marked a turning point, and a temporary reprieve. After being treated in hospital, Javed went to see a GP, who referred him to a Leeds-based refugee charity. They helped find him a place to live, in a house that was donated to LASSN for longer-term stays. For the moment, this has given Javed the basic level of stability he needs to try to resolve his immigration status: with the help of a caseworker from the charity, he is trying to gather evidence that will support a fresh asylum claim.

'Now I have time to think about my case,' he says. 'If I wasn't there [in the home], I would just keep running, I'd be worried about too many things – I'd worry about food, I'd worry about shelter.'

But his situation remains fraught with hazards. Without the right to work or claim benefits, he is entirely reliant on the support of charities. If his asylum claim is refused again, there are few other options, short of remaining undocumented and destitute in the UK until he has been in the country for twenty years – which for Javed, who does not see Pakistan as an option, would mean another nine.

Already, he says, destitution means he has missed out on so much of life. 'The worst thing is that I have been here in the UK for eleven years, but I haven't travelled … I'm thirty-four, so that eleven years is the golden era for a person. After that, how are you going to build your future?'

ABENA

'I started being happy again,' says Abena, a single mother of two and a Londoner, of the moment in 2017 when she received her leave to remain in the UK. 'I could finally have a proper job and get a proper salary.'

Abena has lived in the UK since moving here from Ghana in the early 2000s, but she spent more than a decade undocumented after her initial visa ran out and she was unable to renew it, despite repeated applications. As she describes it, she spent her two sons' early years – one is now eighteen, and the other ten – living 'hand to mouth' to support them. Cash-in-hand work cooking and cleaning for acquaintances was supplemented by loans from friends and family, but it was rarely enough to fully cover the basics. 'There were times I had to starve to make sure my kids had food,' she says.

In 2017, Abena's local MP in east London helped her make an application for leave to remain on human rights grounds. 'I was literally in tears in the local library and he gave me a letter for the Home Office and recommended a solicitor,' she says. Abena was placed on the long and costly ten-year route to settlement and with the unforgiving 'no recourse' conditions attached. But at least she could now work in the formal economy. She took two jobs – one as a school cook, the other as a customer assistant at M&S.

Even so, Abena soon found she was still struggling to make ends meet. 'It was very difficult, because I had debts to pay. In 2017, my oldest son was naturalised as British. But I needed around £6,500 to pay for the [settlement] application for myself and my little one.' Paying off the resulting debts – and saving up for the renewal fees two and a half years later – meant that her take-home pay of around £1,000 a month simply wouldn't stretch, even with a third job, a bit of cooking and cleaning work, on the side. Life was slightly easier than when she had no legal right to work at all, but Abena was still trapped in poverty.

'There have been so many times that I had to go hungry so the kids could eat,' she says. 'Sometimes I would just eat the leftovers from their bowls.' At times, she says,

I'd go for like two weeks where I didn't have money to buy food for all of us – I'd have what was on the sides of their plates and I'd just drink water. I used to go to sleep very early because sometimes I was so hungry I couldn't stay up. It was just… hard. Sorry, I'm being a bit teary now.

Having repeatedly gone short of food over the years means Abena knows various ways to make things stretch. A bag of

rice and some eggs, she says, can feed two children for most
of a week: rice pudding for breakfast and Ghanaian egg stew
for lunch and dinner. But even that wasn't always possible.

> Sometimes I would just buy a bag of chips and they would
> have chips with nothing at all, only mayonnaise or ketchup. If
> I had a bit extra, I would stretch myself and maybe I'd buy a
> value box of chicken or something. I'd just treat them. I'd go,
> 'Oh, I'm treating you today.' And they'd go, 'Yeeeeahh, we're
> having a treat today.' They'd know they were going to have
> food with a bit of protein in it.

There are limited forms of support available for parents with
no recourse to public funds whose children are at risk of destitution. Local councils can provide emergency funds under
a rule known as Section 17,[*4] and specialist food banks exist
in major cities like London to support immigrant families
excluded from the welfare state. At the time, however, Abena
says she didn't know about these options – and, fearful of
a surveillance state that wanted her out of the country, she
would have been too scared to ask for help anyway.

'I didn't know who to call, I didn't know who to talk to,' she
says. 'And I was taking care not to get into any kind of trouble.
Because really and truly, when I got my leave to remain, I

---

* In effect, one part of the state – the Home Office – spends money administering a system
that denies people benefits. Then another part of the state – local government – spends more
money trying to repair the damage.

was frightened. I didn't want anything to ruin my settlement application.'

It was only in 2020, just as her visa was up for renewal, that she discovered it was possible to apply to have NRPF conditions removed.

> I went to a lady's house to cook and she said, 'Why do you work so hard? You work too much.' I remember telling her that I need to survive, my kids need to live. And she said, 'OK, I have a friend who just got her no recourse to public funds taken off. I can get a number for you.'

Through this friend, Abena was put in touch with a caseworker at Praxis, who successfully applied to have the restrictions lifted when she renewed her visa in 2020. As a result, Abena now receives just under £200 a month in Universal Credit and Child Benefit, which she says is vital to keeping her head above water.

Two and a half years on, however, and her visa is up for renewal again – with no guarantee the Home Office will not simply reimpose the restrictions. 'I don't know what's going to come now, so I'm a bit worried,' she says. If NRPF is re-imposed, 'it's going to be working from hand to mouth again'.

'We all pick each other up': Ian Morrison (centre right) with tape over his Deliveroo badge, on strike with his union comrades

CHAPTER 8

ATOMISED, BUT NOT ALONE: WORK AND RESISTANCE IN THE GIG ECONOMY

JEM BARTHOLOMEW

On the cold morning of 7 April 2021, Ian Morrison slipped on his fluorescent teal Deliveroo jacket, fastened the laces of his Nike trainers and pulled a snood over his head. Then Morrison, a courier from south London, ended his usual routine with a new ritual: he tore away a strip of black masking tape and stuck it over his heart, obscuring Deliveroo's logo – an angular kangaroo head known within the company as the 'Roo mark' – on the jacket.

Morrison, thirty-one, wasn't working today. He was driving north of the Thames to demonstrate with scores of other striking riders against the company's employment practices. The strike was planned by the Independent Workers' Union of Great Britain (IWGB) to coincide with Deliveroo's shares opening for public trading. Morrison's blacked-out badge signalled that couriers were angry. 'We're working for you,' Morrison said, 'but what are you doing for *us*?'

As riders gathered to demonstrate outside the City offices of Deliveroo, the London Stock Exchange and Goldman Sachs, which helped list the company, a chorus of honking scooter horns echoed around the empty streets of London's financial district, still half locked down a year into the pandemic. 'Good turnout, innit?' Alex Marshall, the IWGB president and a recent courier himself, said to a colleague. Marshall wore sombre clothing – a black hooded jumper, inky jeans and dark Reeboks – as if in mourning for the insufficient livelihoods of the hundreds of workers gathered around him. As he cycled at the head of the procession, Marshall sparked a flare, enclosing the riders in a shroud of red mist. Photographers jostled for the best picture. Chants went up of 'Shame on Roo' and 'Shame on Shu', referring to the co-founder and chief executive of the company, Will Shu. Some demonstrators wore masks of Shu's face, alongside signs reading: 'You're Taking Us For A Ride'.

Shu, a former Morgan Stanley analyst, set up Deliveroo from his Chelsea flat in 2013 – along with developer Greg Orlowski – based on a compelling idea: deliver good food fast. A year later, Shu attracted venture capital to expand to Paris and Berlin. Around that time, politicians like Chancellor George Osborne were positioning Britain as a global leader in the 'gig economy', or, as they sometimes called it then, the 'online sharing economy'.[1] In cities like London, Deliveroo became a household name. By 2021, it valued itself at around £8 billion and was shooting for Britain's largest initial public offering (IPO) in a decade.[2] The then eight-year-old company, with few physical assets, was sold as being more valuable than Sainsbury's and having more than double the market capitalisation of Marks & Spencer.

But by the day of the strike, the shine was wearing off. The small and sparky IWGB union was determined to disrupt the party for Deliveroo, like a barnacle affixed to the boat's hull, threatening to bore a hole in the bottom of the vessel. In the immediate run-up to the float, around £1 billion had been shaved off Deliveroo's valuation range – with much worse to come. Deliveroo's IPO saw its shares drop by as much as 31 per cent, with the *Financial Times* reporting that the float was perhaps 'the worst in the history of the London market'.[3] Things have hardly improved since; the company's share price collapsed in 2022, with a one-year change at the time of writing of minus 62 per cent.[4]

So what went so wrong? Well, despite the great boost to its revenues from a pandemic which made it the gatekeeper to restaurant food, Deliveroo has never actually made an annual profit. Still, investors are very patient with tech start-ups, and in 2021 the company was continuing to grow apace: between January and December that year, it was targeting expansion to 100 new UK towns and cities. The firm was listed with a so-called dual-class share structure – allowing Shu to raise cash but retain control. That blocked some funds from investing. But other tech firms worldwide had taken the same route and still managed to thrive. The root problem that scuppered Deliveroo's plans was something else – something far simpler than financial projections or stock-and-share structures: workers' rights. Concerns were emerging about the company's relationship to the people, like Morrison, who try to make a living by doing its delivery driving.

TAKING TO THE ROAD

When Morrison began driving for Deliveroo and Uber Eats, in 2018, he loved it. The freedom of riding a moped across London beat shuffling between tables at his old restaurant job. His feet no longer ached. His hours were enviably flexible. He was comfortably making £500 to £600 a week. It barely felt like work at all. Morrison recalls a memory of scooting past Big Ben as it counted out the hours and feeling 'like, wow, this is amazing' – the driving gave him a new sense that even though he had grown up here, he was now thriving at the centre of things in London, his city. But Morrison said a series of changes enacted by Deliveroo across 2018 and 2019 – gradually replacing a system whereby shifts in many London zones were pre-booked, which provided some reliability for regular drivers, with more free-for-all zones, governed by competition for orders – roughly halved his wages. His honeymoon phase came to an end. 'That's when it started feeling like work,' he told me.

Morrison, raised in West Norwood, has had to bring home an income to support his siblings since his mother died a few years ago. Even before fuel prices surged by half in the year to summer 2022, a third of Morrison's pay cheque was going on operating costs such as petrol and work-related loan repayments, which, if he was a conventional employee, his company would bear.[5] He took out a £2,000 loan to pay for his Peugeot 125 scooter, worth around £1,200, he said, and other equipment. Money was tight. 'It's just impossible,' he told me, even before the energy price hikes. 'How can anybody live like this, you know?'

Multiple full-time couriers told me the same story: they initially enjoyed the job and its flexibility, but low and increasingly precarious pay made it an uphill struggle simply to cover costs. Each day at around 11 a.m., Ismail Eloued leaves his Mile End house-share and logs on to the Deliveroo app. He rides his electric bicycle for roughly four hours, ferrying food in his backpack to homes and offices over lunchtime. Then his bike's battery dims. He returns home to charge up – 'to maximise the hours' – before hitting the streets again around 7 p.m. Eloued, in his early twenties and originally from Morocco, said he moved to the UK in 2018 from Italy and first worked for a gig economy platform doing kitchen portering jobs. He then started working as a delivery rider in 2020. 'I'm working basically every day,' he told me in 2021.

Most people I spoke to rarely took a day off. It was six or seven days a week, often 12 p.m. to 12 a.m., of cycling, collecting, delivering – working with a sense of panic until legs burned and eyes drooped. One self-employed courier who worked in a Mayfair restaurant's in-house delivery service, whose name is not being disclosed to protect their identity, told me, 'Sometimes in my dreams I'm still doing the deliveries.'

When Morrison's head finally hits the pillow, he delivers orders in his dreams, too. Sometimes it's just dropping packages. Other nights, he's plagued by recurring nightmares. There's one panicked dream where his pay cheque arrives as usual but the payment amount is, inexplicably, £0. Or another dream where he's running and bailiffs are chasing him, demanding his possessions; he wakes up after begging them to leave him alone. Hour by hour, all across Britain, the gig economy is exacting a punishing toll.

Weekends seeing friends soon evaporated for Morrison. It was a lonely slog. But then one day, as he was waiting on the street outside a restaurant, a courier friend said to him, 'You should join the union. If we've got the union on our side, we've got a much better chance.' He signed up, attending a demonstration criticising Deliveroo for its low pay and lack of protections. It was his first dip into activism. Morrison

was new to politics, but the speeches chimed with him. He
suddenly realised how many others felt exactly the same way
about working ever harder for vanishing rewards. But he
didn't know, that day on the street, what a profound turning
point this would be in his life.

CONTESTED TERRITORY

Morrison's journey from enthusiasm to disillusion in his work
mirrors a wider shift in attitudes towards the whole model of
his industry. Not long ago, the gig economy felt like the future,
with every industry primed for tech-enabled 'disruption' as
inevitably as a train barrelling towards its destination. Empty
flats, underused cars, flexible workers and more were to be
matched via app-based platforms with whoever had the most
demand for them. For evangelists like Wingham Rowan, the
social entrepreneur behind non-profit Modern Markets for
All, gig efficiencies promised to be empowering for everybody
– from lone parents who wanted to work odd hours to cafes
that needed hired hands at short notice.[6] And many consum-
ers enjoyed the new flexibility. Booking an Uber through a
smartphone soon felt as natural as hailing a cab.

While the engine of this new model was Silicon Valley, British politicians latched onto Deliveroo as their home-grown
exemplar. Even a few weeks before Deliveroo's disastrous flotation, the current Conservative Prime Minister Rishi Sunak,

then serving as Chancellor, praised the firm as a 'true British tech success story'.[7]

And yet as early as 2016, the realities experienced by some workers and couriers were beginning to intrude on the hype. There were murmurs that the gig economy employment model was sickly – and that political treatment may be required. After a wave of strikes from Uber Eats and Deliveroo couriers in 2016, Conservative Prime Minister Theresa May was pressured into setting up an independent review of working practices. Led by Matthew Taylor, a think-tanker and former Tony Blair aide, the commission's July 2017 report sought to chart a middle way, with proposals aiming to balance the gig economy's dynamism with greater stability for workers.[8] But even if it had been immediately implemented, instead of being hampered by drift and delay, it wouldn't have shut down the argument: unions criticised the recommendations as weak and inadequate.

Later in 2017, the Labour Mayor of London Sadiq Khan supported Transport for London (TfL) in what at the time seemed like a shocking decision to strip Uber of its licence in the city, over concerns the company was failing to vet its drivers adequately on passenger safeguarding. Although Uber eventually won that court battle with TfL in September 2020 – and had continued to operate while appealing the decision – the years-long saga had shown that gig companies could not forever rely on skirting regulatory oversight or avoiding the political heat.

Then, in February 2021, the UK Supreme Court lit a match under the sector's employment model, by ruling that Uber drivers should be classified as 'workers' instead of 'contractors' – entitling them to minimum wage and holiday pay – because they are in a 'position of subordination to Uber'.[9] The ruling placed them in a sort of halfway category, known formally as 'limb (b) workers', between fully protected employees and unprotected self-employed people under the 1996 Employment Rights Act.[10] The status argument goes to the heart of the controversy: it pits the gig companies' claims that workers enjoy self-employed-style autonomy over their time against the workers' argument that they are under the control of the firm in other ways.[11]

From couriers to care home workers to waiters, it seemed as if consequences from the ruling could soon ripple across the gig economy, which had now grown to the point where – a 2019 Ipsos MORI survey found – it employed nearly one in ten Britons aged sixteen to seventy-five at least once a week.[12] The Supreme Court cast once-shiny start-ups in an unforgiving light: gig economy workers were never really their own boss, and companies had thrived by offloading risk onto workers.[13] Its ruling wrenched away the automatic assumption that tech platforms could dispense with employer worker obligations with clever contracts.

And yet winning one battle is very different from winning the war. The Supreme Court's Uber ruling was not a gig economy-wide reboot: everything still turns on the exact details of the particular economic relationship. Employment lawyers got busy, and further cases followed. In a parallel case concerning union rights just a few months later, in June 2021, the Court of Appeal sided with Deliveroo, finding that drivers were not entitled to have their membership of the IWGB recognised.[14] The company at the time declined to comment to me, but its spokesperson was reported as saying, 'This small self-appointed union does not represent the vast majority of riders.'[15]

But again, this ruling proved to be a less than final word. It relied on, without fully reassessing, a previous judgment that had found that couriers were contractors, not workers. In September 2022, the IWGB took Deliveroo to the Supreme Court to challenge the denial of collective bargaining rights.[16] And even when that verdict arrives, others will surely follow, as the messy struggle to figure out how twentieth-century employment laws apply to 21st-century labour markets inches along, case by case.

Through the fog of legal and ethical uncertainty, one thing cuts through: the gig model of contracting with workers is now contested terrain. For some firms, this poses questions of regulatory legitimacy that could become existential: 'If a company isn't able to function without paying at least the minimum wage to its workers and respecting very basic working-time protections,' says Alan Bogg, professor of labour law at the University of Bristol, then 'I don't think we should lament businesses that struggle to function.'

It was this uncertainty, more than anything else, that stymied Deliveroo's momentum in 2021. Nobody can be sure how sustainable or profitable the company will be until there is clarity about what obligations it has – or doesn't have – towards its tens of thousands of drivers. A few days before the April 2021 flotation, Aviva Investors, one of the UK's ten largest asset managers, told the BBC's *Today* programme that it would not invest because, among other things, Deliveroo riders were not guaranteed the minimum wage, sick leave and holiday pay.[17]

The uncertainty is not just legal, about the application of existing laws, but political, concerning the writing of new ones. Across the political spectrum there is a sense that reforms to protect workers might be required. Just after winning the December 2019 election, Boris Johnson's Conservative government promised an Employment Bill to ensure the 'security that workers deserve', with special reference to the 'gig economy'.[18] Three years on, no bill had materialised. A government spokesperson tells me that the Johnson Employment Bill is 'no more' but that the Sunak administration is supporting other private members' bills to 'increase workforce participation, protect vulnerable workers and level the playing field, ensuring unscrupulous businesses don't have a competitive advantage'. Workers, however, are not waiting – a fightback is under way.

Morrison is not alone in getting active. Union membership overall had for decades been declining remorselessly, cumulatively roughly halving since the 1979 peak of 13.2 million. But it edged back up in the four years preceding the pandemic (before slipping back very slightly in Covid's unique circumstances); the tally of union members stood at 6.44 million in 2021,[19] with small nimble 'start-up' unions like the IWGB reinvigorating the scene.

As the couriers arrived at Deliveroo's locked-down offices during the April 2021 strike, Marshall, a belligerent campaigner, sounded defiant addressing the crowd through a megaphone. 'You guys are all absolute heroes,' he said to cheers. Streets that had been empty were buzzing with an electric atmosphere; the boisterous noise ricocheted off the glass windows of corporate offices. 'We want better pay, we want better rights and we want better safety,' Marshall said. 'You guys do not deserve to be doing such a dangerous job for less than minimum wage.'

FREE FALL

Throughout 2019, Morrison was slowly becoming more involved with the IWGB union. But it wasn't until an evening that November that he felt its true importance. Around the time Deliveroo began gradually expanding its free-for-all login system across London, Morrison found that he was having to travel further afield on delivery drops.

He recalls shuttling from Waterloo to Greenwich at around 9 p.m. to deliver a kebab to a block of flats. The location felt a little sketchy. His fluorescent uniform stuck out in the dark. The next thing Morrison knew he was being attacked by a gang of eight. They kicked him off his bike. They seized his moped and, with the key still in the ignition, started driving away. In the moment Morrison forgot all sense of danger and his legs started pursuing them. An adrenaline rush surged through him and his heart was thumping like mad. Now he was catching up with his attackers. The only thought in Morrison's mind was 'I need to pay my bills, I can't afford to lose this,' he said. Suddenly they were in front of him. He tried wrestling the moped back. But the men scattered, and, as he watched, the red tail light of his bike sailed away into the night.

Morrison rang the police, but they couldn't catch the thieves. His insurance did not cover theft. When he called Deliveroo, they were sympathetic, telling him not to work in that area in the future. But he sensed a disconnect between the company's words and actions – its app, after all, had sent him there. It was 'a sense of betrayal', he later said. There is not and has never been any suggestion that Deliveroo is legally responsible for couriers' bikes. In 2021, when I reported on this topic for *Prospect* magazine, Deliveroo did not reply to repeated enquiries. When I contacted them for this book, a spokesperson told me riders have access to safety tools, like the app Flare, and to insurance, which began rolling out in 2018, covering accident and sick pay; but Deliveroo conceded that this insurance does not cover theft.

Yet for couriers like Morrison, vehicle robbery can be a catastrophe: the loss of an asset – which they might still be paying for – which also spells the disappearance of income. Morrison saw debts pile up, falling a month behind on rent, which, he said, provoked threats of eviction from his landlord.

Listen out for them and you will hear many more stories like Morrison's. When 35-year-old Bora Radu, who drives for Uber Eats and Just Eat in Swindon, had his Yamaha T-150 stolen at knifepoint in January 2021, he told me he'd lost around £1,000 in income by the time police retrieved it. Not only was it a terrifying experience but he was pushed into debt just to cover his rent for the one-bed he shares with his wife. 'That bike is my bread,' he told me. Radu didn't even think to ask Uber Eats for support, assuming it would be hopeless to ask.

As for Morrison, whatever the law says and contrary to Deliveroo's line, his feelings were clear. 'I felt abandoned,' he told me. The only practical support Morrison felt he received was not from Deliveroo but instead from the IWGB, which offered him an electric bike for a week while he got back on his feet – but he declined the offer. He became unwell, spiralling into depression. The city he'd grown up in had overnight become dark and frightening. The experience played over and over in his head. He was not entitled to typical sick pay for employees, so to cushion his freefalling bank balance, he signed up for Universal Credit. (In this way, the gig economy passes risks not just on to workers but on to the taxpayer, too.) In the end, Morrison was forced to stop working as a courier for over six months and returned to the old waitering job he had once been so relieved to escape. But he did keep in touch with people at the IWGB.

WAGES OF DISCORD

When the company and the IWGB union that it refuses to recognise talk about the gig economy, they sound like they are describing entirely different worlds. Deliveroo claimed it conducted a survey of 8,500 riders in 2021 which found that 89 per cent were 'satisfied' with their job and said that workers 'value the total flexibility they enjoy'.[20] (The IWGB disputed the survey and its findings.) The two sides even disagree on what one might hope would be a basic and verifiable fact: hourly pay. Deliveroo said drivers have 'the ability to earn over £13 an hour', whereas the IWGB claimed the rate can fall to just £2 when demand for deliveries falls, less than a quarter of the headline minimum wage.

The crux of the issue is the definition of 'clocking in'. Gig economy couriers are often paid a fee only when they accept a passenger or food order. The firms say they are not working (or even 'on call', a state that carries some protection for employees) until this moment. Up until that point, the companies say, drivers are free to decline trips. For their part, unions say that time spent logged into an app and ready to go, waiting outside a McDonald's, should also count as work. If the companies don't need them, then – from the workers' point of view – they should fix their algorithms to prevent drivers sitting idly by the curb. 'If you're working in a pub,' IWGB's Marshall told me, 'do you only get paid every time you pour a pint?'

In March 2021, the Bureau of Investigative Journalism published an analysis of 318 Deliveroo invoices covering 34,000 working hours. They found that 17 per cent of riders were earning below £6.45 an hour – until April 2021 the minimum wage for 18–20-year-olds – and 41 per cent were earning below the full £8.72 pay floor for those over twenty-five.[21] The company told the bureau that 'time logged on does not mean they are working'. Deliveroo calculates average pay 'from the moment a rider accepts a Deliveroo order until they complete the order. This is more than the national minimum wage.' But Frank Field, former chair of the Work and Pensions Select Committee, looked at dead time, and in a 2018 report likened Deliveroo's business model to Britain's early twentieth-century ports, 'where workers would gather around the dock gate desperately hoping that they would be offered work'.[22]

For Uber drivers, at least, the 2021 Supreme Court ruling has moved the argument on: their working time now begins when a driver is logged onto the Uber app.[23] The ruling is already influencing lower courts, raising the spectre of large liabilities concerning backdated wage claims, holiday and sick pay over years for thousands of workers. For Chris

Beauchamp, head of market analysis UK at IG Group, this 'does call into question this growth-at-any-cost, high-cash-burn kind of [start-up] model'. To critics, reality is finally catching up with the tech utopians who they say have long manipulated the rules on employment law – and built businesses on the backs of exploited workers.

AGAINST THE MACHINE

The fightback has been driven by scrappy upstart unions like the IWGB, which has over 6,000 members, and others. 'Those new forms of organising are a response to new forms of employment that appear to be designed to avoid traditional employment law and organising methods,' Paddy Bettington, research officer at the union-sponsored think tank the Centre for Labour and Social Studies (CLASS), told me. Small independent unions see their role as different from Labour Party-affiliated giants like Unite (1.4 million members), Unison (1.3 million) or GMB (570,000); they are political outsiders and often deploy more combative tactics.

The newer organisations worry that employers will move to cut deals with bigger and more familiar unions with minimal boots-on-the-ground organising density. Since Uber lost its Supreme Court fight over drivers' status and rights to the small App Drivers and Couriers Union (ADCU), for instance, the company has struck a recognition deal of sorts with the

GMB. (The ADCU did not seek recognition; a source told me in 2021 it would only seek to bargain with Uber after it adhered to basic statutory employment rights.) A few years ago, it would have been unimaginable for a gig platform to buckle to a union on behalf of people who it insists are not employees. The GMB says the deal has created a safety net that drivers cannot fall through. But it's equally striking that this deal does not cover pay bargaining.

By contrast, in May 2022, a year on from the IWGB strike, the GMB signed a voluntary agreement with Deliveroo which did include collective bargaining on pay. A Deliveroo spokesperson told me the agreement is clear that riders are guaranteed the National Living Wage, with the majority earning 'significantly more than this'. Again, this would have been unimaginable until recently. Yet the GMB–Deliveroo agreement was attacked as 'hollow and cynical' by the IWGB. The small union not only felt undercut by its bigger cousin and the company; it was aggrieved by how the deal classified drivers as self-employed and did not cover those crucial waiting times, which the IWGB insists can cause pay to plummet below minimum wage.[24] (The GMB did not agree to an interview.) Experts told me these clashes between large and small unions will likely accelerate in the future.

Proponents of small unions say they are faster and freer. Big unions' bureaucracies can create a barrier between officials and workers, said Alberto Durango, co-founder and former president of the IWGB, now national organiser at the tiny Cleaners and Allied Independent Workers Union. Only unions of a few thousand members, he told me, can strike the right balance, being able to crowdsource the resources to make an impact while remaining truly worker-led.

Before being elected IWGB president in November 2020, Marshall himself worked as a courier for a laboratory, depositing medical equipment across London. In February 2020, 'we started to see specimens with these little yellow stickers on them saying "Covid-19 Specimen"', he recalls. 'We were like, "What?"' When his confusion lifted, he was alarmed. A few weeks later, the country was in lockdown and the roads were ghostlike. Marshall remembers crying as he cycled to work through the empty city – the fountains of Trafalgar Square splashing away with no one to hear them – initially without PPE or masks. He has asthma. 'Would I be on a ventilator?' Marshall recalls wondering in those scary first weeks. He tells me that such recent direct experience of hitting the streets, which would be unlikely in a larger union where it takes time to rise through the ranks, colours the way he runs the IWGB.

LEVELLING DOWN

So if campaigners can finally secure the Employment Bill which has, as things stand, been abandoned by Sunak, what would they want to see in it? First, they want to make sure *existing* protections can be counted on. 'We have massively underinvested in our enforcement capacity over decades,' Tony Wilson, director of the Institute for Employment Studies (IES), told me. A January 2021 IES report found that, on average, UK employers can expect a knock on the door from wage enforcers only 'once every 500 years'.[25] The problem is all the more pressing in an economy swimming with contracts for labour whose very form is disputed; this uncertainty makes it difficult for workers even to know what their rights are. One idea Wilson supports is to create a single enforcement agency – with a big budget and a stiff mandate – streamlining powers that sit siloed across a handful of Whitehall departments, and ideally armed with the ability to issue punitive fines to deter employers from bending the rules.

At the same time, campaigners want it made much easier for workers to assert their rights. The Uber ruling took five years of fighting through the courts, expending time and resources many workers cannot access. This tilts the scales in favour of corporations, with their deep pockets. Another demand is easier union recognition. Currently, employers must grant unions recognition. If denied, unions must seek arbitration.

For Wilson, the very category of 'worker' – which the courts have now applied to Uber drivers – is 'a real fudge of a grey area'. It could be scrapped, establishing a legal presumption that someone whose labour is being deployed by a firm is a full 'employee', unless and until they are shown to be self-employed.

As things stand, the gig economy has grown very large, but

the government drags its feet in ensuring the law keeps pace. The result, Wilson said, is 'allowing employers to level down on standards and level down on protection'. And the threat to workers isn't just from dither and delay. Amid the discontented winter of 2022–23, with a wave of strike action by employees seeking to tackle a cost-of-living crisis and inflation that rocketed over 11 per cent,[26] Sunak's government – cheered on by right-wing newspapers – seemed more interested in restricting union rights to get organised in the public sector than in extending them elsewhere.

Meanwhile, the bet for gig economy executives is that habits built during lockdown – ordering much more restaurant food or groceries with the swipe of a finger – will persist like muscle memory far beyond it. That may happen and would presage still more growth. The gig economy's critics, however, fear that the corollary will be even more precarious jobs. In a fragile recovery from Covid and a spiralling cost-of-living crisis, in which many traditional employers on the high street and elsewhere may not survive, even more people could soon find gig work the only way to put food on the table.

POWER UP

After the November 2019 robbery, Morrison's depressive episode lasted months. He eventually began delivering again in summer 2020. It wasn't the same. He deliberated over orders at night, anxiously checking the postcode to assess its safety. When he was sent back to Greenwich on an assignment, his heart pounded, his pulse drummed. What had once seemed exciting and hopeful now felt scary, uncertain, no good. But something had shifted in Morrison. For one, he was determined not to let his attackers win. Yet there was also something bigger than that. He began to realise that it was the job that made him sick. The guilt of taking a single day off, the stress of upkeeping expensive gear, the precariousness of no protections, the panic when more couriers are hired and wages driven down, the utter powerlessness of changing it all – the job *itself* was in a state of sickness, not just him. He felt like the world of work was being poisoned by an invisible cancer. 'You feel powerless,' he said.

The way Morrison wrestled power back was through the union. 'It's a massive difference, honestly,' he said when I caught up with him at April 2021's Deliveroo strike. For that he thanks the friend who nudged him to join, on that street corner, years ago. 'I feel empowered, because I know I'm not alone and I've got other people fighting for the same thing.' He went on, a hand hitting his knee for emphasis. 'We're always there for one another, you know. If one person's down, we all pick each other up.' His new confidence was followed by a positive work development. A few months after the strike, Morrison landed a formal employment contract with Getir, a grocery courier firm, which means more stable hours and a chance to tackle his debts.

Morrison's journey – from hope to disarray to empowerment through the union – furnished him with a desire to help other riders, too. A couple of years back, someone at the IWGB wondered if Morrison might like to run for the committee. He was elected disability officer and, while serving, campaigned for accessibility adjustments such as for hard-of-hearing or menstruating couriers. Often, nowadays, when Morrison is stood waiting on the street with other couriers, he'll tell them, 'You should join the union.'*

---

* A version of this piece appeared in *Prospect* in 2021. It has been expanded and fully updated for this volume.

CONCLUSION

A FIX FOR BEING BROKE? FROM INSIGHT TO ACTION

TOM CLARK

Well before the pandemic and energy crisis, as austerity ground on, the progress we used to take for granted on life expectancy was petering out: women in poorer parts of England had actually started dying earlier.[1] Other trends, like an 80 per cent increase in drug deaths (far worse in Scotland), hinted at a connection with despair and social distress.[2] But isolating causes using statistics is devilishly difficult at the best of times – and with slow-building problems like chronic disease and premature death, we are always looking deep in the rear-view mirror.

Walking into homes and communities with ears and eyes open is another matter. The human beings in the midst of the poverty crisis can immediately point to the precise privations that sink the spirit and batter the body – as well as the snares that prevent any easy escape. They don't have to wait for any statistical test to elucidate exactly how each of these issues inflames others.

Just recall, in no particular order, how 'Sandra's' lack of a decent bed in High Wycombe aggravated her asthma to the point where her heart stopped, and how even now – long since out of intensive care – her struggle to afford electricity leads to her switching off the air conditioning that keeps the air moving through her lungs on warmer days; recall, too, how when it's colder she – just like indebted Phoebe in Manchester – skimps on warm showers; how destitute 'Javed' in Leeds has often been unable to wash at all, save perhaps in the rain; how his material condition contributed towards his suicidal breakdown; and how – 400 miles north in Orkney – Lindsay lay helplessly under sheets damp with condensation, feeling not only cold but also 'mad'; how the reticence of 'Sophie' in Manchester, Lowri in Blackpool and 'Yvonne' in Tottenham in coming clean with colleagues, friends and family about the hunger they suffer has distanced them from the very people who should be there to support them; how one loan from the shark soon begot many more for 'Kelly' in Cheshire; how the slavish hours of Ismail in Mile End leave him none of the spare time that he might otherwise use to plot an escape from the gig economy; how the empty days of Francis in Glasgow led him to seek comfort in drink, which in turn left him with too little money for the right food, thus too little iron, and too few healthy red blood cells; and how Tracy's eviction notice in Bideford, Devon, led to her treasured garden, which used to provide some peace of mind, running to seed.

As Matthew Desmond – the American sociologist who went so far as to move into a Milwaukee trailer park to secure a close view of the hardships he wrote about – has summed things up, 'poverty isn't a line' but 'a tight knot of social maladies', 'a relentless piling on' of difficulties.[3] All this makes poverty an extraordinarily complex *phenomenon*, but it is at the same time also an extremely simple *problem*: very many people in Britain today don't have enough money. Not all the troubles listed in the previous paragraph would completely disappear if the people involved had some extra resources, though a lot would. All of them would be soothed.

So, in a world where money is always – or at least always claimed to be – scarce, when it comes to 'fixing' the poverty crisis, there is in truth just one fundamental question. Namely, what needs to change for the millions of Britons who currently lack the basic resources for life to acquire them? Prod it, however, and this turns out to conceal several other questions. For example, how can public policy best concentrate the resources at hand where they are most urgently needed? At the same time, which sort of policies are most likely not only to relieve want but also to support a virtuous cycle of dignity, confidence and habits that can help to hold it at bay? Third, what balance to strike between these first two objectives, of relieving the worst consequences of poverty and addressing the deepest causes? Fourth, what are the most promising political avenues to expand the total public resources available for dealing with both halves of the problem? Fifth, what needs to happen to empower all those suffering from deprivations today to rise up and secure adequacy for themselves?

A whole book could be written about every one of these questions, and in these closing pages I can do no more than offer a few thoughts relating to each. In every case, however, I will draw on our dispatches from the hard end of an unfolding emergency, highlighting the insight that our interviewees have shared. Throughout, in addition to emphasising the more promising prospective solutions, I'll also stress the small things we can all do to try to make life a little more tolerable for all those in our communities and our streets who are on the wrong side of this crisis right now. In case you either find yourself in need of somewhere to turn or are moved to donate money or time, a Resources section at the back of this book provides full details of the various charities whose practical and sometimes life-saving support has cropped up in the course of our reportage. In the same spirit, I'm delighted that the Joseph Rowntree Foundation have not only made this book possible but also agreed to donate all royalties to the Leeds Asylum Seekers' Support Network, whose invaluable efforts are documented in the stories of 'Mary' and Javed in Chapter 7.

TAKE BACK CONTROL

Simply listening to families in hardship would suggest a few immediate priorities for relatively low-cost action that might otherwise be missed. If there is one theme that has rattled right through these pages, it is control – or rather the lack of it. When money is tight, most people soon become expert at budgeting. It is when costs suddenly swell or income disappears in unpredictable ways that planning becomes impossible and the pile-on of problems truly starts, including, sometimes, the loss of the confidence to even attempt to grip the situation. The story of 'Mike' in High Wycombe, who had been making gains with his agoraphobia but was soon knocked back down to 'rock bottom' by the threat to his benefit lifeline that came when the system ruled him 'fit to work', is one case in point.

In the context of benefits, one obvious tweak, which the Labour opposition has recently expressed interest in, is reassuring claimants that if they try out a job and it doesn't work out, they will quickly be free to return to all the same payments they had previously, without facing all the uncertainties of a fresh application.[4] Freeing people to experiment with changing their circumstances without risk not only creates a sense of control but could well – if it encourages more people to take the plunge into work – pay for itself.

More generally, public policy and public administration have to put much more of an onus on the avoidance of nasty surprises. Think of Becca in Glasgow, suddenly told that because different computer systems hadn't spoken to each other when her child came of age, she suddenly owed the Department for Work and Pensions over £1,500; or Sophie in Manchester, who faced a devastating sudden interruption in her money when she was 'migrated' from the old benefits to Universal Credit, with its built-in five-week wait. These are exactly the sort of shocks that push people from hardship into destitution, and which indeed turned Sophie from a food bank volunteer into a food bank user. When systems are being designed, a premium ought to be placed on avoiding such disruptions. And to the extent that some shocks are unavoidable in life, a proper, nationwide scheme of crisis loans urgently needs to be reinstated. The Cameron coalition's 2012 decision to delegate this function to councils with only cut-priced grants to cover it shredded the ultimate safety net – and virtually guaranteed that hardship would translate into outright destitution of the sort we increasingly witness.[5]

Unmanageable debts are perhaps the single biggest reason why people end up losing control. Remember Phoebe in Manchester, who despite convening a debt support group herself admits to struggling to keep track of the repayments to her many lenders. Many others we have met, including 'Stella' in London, who had to borrow to fund the visas that secure her immigration status, Becca in Glasgow and Mike and Sandra in High Wycombe, all conveyed the panic that comes with juggling repayments and fretting about how long they'd be able to keep all the balls up in the air. Calm, expert assistance could often make all the difference. In the context of the £200 billion-plus the government directly hands out through the pension and benefits system, the few tens of millions spent on debt advice is a rounding error. The government points out that resourcing in

England is higher than before the pandemic, but it remains far too low, especially as the rising prices that are pushing so many families into debt are also eating up the real value of the grants.[6]

It is also important to recognise the direct role the government has as a creditor itself: sometimes, as with Sandra, the demands to repay benefits are merely one of several competing problems, but sometimes, as with Becca, they are the most frightening problem of all. At the very least, the onus should be on the state to communicate early and clearly in such cases, and show flexibility about the timing of any repayments due. At the moment, it too often fails to do this.

But money isn't everything – even when it comes to coping without having enough of it. One unmistakable refrain echoing through our dispatches with a force that surprised me is the importance of nature and the great outdoors in giving those in hardship the space they need to confront – and take mindful charge of – their situation. Recall, once again, Tracy's garden in Devon, but also the importance David in Drumchapel puts on 'getting my hands dirty' in the community allotment to keep his despair and health problems in check, and then too the solace that Dieter draws from feeding the birds and watching the 'slow maturing' of trees, as he battles the chill winds of adversity on the Isle of Lewis. Green spaces obviously aren't a complete answer to the poverty crisis, but if we are to take seriously what we have heard in *Broke*, preserving and promoting access to them is one modest and worthwhile thing public policy can do to help people endure it.

Far too many people in 21st-century Britain are entirely at the mercy of events, both at home and at work. Obvious and overdue reforms could help in both contexts. Indeed, the Westminster government did pledge an Employment Bill, which it is hoped will provide more predictable shifts for zero-hour and gig workers, and has also vowed to abolish so-called Section 21 no-fault evictions, which can see English tenants like Tracy in Bideford rapidly booted out on a landlord's whim. But as I write, both reforms have been postponed, with the government at one point even floating giving up on the Section 21 change altogether. I suspect something will be done in respect of both before the next election – these are, after all, popular causes – but everything will then turn on the detail.

Gig drivers like Ismail in Mile End and Bora in Swindon don't want to hear about some theoretical right to more stable earnings; they want to know exactly how many hours they have to do for how long before the platforms that rely on their efforts are forced to provide them with a living that they can rely on in turn. Likewise, for the next wave of English tenants facing Section 21 notices, what matters isn't just seeing those orders banished but also the exact alternative grounds on which landlords will be allowed to kick them out in future. If the right for a landlord to move themselves or a relative in, even for a temporary spell, is drawn too widely, then there will be many circumstances in which nothing much changes – as Jo discovered in Scotland, where no-fault evictions have already been abolished.

EXPANDING THE POSSIBLE

Looking further ahead, the route to more secure homes has to involve resetting the tenure mix, with more social housing and new taxes on property which diminish its attractions for speculative investment and thereby increase the affordability of ownership for everyone else. But in a world where older people both turn out to vote and own homes in very large numbers, and in a country where the great austerity Chancellor could quip to the Cabinet that 'hopefully we will get a little housing boom and everyone will be happy as property values go up', to call the politics of this fraught is an understatement.[7]

The key to unlocking the housing problem is, somehow, engendering empathy among those who own homes for those who do not. Empathy is also the missing ingredient when it comes to summoning the resources needed to fix the many holes in our benefit safety net, and indeed to weave protection from scratch for those – like the migrants Javed, Mary and tent-dwelling 'Zhenya' – who currently have no safety net at all.

The top priorities for extra expenditure on social security are a subject well covered in endless think tank reports. For transparency, I should just register that the most important principle as I see it is re-establishing the broken link between needs and assistance. This specifically requires ditching the two-child limit, which ignores the number of mouths a family must feed; boosting Local Housing Allowance so that it no longer leaves half of its private renting claimants facing a shortfall of £150 a month simply to keep their roof over their head; and ditching the arbitrary household benefit cap.[8]

But the deeper issue is, of course, that the basic rates of benefits no longer provide adequately for the basics of life. It is, for example, not any detail of the social security system but rather the sheer stinginess of the £69 a week Carer's Allowance Mike receives that means he is always living close to the edge – and so always liable to topple over it.

The real prize would be an indexation regime which slowly but surely ratchets up all the rates towards adequacy. Long ago, I worked on analysis of the great inequality increase in 1980s Britain, which found that as much as *half* the total rise was explained by the quiet switch away from the pre-1979 practice of raising benefits roughly in line with general prosperity and instead freezing them in real terms.[9] More recently, the 'triple lock' on the annual pension increase (and earlier incremental rises in the means-tested Pension Credit) played a big part in reducing rates of poverty among the elderly. Conversely, it is after repeated freezes and squeezes on basic benefit rates – which lost value in eight of the ten years between 2013 and 2022 – that extreme hardship has crept up across younger age groups, just as it crept up on Kelly, Lowri, Sophie and so many of the other people we have met in these pages.[10] Incrementally ratcheting benefits up would eventually make a huge difference, while avoiding landing taxpayers with one big, sudden bill.

There is, however, no escaping the reality that both the

immediate fixes of the system's worst gaps and then the steady improvement in its adequacy will require new and ultimately substantial public funds. Which means there can be no ducking the task of persuading taxpayers to consider this as priority spending and stump up. So how to do that?

First, launch an unremitting assault on the political lie that a neat line can be drawn between the 'working' and 'shirking' (or 'striving' and 'skiving') elements of society. Having grown up in a middle-class family but with a mostly unemployed dad, I've always known that the whole idea of this clean divide is grotesque distortion, and I have no doubt that the complexities of real life will have likewise taught very many Britons to see straight through it. But even in a world of rising in-work poverty, others will still need disabusing of it – which is where the meticulous arithmetic of the late LSE Professor John Hills comes in handy. In his 2015 book *Good Times, Bad Times*, he demonstrated that the great bulk of the work the welfare state does is redistributing not between people of irreconcilably different sorts, but rather across the life cycle of all of us.[11] The upshot is that it is worth us paying for social security, because there will come a time – whether that be due to illness, parenthood or infirmity – when most of us will need to fall back on it. As a campaigning strategy, the argument for a (real) 'all in it together' approach has the additional advantage of fighting back directly against the sort of demonisation encountered by Mike and Sandra, and also tackling the stigma that has gnawed at Yvonne and so many others we have met.

Second, make the argument for social security in a confident, full-throated manner. The doyen of British pollsters, John Curtice, has demonstrated how public attitudes to benefit claimants markedly hardened in the mid-1990s, immediately after Tony Blair's opposition diluted the party's traditionally strong pro-welfare state stance, adopting a more questioning and judgemental attitude towards some who relied on state benefits. Moreover, Curtice found that this hardening of attitudes was most marked among Labour not Conservative supporters, suggesting a role for politicians in shaping, rather than merely reacting to, the attitudes of their own followers.[12]

More recently, whereas the frequently hesitant Labour opposition of 2010–15 was unable to stop a whole run of benefit cutbacks, once the party took a strident turn in September 2015 and began opposing all cuts unapologetically, multiple government U-turns were forced – affecting, for example, tax credits and disability benefits.[13] Of course, Jeremy Corbyn ultimately led Labour to heavy defeat and left it a long way from the levers of power. But while Keir Starmer has been desperate to distance himself from his predecessor on most questions, he hasn't yet reverted to New Labour triangulation on benefits. True, the opposition is making few hard promises – and campaigners must press them strongly for more – but at least it is asking the right questions concerning, for example, the dismal 'two-child' policy. The existence of a firm flank defending social security on one side of the political pitch creates room for individual politicians on the other side concerned about poverty to make a stand. Indeed, when the government moved to withdraw its emergency pandemic £20 a week 'uplift' in Universal Credit, disquiet right across the House jolted the then Chancellor Rishi Sunak to markedly increase support for poorer working families.[14]

Standing up for decent benefits, then, has been proven to make a difference. The opposition must do it, and it must also avoid the great danger of tying its own hands in a way that precludes acting in power. Amid a desperate need for public resources, any pledge not to raise this or that tax or to restrict borrowing needs to be carefully weighed, not thrown around casually in a dash for 'sound money' respectability. Yes, things need to be paid for, but some things are worth paying for.

Finally, as well making the case for social security vigorously, we need to strike a note of optimism about what a remarkable difference it can make. 'The poor are always with us' is an attitude as old as the Bible, so resignation can be tough to shrug off. Exactly as Matthew Desmond has written of the US, progressives in the UK are in danger of being so 'fluent in the language of grievance and bumbling in the language of repair' that they miss spectacular successes. In the US, they too rarely point to the sharp reduction in rates of hardship that steadily followed Lyndon Johnson's supposedly losing 'War on Poverty' and – more recently – the marked falls in evictions, homelessness and hardship during the pandemic period of policy activism.[15] Here in the UK, too, as Covid-19 shut down the economy there were widespread fears of unprecedented penury, and many people certainly struggled. But overall, thanks to a raft of imaginative policies put in place – including furlough, a temporary ban on evictions and above all that crucial 'lifeline' in the form of a £20 a week Universal Credit uplift – on all the main definitions, overall poverty actually *fell* during 2020/21.[16]

In a time of adversity, that is a heroic achievement and something to build on. The political failure to shout about it, and campaigners' understandable tendency to focus only on those people who have fallen through the gaps, can only encourage the sort of helplessness aired by Phoebe in Manchester when she relayed that since 'the people with all the money do not care about the rest of us' she just couldn't imagine meaningful change.

NOT WAITING, BUT TAKING

There is, of course, a great deal of truth in what Phoebe says: life's haves are always unlikely to care as much about the plight of the have-nots as they do themselves. Which is why, in the end, a huge part of fixing the problem of people being broke involves those very same people taking charge of the situation. From the five-day week to equal pay laws to collective bargaining and even the right to vote, the entitlements we enjoy as citizens are historically something that have been taken as much as given. So it will also be if 21st-century Britain is finally to secure the ideal, described over eighty years ago by Franklin Roosevelt, of 'freedom from want'.[17]

It is not for me or anyone else to tell renters like Lizzie or couriers like Ian and the many allies both have found in their tenants' and workers' unions how to organise their campaigns. Instead, we can draw heart from their accounts, which demonstrate how their activism has not only advanced their material interest but also done something to restore that crucial sense of control. Recall Lizzie talking about the 'joyful aspect' of 'collective power' that she felt after overcoming her nerves and heading to Elephant and Castle with fifteen others who, simply by making life a bit awkward for the bailiffs, were able to buy a tenant threatened with eviction precious time. Recall, too, in the words of her housemate, just how 'full of fight' she then turned out to be when the time came to contest her own eviction.

In a world where business interests are deeply wired into policy-making processes, and where landlords are – as Chapter 1 detailed – heavily represented in Parliament and government, thoughtful establishment commentators increasingly recognise that, simply in the interests of balance, organisations representing workers and tenants need to be given more of a voice.[18] As of early 2023, however, the government is moving towards new restrictions on both the right to protest and the right to strike.[19] The role of public policy should instead be to facilitate and empower grassroots collectives and listen carefully to them. After all, a jobs and housing market that worked better for tenants and workers should also leave a lot less work for the welfare state to do – and so a smaller bill for the taxpayer.

Sometimes, the importance of the collective doesn't lie in taking action, as such, still less in lobbying on particular policies, but simply in letting people know they're not alone. Recall Phoebe's take on why the debt support groups she and Nicola run in Greater Manchester matter so much: 'There is a need for people to talk. But me and Nic are those people as well.' The contribution of policy here, which can't be taken for granted in an austerity state, is simply to make sure there are safe, warm and accessible halls or community centres for people to meet in.

But to fix many of the problems that leave so many in Britain both broken and broke will involve bigger, more difficult and expensive decisions. Bringing the voices of those with direct experience of hardship to bear is crucial to getting those decisions taken. Simply paying heed to the sort of testimony that is collected in this book is a good place to start, but the real prize is getting more people who know what it's like to face hardship into positions of power. As Darren McGarvey, the writer and rapper who grew up in Glasgow communities with many of the same problems as those Dani Garavelli reported on in Chapter 5, has recently put it:

Why does a tradesman have to look at a blocked toilet or a burst pipe before he lets loose with the tools? Why does a GP need to see you in person? … These conventions exist because it would be absurd and even dangerous to do otherwise. Yet decisions about Britain's most pressing social problems in the 21st century are often devised remotely, behind closed doors, with no meaningful input for those the decisions affect.[20]

Among the many efforts made to secure 'diverse' and gender-balanced political representation, experience of the rough edges of life remains an afterthought. The awkwardly independent journalist Michael Crick is keeping tabs on candidate selections for the next general election and noted in November 2022 that Labour had 'now picked 40 candidates for winnable seats', of whom only one had a working-class job.[21] The old ladder up into public life that used to be provided by the trade union movement is not, for the moment, what it was in the days when half the workforce carried a union card. Which is all the more reason for anyone concerned with recruitment to concern themselves with the class and hardship angles of diversity, on top of all the others. And all the more reason, too, to support those grassroots movements of tenants, workers and activists that can supplement the experience of hardship with the experience needed to lead.

It isn't so long since the pandemic made the unthinkable unarguable. A sharp reminder of the myriad ways in which our fates – physical as well as financial – are intertwined, it persuaded us collectively to depart from long years of austerity and embrace the furloughs and emergency benefit boosts that prevented pestilence from automatically translating into mass penury. Although the British state rapidly lapsed back into its callous old habits as soon as the vaccine was rolled out, it is the same heads and hearts that were persuaded back then that things had to be different that now need be won over to a more permanent fix for being broke.

Those same heads are well capable of looking at the worrying numbers of Britons who have withdrawn from the labour market on health grounds, and processing Mike's story of being not only impoverished but also incapacitated by the cruel perversities of the system.[22] Those same hearts will surely be moved by the story of Mary, who, after twenty years in this country, can only sleep dry by hiding in St James's Hospital or picking up a discarded ticket and boarding the overnight Megabus from Leeds to London and back. Those heads and hearts alike will surely grasp that expecting 'Abena's' children to grow up without adequate protein, and Lowri's thirteen-year-old daughter to live in a home where there's sometimes been 'no money for food', is both wrong in itself and at the same time runs unacceptable risks with health and learning which are dangerous for our future society. Whatever our failings as a nation, we are not so broken that we can't see it. The argument is there to be won.

NOTES

A NATION DISTURBED: WHERE THINGS STAND IN 2024

1   Available at: https://www.youtube.com/watch?v=2Kf8gzqjbOo
2   Frankie Lister-Fell, 'Staff throw away tents of people sleeping rough outside hospital', *Camden New Journal*, 9 June 2023.
3   'Homeless tents destroyed during Met Police operation', BBC News, 12 November 2023.
4   'Camden Council admits role in removal of homeless tents', BBC News, 15 November 2023.
5   Margaret Davis, 'Officers who cleared homeless people's tents acted unlawfully, say Met Police', *The Independent*, 17 January 2024.
6   @SuellaBraverman, 4 November 2023. Tweet available at: https://twitter.com/ SuellaBraverman/status/1720730450556006714?lang=en
7   Tevye Markson, 'Braverman sacked as home secretary after policing row', *Civil Service World*, 13 November 2023.
8   Olivia Barber, 'Conservative MPs set to revolt against government plans to criminalise rough sleeping', Housing Today, 2 April 2024.
9   House of Commons, Criminal Justice Bill [as amended in Public Bill Committee], 30 January 2024, available at: https://publications.parliament.uk/pa/bills/cbill/58-04/0155/230155.pdf
10   Eleni Courea, 'Tory rebels plan to decriminalise rough sleeping by repealing 200-year-old law', *The Guardian*, 1 April 2024.
11   'Consumer price inflation, UK: April 2024', Office for National Statistics, 22 May 2024, available at: https://www.ons.gov.uk/economy/inflationandpriceindices/bulletins/consumer priceinflation/april2024
12   Katie Schmuecker, 'As cost of living support ends, people still can't afford life's essentials', Joseph Rowntree Foundation, 22 February 2024, available at: https://www.jrf.org.uk/ social-security/as-cost-of-living-support-ends-people-still-cant-afford-lifes-essentials
13   Trussell Trust, 'Emergency food parcel distribution in the UK 1 April 2023 to 31 March 2024', 15 May 2024, available at: https://www.trusselltrust.org/wp-content/uploads/sites/2/2024/05/ EYS-UK-Factsheet-2023-24.pdf
14   Hannah Corbett and Karen Turner, 'Ofgem price cap announcement: Energy prices are going down, but the burden on those least able to pay remains too high', University of Strathclyde, February 2024, available at: https://www.strath.ac.uk/humanities/centreforenergypolicy/ newsblogs/2024/ofgempricecapannouncement/
15   Tom Clark, 'Scars and stripes: the horror of US poverty', *Prospect*, 10 May 2023.

16 Department for Work and Pensions, 'Households below average income: for financial years ending 1995 to 2023', 21 March 2024, available at: https://www.gov.uk/government/statistics/households-below-average-income-for-financial-years-ending-1995-to-2023

17 Joseph Rowntree Foundation, 'Destitution in the UK 2023', 24 October 2023, available at: https://www.jrf.org.uk/deep-poverty-and-destitution/destitution-in-the-uk-2023

18 Noah Vickers, 'London rough sleeper numbers at highest seen in count', BBC News, 11 November 2023.

19 Department for Levelling Up, Housing and Communities, 'Rough sleeping snapshot in England: autumn 2023', 29 February 2024, available at: https://www.gov.uk/government/statistics/rough-sleeping-snapshot-in-england-autumn-2023/rough-sleeping-snapshot-in-england-autumn-2023

20 @PeteApps, 29 February 2024. Tweet available at: https://twitter.com/PeteApps/status/1763160269109198926

21 Department for Levelling Up, Housing and Communities, 'Statutory homelessness in England: July to September 2023', 30 April 2024, available at: https://www.gov.uk/government/statistics/statutory-homelessness-in-england-july-to-september-2023/statutory-homelessness-in-england-july-to-september-2023#temporary-accommodation

22 John Burn-Mudoch, 'Why Britain is the world's worst on homelessness', *Financial Times*, 17 May 2024.

23 Department for Work and Pensions, 'Households below average income: for financial years ending 1995 to 2023', 21 March 2024. Go to https://www.gov.uk/government/statistics/households-below-average-income-for-financial-years-ending-1995-to-2023, select 'HBAI data tables' then pick 'food-security-hbai-timeseries-2019-20-2022-23-tables.ods' and finally select 'Tab 9_1ts'.

24 Ibid.

25 Ofgem, 'Changes to energy price cap between 1 April to 30 June 2024', 23 February 2024, available at: https://www.ofgem.gov.uk/publications/changes-energy-price-cap-between-1-april-30-june-2024

26 National Energy Action, 'Energy Crisis', available at: https://www.nea.org.uk/energy-crisis/

27 National Energy Action, '6.5 million UK households will be in fuel poverty from January as new polling shows 2 million have gone without energy in the last three months', 29 November 2023, available at: https://www.nea.org.uk/news/30096/

28 Kevin Peachey, 'Debt avoided by cutbacks on dining out and clothes, banks' data shows', BBC News, 9 March 2023.

29 Jon Ungoed-Thomas, 'Fears of spiralling debt as "buy now pay later" credit quadruples in UK', *The Guardian*, 6 April 2024.

30 Will Fyfe and Catriona Aitken, 'Crime: Shoplifting spike sees charity shop move items online', BBC News, 8 February 2024.

31 Reemul Balla, 'Shoplifting "epidemic" hits record high as abuse against shop workers also soars, survey shows', Sky News, 14 February 2024.

32 Robyn Vinter, 'Britons increasingly turning to food black market, experts say', *The Guardian*, 22 December 2023.

33 Laura Onita, 'Theft and violence in UK's small shops soars to record levels', *Financial Times*, 4 March 2024.

34 'Average weekly earnings in Great Britain: March 2024', Office for National Statistics, 12 March 2024, available at: https://www.ons.gov.uk/employmentandlabourmarket/peopleinwork/employmentandemployeetypes/bulletins/averageweeklyearningsingreatbritain/march2024

35 'EMP17: People in employment on zero hours contracts', Office for National Statistics, 14 May

2024, available at: https://www.ons.gov.uk/employmentandlabourmarket/peopleinwork/employmentandemployeetypes/datasets/emp17peopleinemploymentonzerohourscontracts

36 Louise Murphy, 'A U-shaped legacy', Resolution Foundation, 23 March 2024, available at: https://www.resolutionfoundation.org/app/uploads/2024/03/U-shaped-legacy.pdf

37 'Long-term international migration, provisional: year ending June 2023', Office for National Statistics, 23 November 2023, available at: https://www.ons.gov.uk/peoplepopulationand community/populationandmigration/internationalmigration/bulletins/longterm internationalmigrationprovisional/yearendingjune2023

38 'Destitution in the UK 2023', op. cit, p. 2.

39 'National life tables – life expectancy in the UK: 2020 to 2022', Office for National Statistics, 11 January 2024, available at: https://www.ons.gov.uk/peoplepopulationandcommunity/birthsdeathsandmarriages/lifeexpectancies/bulletins/nationallifetablesunited kingdom/2020to2022

40 'Health state life expectancies by national deprivation deciles, England: 2018 to 2020', Office for National Statistics, 25 April 2022, available at: https://www.ons.gov.uk/people populationandcommunity/healthandsocialcare/healthinequalities/bulletins/health statelifeexpectanciesbyindexofmultipledeprivationimd/2018to2020#:~:text=Males%20 living%20in%20Decile%201,2017%2C%20and%202018%20to%202020

41 Ann Raymond et al., 'Health inequalities in 2040', Health Foundation, April 2024, available at: https://www.health.org.uk/publications/health-inequalities-in-2040

42 Hannah Devlin, 'Surge in number of people in hospital with nutrient deficiencies, NHS figures show', The Guardian, 21 December 2023.

43 'British children shorter than other five-year-olds in Europe, study finds', ITV News, 21 June 2023.

44 Michael Marmot, 'Britain's shorter children reveal a grim story about austerity, but its scars run far deeper', The Guardian, 25 June 2023.

45 'Exclusive: 55 homeless children have died in temporary accommodation since 2019', ITV News, 4 March 2024.

46 Gordon Brown with Tom Clark, 'Partnership to end poverty', National Family Centre, 13 May 2024, available at: https://gordonandsarahbrown.com/wp-content/uploads/2024/05/PovertyUK090524.pdf

47 Tom Weekes, 'The State of Hunger – a foundation for a plan to end the need for food banks', Trussell Trust, 14 May 2021, available at: https://www.trusselltrust.org/2021/05/14/the-state-of-hunger-a-foundation-for-a-plan-to-end-the-need-for-food-banks/

48 Liam Geraghty, 'No-fault evictions put households at risk of homelessness over 80,000 times since Tory ban pledge', Big Issue, 15 April 2024.

49 @hoffman_noa, 28 March 2024. Tweet available at: https://twitter.com/hoffman_noa/status/1773328763914248486

50 Faye Brown, 'Renters Reform Bill shelved as Tories accused of "caving into vested interests"', Sky News, 24 May 2024.

51 NRLA, 'Win for NRLA as Labour u-turns on rent controls', available at: https://www.nrla.org.uk/news/monthly-bulletin/202307/win-for-nrla-as-labour-u-turns-on-rent-controls

52 Labour, 'Just Announced: Labour will build 1.5 million homes to save the dream of homeownership', 11 October 2023, available at: https://labour.org.uk/updates/stories/just-announced-labour-will-build-1-5-million-homes-to-save-the-dream-of-homeownership/

53 Samantha Eckford, 'Government amends Bill to allow councils to buy land for affordable housing at existing use value', Planning, 28 March 2023, available at: https://www.planningresource.co.uk/article/1817953/government-amends-bill-allow-councils-buy-land-affordable-housing-existing-use-value#:~:text=The%20government%20has%20tabled%20an,existing%20use%20of%20their%20land

54 Matilda Battersby, 'Labour planning overhaul of compulsory purchase rules to make owners sell land more cheaply', Building Design, 8 June 2023, available at: https://www.bdonline.co.uk/news/labour-planning-overhaul-of-compulsory-purchase-rules-to-make-owners-sell-land-more-cheaply/5123513.article

55 Geraldine Scott, 'Labour lays out plan to protect "buy now, pay later" customers', The Times, 6 November 2023.

56 Rachel Reeves, 'Securonomics' speech to Peterson Institute, Washington DC, 24 May 2023, full text available at: https://labour.org.uk/updates/press-releases/rachel-reeves-securonomics/ https://labour.org.uk/updates/press-releases/rachel-reeves-securonomics/

57 'May denies reheating Labour policy as she explains Tory bid for cap to stop "rip off" energy prices', ITV News, 8 May 2017.

58 Low Pay Commission, 'The National Minimum Wage in 2024 and forecast National Living Wage in 2025', March 2024, available at: https://assets.publishing.service.gov.uk/media/66043e0991a320001a82b0e7/The_National_Minimum_Wage_in_2024.pdf

59 Matthew Taylor, 'Good work: the Taylor review of modern working practices', Department for Business and Trade and Department for Business, Energy and Industrial Strategy, 11 July 2017, available at: https://www.gov.uk/government/publications/good-work-the-taylor-review-of-modern-working-practices

60 Hopson Solicitors, 'Uber case – What does the Supreme Court's decision mean for employers?', 24 March 2021, available at: http://www.hopsonsolicitors.co.uk/uber-case-what-does-the-supreme-courts-decision-mean-for-employers/

61 Lucy Fisher, Michael O'Dwyer and Jim Pickard, 'Labour rows back on workers' rights to blunt Tory "anti-business" claims', Financial Times, 17 August 2023.

62 Labour, 'A New Deal for Working People', 1 January 2024, available at: https://labour.org.uk/updates/stories/a-new-deal-for-working-people/

63 Department for Work and Pensions, 'Work Capability Assessment Reform: update to estimated number of claimants affected', 18 April 2024, available at: https://www.gov.uk/government/publications/work-capability-assessment-reform-estimated-number-of-claimants-affected/work-capability-assessment-reform-update-to-estimated-number-of-claimants-affected

64 Office for Budget Responsibility, 'Supplementary forecast information on work capability assessment reform', 17 April 2024, available at: https://obr.uk/supplementary-forecast-information-on-work-capability-assessment-reform/

65 Department for Work and Pensions, 'Disability Benefits system to be overhauled as consultation launched on Personal Independence Payment', 29 April 2024, available at: https://www.gov.uk/government/news/disability-benefits-system-to-be-overhauled-as-consultation-launched-on-personal-independence-payment--2#:~:text=Prime%20Minister%20Rishi%20Sunak%20said,who%20genuinely%20need%20it%20most.

66 Gordon Brown, 'Tables without food, bedrooms without beds. Grinding child poverty in Britain calls for anger – and a plan', The Guardian, 8 February 2024.

67 HM Treasury, 'Spring Budget 2024', March 2024, available at: https://assets.publishing.service.gov.uk/media/65e8578eb559930011ade2cb/E03057752_HMT_Spring_Budget_Mar_24_Web_Accessible__2_.pdf

68 @BBCPolitics, 16 July 2023. Tweet available at: https://x.com/BBCPolitics/status/1680534792171933697

69 Tom Clark, 'Amber Rudd's so-called "u-turn" on the two child benefit cap isn't good enough', Prospect, 11 January 2019.

70 Resolution Foundation, 'Catastrophic caps', 31 January 2024, available at: https://www.resolutionfoundation.org/publications/catastrophic-caps/#_ednref5

71 @djmgaffneyw4, 23 March 2023. Tweet available at: https://twitter.com/djmgaffneyw4/status/1777994149179846810

72 Resolution Foundation, 'Catastrophic caps', op. cit.

73 Sarah Young, 'UK's Labour Party aims to boost defence spending to 2.5% of GDP', Reuters, 12 April 2024.

74 BBC Radio 4, *Today* programme, 24 May 2024.

75 HM Treasury, 'Autumn Statement 2023', November 2023, Table 5.1, available at: https://assets.publishing.service.gov.uk/media/6568909c5936bb00133167cc/E02982473_Autumn_Statement_Nov_23_Accessible_Final.pdf and HM Treasury, 'Spring Budget 2024', op. cit., Table 5.1.

76 Benefit cap amounts available at: https://www.gov.uk/benefit-cap/benefit-cap-amounts

77 Henry Dimbleby and John Vincent, 'The School Food Plan', July 2013, pp. 115–16, especially Figure 13, available at: https://www.schoolfoodplan.com/wp-content/uploads/2013/07/School_Food_Plan_2013.pdf

78 Labour, 'Labour's plan for schools', 9 January 2024, available at: https://labour.org.uk/updates/stories/labours-plan-for-schools/

79 See: https://stats.oecd.org/Index.aspx?DataSetCode=NRR

80 Trussell Trust and Joseph Rowntree Foundation, 'An Essentials Guarantee', 27 February 2024, available at: https://www.jrf.org.uk/social-security/guarantee-our-essentials-reforming-universal-credit-to-ensure-we-can-all-afford-the (select 'Full report').

81 Centre for Economic Performance, Resolution Foundation and Nuffield Foundation, 'Ending Stagnation: A New Economic Strategy for Britain', 4 December 2023, Figure 52, available at: https://economy2030.resolutionfoundation.org/wp-content/uploads/2023/12/Ending-stagnation-final-report.pdf

82 See the flood of stories in the *Telegraph*, in particular, e.g. Lauren Shirreff and Daniel Martin, '"Bad nerves" is not a reason for claiming sickness benefit, says former Tory minister', *Daily Telegraph*, 7 March 2024; Tim Wallace, Eir Nolsøe and Szu Ping Chan, 'Sickness benefits bill to surge by a third as worklessness crisis deepens', *Daily Telegraph*, 21 March 2024.

83 Josh Halliday, '"DWP are the real criminals": carer in tatters after "brutal" fraud prosecution', *The Guardian*, 7 April 2024.

84 On IDS: Eleni Courea and Josh Halliday, 'Iain Duncan Smith urges ministers to pause carers' fines', *The Guardian*, 9 April 2024. On Starmer: Patrick Butler, 'Carers having to pay back thousands is very wrong, says Keir Starmer', *The Guardian*, 15 April 2024.

85 @SkyNews, 16 November 2023. Tweet available at: https://twitter.com/SkyNews/status/1725189799793877311

86 Jeremy Hunt, Autumn Statement speech, 2023, full text available at: https://www.gov.uk/government/speeches/autumn-statement-2023-speech

87 @tonywilsonIES, 22 November 2023. Tweet available at: https://twitter.com/tonywilsonIES/status/1727326102602010720

88 @Alison_McGovern, 14 November 2023. Tweet available at: https://twitter.com/Alison_McGovern/status/1724385759161942061

89 Department for Work and Pensions, 'Social Security Advisory Committee to Secretary of State for Work and Pensions: The Universal Credit and Jobseeker's Allowance (Work Search and Work Availability Requirements – limitations) (Amendment) Regulations 2022', 6 July 2022, available at: https://www.gov.uk/government/publications/uc-and-jsa-work-search-and-work-availability-requirements-limitations-amendment-regulations-2022/ssac-to-secretary-of-state-for-work-and-pensions-the-universal-credit-and-jobseekers-allowance-work-search-and-work-availability-requirements-lim

90 @tonywilsonIES, 5 February 2024. Tweet available at: https://twitter.com/tonywilsonIES/
    status/1754525519985447053

91 Sophia Sleigh, 'SIR SOFTIE: Sir Keir Starmer's "soft touch" approach to benefits "could cost
    taxpayers £450m a YEAR"', *The Sun*, 3 February 2024.

INTRODUCTION: FACE TO FACE WITH BRITAIN'S NEW PENURY

1   The growth referred to is of secondary diagnoses for malnutrition, relating to admissions
    that were originally for something else. Primary admissions specifically for malnutrition,
    which are far rarer, have also risen sharply, though not quite so fast. Both sets of figures
    from NHS Digital, 'Admissions for scurvy, rickets and malnutrition', 21 October 2021,
    available at: https://digital.nhs.uk/supplementary-information/2021/admissions-for-scurvy-
    rickets-and-malnutrition-2007-08-to-2020-21

2   The Ministry of Housing, Communities and Local Government estimates – 'Rough sleeping
    snapshot in England' – registered a rise from 1,768 in 2010 to 4,266 in 2019, after which
    there was a sharp fall in 2020, almost certainly attributable to the emergency 'Everyone
    In' pandemic policy, which asked councils to bring anyone at risk of sleeping rough into
    accommodation. All figures up to 2020 reported at ONS, 'Rough sleeping in the UK: 2002
    to 2021', 10 June 2021, available at: https://www.ons.gov.uk/peoplepopulationandcommunity/
    housing/articles/roughsleepingintheuk/2002to2021

3   The UK's largest network of food banks, the Trussell Trust, has emphasised different statistical
    currencies at different times. But successive reports demonstrate: first, the number of people
    receiving at least three days of emergency food grew from 41,000 in 2009/10 to 347,000 in
    2012/13, suggesting an eight-fold increase; secondly, that between 2014/15 and 2020/21 the
    number of emergency food parcels distributed grew from 1.1 million to over 2.1 million,
    suggesting a further doubling. See: Trussell Trust, 'Biggest Ever Increase in Foodbank Use', 24
    April 2013, available at: https://www.trusselltrust.org/wp-content/uploads/sites/2/2015/06/
    BIGGEST-EVER-INCREASE-IN-UK-FOODBANK-USE.pdf. Trussell Trust, 'End of
    Year Stats', 2022, available at: https://www.trusselltrust.org/news-and-blog/latest-stats/
    end-year-stats/

4   The *Good Morning Britain* broadcast was on 3 May 2022, and is available to view online
    at: https://twitter.com/gmb/status/1521402532857274370. There were many write-ups in the
    press, including: 'Good Morning Britain viewers "heartbroken" for pensioner who uses free
    pass to ride buses all day to keep warm', *Manchester Evening News*, 3 May 2022.

5   Quoted in Jack Simpson, 'Awaab Ishak death: the coroner's verdict in full', *Inside Housing*, 16
    November 2022.

6   See: John Steinbeck, *The Grapes of Wrath*, Pan Books, 1975 (1939) and Barbara Ehrenreich,
    Nickel and Dimed: On (not) getting by in America, Henry Holt, 2002.

7   See, for example, BBC News, 'Migrant crisis: Photo of drowned boy sparks outcry', 3
    September 2015.

8   This book very deliberately emphasises individual human stories over analysis of public
    policy. But I've previously written at length about the rhetoric and the arithmetic of the
    retrenchment of the 2010s in: Tom Clark with Anthony Heath, *Hard Times: Inequality,
    Recession, Aftermath*, Yale University Press, 2015. For a more up-to-date audit, I would
    recommend: Jonathan Portes and Howard Reed, 'The cumulative impact of tax and welfare
    reforms', Equality and Human Rights Commission, Research Report 112, available at: https://
    www.equalityhumanrights.com/sites/default/files/cumulative-impact-assessment-report.
    pdf

9   The leading academic analysis asserts a strict, two-part definition of destitution: *either*
    going without two or more of six essentials – shelter, food, heat, light, weather-appropriate

clothing and basic toiletries. – because of lack of money *or* having an extremely low income which would leave someone unable to purchase these things for themselves. It then applies this definition to data collected, principally, by surveying users of over 100 'crisis services', such as food banks, housing rights services and Citizens Advice Bureaux. On this basis, it estimated that 2.4 million people, of whom 550,000 were children, were in households that had experienced destitution in 2019. The count of such households was up by over a third (35 per cent) over the two years since 2017. See: Suzanne Fitzpatrick et al., 'Destitution in the UK', 9 December 2020, available at: https://www.jrf.org.uk/report/destitution-uk-2020

10 George Eliot, *Middlemarch*, Wordsworth Classics, 1993 [1871–72].

11 Charles Booth's famous study and maps were published in multiple editions from 1889 onwards, culminating in the seventeen-volume Charles Booth, *Life and Labour of the People in London*, Macmillan, 1902. His studies led to a special interest in the elderly, and the influential book Charles Booth, *Old age pensions and the aged poor: a proposal*, Macmillan, 1899. Seebohm Rowntree's series of studies in York started with Seebohm Rowntree, *Poverty: A Study in Town Life*, Macmillan, 1901.

12 Jobseeker's Allowance for adults aged up to twenty-four in 2022/23 is worth £61.05 per week (the equivalent rate of Universal Credit, calculated on a calendar monthly basis, is £265.31). By contrast, Pension Credit guarantees a single person £182.60 a week.

13 Department for Work and Pensions, 'Households below average income: for financial years ending 1995 to 2021', HBAI summary results file, available at: https://www.gov.uk/ government/statistics/households-below-average-income-for-financial-years-ending-1995-to-2021. Table 1.3a shows the proportion of all individuals in households with disposable incomes (i.e. after housing costs) of less than 60 per cent of the contemporary median was 22 per cent in 2019/20, and 20 per cent in the special circumstances of the pandemic in 2020/21. Table 1.6a shows the respective figures for pensioners were 18 per cent and 15 per cent.

14 A recent study of 'very deep poverty' found that just one in ten cases were pensioners, about half their weight in the population as a whole. See: Katie Schmuecker et al., 'Going without: deepening poverty in the UK', Joseph Rowntree Foundation, 25 July 2022, p. 8, available at: https://www.jrf.org.uk/report/going-without-deepening-poverty-uk

15 Department for Work and Pensions, 'Households below average income'. Table 1.4b shows the total number of children in households with less than 60 per cent of the contemporary median income (after deducting housing costs) rose from 3.6 million in 2011/12 to 4.3 million in 2019/20, matching previously recorded peaks back in the 1990s. The time series is disrupted by the switch from a Great Britain-only to a UK-wide basis in 2002/03, but given the small relative size of the Northern Irish population the big picture is little affected.

16 Tom Clark and Peter Matejic, 'From disability to destitution', Joseph Rowntree Foundation, 26 July 2022, available at: https://www.jrf.org.uk/blog/disability-destitution

17 Contact surveyed 3,893 families with disabled children online between 25 August and 5 September, of whom 2,772 answered a question about whether they had had to cut back on health or disability equipment because of the electricity cost. Thirty-nine per cent said yes: triple the proportion that had said the same when the organisation ran a similar survey just a few months earlier. Contact, 'Out of Energy', 2022. Full survey results available online: at https://view.officeapps.live.com/op/view.aspx?src=https%3A%2F%2Fcontact.org.uk%2Fwp-content%2Fuploads%2F2022%2F11%2FContact-Energy-Survey-NOV-2022-Tables-by-AreaFINAL.xlsx&wdOrigin=BROWSELINK

18 The official data consistently points to a poverty rate for the white group of about 20 per cent, compared to about 40 per cent for the black group. While the comparable figure for Bangladeshis declined a long way after the 1990s, it has since crept back up and remains at around 50 per cent. For a time-series of poverty rates for each ethnic group see: 'UK Poverty

2022: The essential guide to understanding poverty in the UK', Joseph Rowntree Foundation, 18 January 2022, p. 55, available at: https://www.jrf.org.uk/report/uk-poverty-2022

19 Setting pensioners to one side, the proportion of poor adults who lived in a household where someone was working was less than half in the mid-1990s. But it has risen sharply since, remorselessly so in the years running up to the pandemic, to peak at 68 per cent in 2019/20. From Joseph Rowntree Foundation analysis of the official 'Households below average income' data up to financial year 2019/20, in: 'UK Poverty 2022: The essential guide to understanding poverty in the UK', Joseph Rowntree Foundation, 18 January 2022, available at: https://www.jrf.org.uk/report/uk-poverty-2022. See especially p. 31.

CHAPTER 1: UPROOTED: NO PLACE LIKE HOME

1 Department for Levelling Up, Housing and Communities, 'Statutory homelessness in England: financial year 2021–22', 22 September 2022, available at: https://www.gov.uk/government/statistics/statutory-homelessness-in-england-financial-year-2021-22

2 Ministry of Housing, Communities and Local Government, 'English Housing Survey 2019 to 2020: headline report', 17 December 2020, available at: https://www.gov.uk/government/statistics/english-housing-survey-2019-to-2020-headline-report

3 Ministry of Housing, Communities and Local Government, 'Statutory homelessness in England: October to December 2019', available at: https://www.gov.uk/government/statistics/statutory-homelessness-in-england-october-to-december-2019

4 Social housing refers here to properties rented from local authorities (council housing) in addition to those rented from private registered providers of social housing, such as housing associations or registered social landlords.

5 Wendy Wilson, Cassie Barton and Hannah Cromarty, 'The end of "no fault" section 21 evictions (England)', House of Commons Library, 24 October 2022, available at: https://researchbriefings.files.parliament.uk/documents/CBP-8658/CBP-8658.pdf

6 Aled Davies, '"Right to Buy": The Development of a Conservative Housing Policy, 1945–1980', *Contemporary British History*, 2013, Volume 27, Issue 4, pp. 421–44. Cabinet Secretary for Social Justice, Housing and Local Government, 'Housing Statistics 2020 & 2021: Key Trends Summary', 10 May 2022, available at: https://www.gov.scot/publications/housing-statistics-2020-2021-key-trends-summary/pages/2/

7 Department for Levelling Up, Housing and Communities and Ministry of Housing, Communities and Local Government, 'Live tables on dwelling stock (including vacants)', Table 104: by tenure, England (historical series), last updated 15 December 2022, available at: https://www.gov.uk/government/statistical-data-sets/live-tables-on-dwelling-stock-including-vacants. Department for Levelling Up, Housing and Communities, 'English Housing Survey 2020 to 2021: headline report', 9 December 2021, available at: https://www.gov.uk/government/statistics/english-housing-survey-2020-to-2021-headline-report. The figure for social housing remains higher in Scotland, at 23 per cent of dwellings (see: Cabinet Secretary for Social Justice, Housing and Local Government, 'Housing Statistics 2020 & 2021').

8 Wendy Wilson et al., 'Extending home ownership: Government initiatives', House of Commons Library, 30 March 2021, available at: https://researchbriefings.files.parliament.uk/documents/SN03668/SN03668.pdf

9 Julie Rugg and Alison Wallace, 'Property supply to the lower end of the English private rented sector', Centre for Housing Policy funded by Nationwide Foundation and University of York, June 2021.

10 Carolin Schmidt, 'Strong tenant protections and subsidies support Germany's majority-renter housing market', Brookings, 20 April 2021, available at: https://www.brookings.edu/essay/germany-rental-housing-markets/

11 Emma Bimpson, Hannah Green and Kesia Reeve, 'Women, homelessness and violence: what works?', Centre for Homelessness Impact produced in partnership with Sheffield Hallam University's Centre for Regional Economic and Social Research, July 2021.

12 Maeve McClenaghan, 'Evicted in less than 10 minutes: courts fail tenants broken by pandemic', Bureau of Investigative Journalism, 23 September 2021, available at: https://www.thebureauinvestigates.com/stories/2021-09-23/evicted-in-less-than-10-minutes-courts-fail-tenants-broken-by-pandemic

13 Steven Kennedy et al., 'Briefing Paper: The Benefit Cap', House of Commons Library, 21 November 2016, available at: https://researchbriefings.files.parliament.uk/documents/SN06294/SN06294.pdf

14 See: Alexandra Goss, 'The rise of the four-figure rent bill', *Sunday Times*, 13 January 2019.

15 Ministry of Justice, 'Mortgage and landlord possession statistics', 8 August 2013 (last updated 9 February 2023), available at: https://www.gov.uk/government/statistics/mortgage-and-landlord-possession-statistics-october-to-december-2022. In particular, Table 5 within 'Mortgage and landlord possession accessible statistical tables: October to December 2022' records 78,947 possession orders for 2019 and 22,834 repossessions by county court bailiffs. For wider implications, see: Vickie Cooper and Kirsteen Paton, 'Accumulation by repossession: the political economy of evictions under austerity', *Urban Geography*, 2021, Volume 42, Issue 5, pp. 583–602.

16 Ministry of Housing, Communities and Local Government, 'Government announces end to unfair evictions', 15 April 2019, available at: https://www.gov.uk/government/news/government-announces-end-to-unfair-evictions

17 Ministry of Justice, 'Mortgage and landlord possession statistics', October to December 2022, available at: https://www.gov.uk/government/statistics/mortgage-and-landlord-possession-statistics-october-to-december-2022

18 Department for Levelling Up, Housing and Communities, 'A fairer private rented sector', June 2022 (last updated 2 August 2022), available at: https://www.gov.uk/government/publications/a-fairer-private-rented-sector/a-fairer-private-rented-sector

19 'English Housing Survey Private rented sector, 2019-20', Ministry of Housing, Communities and Local Government, July 2021, available at: https://assets.publishing.service.gov.uk/government/uploads/system/uploads/attachment_data/file/1000052/EHS_19-20_PRS_report.pdf

20 Darren Baxter and Luke Murphy, 'Sign on the dotted line? A new rental contract', Institute for Public Policy Research, January 2019, available at: https://www.ippr.org/files/2019-01/sign-on-the-dotted-line-jan19.pdf

21 The Joseph Rowntree Foundation has provided funding for reporting in this book.

22 Department for Levelling Up, Housing and Communities and Ministry of Housing, Communities and Local Government, 'Live tables on homelessness', updated 24 November 2022, available at: https://www.gov.uk/government/statistical-data-sets/live-tables-on-homelessness

23 '"I Want Us to Live Like Humans Again": Families in Temporary Accommodation in London, UK', Human Rights Watch, 17 January 2022, available at: https://www.hrw.org/report/2022/01/17/1-want-us-live-humans-again/families-temporary-accommodation-london-uk

24 Shelter, 'At least 271,000 people are homeless in England today', 11 January 2023, available at: https://england.shelter.org.uk/media/press_release/at_least_271000_people_are_homeless_in_england_today

25 Guy Ortolano, *Thatcher's Progress: From Social Democracy to Market Liberalism through an English New Town*, Cambridge University Press, 2019.

26 Department for Levelling Up, Housing and Communities, 'English Housing Survey 2020 to

2021: headline report', Annex Table 1.5, Annex Table 1.4, updated 13 December 2022, available at: https://www.gov.uk/government/statistics/english-housing-survey-2020-to-2021-headline-report

27 Department for Levelling Up, Housing and Communities, 'English Private Landlord Survey 2021: main report', 26 May 2022, available at: https://www.gov.uk/government/statistics/english-private-landlord-survey-2021-main-report

28 McKee has researched the profoundly alienating consequences of this set up, in Kim McKee, Adriana Mihaela Soaita and Jennifer Hoolachan, '"Generation rent" and the emotions of private renting: self-worth, status and insecurity amongst low-income renters', *Housing Studies*, 2020, Volume 35, Issue 8, pp. 1,468–87.

29 Department for Levelling Up, Housing and Communities, 'English Housing Survey: Household Resilience Study, Wave 3 April–May 2021', available at: https://www.gov.uk/government/statistics/household-resilience-study-wave-3

30 House of Commons Publications, 'Register of Members' Financial Interests', as at 9 January 2023, available at: https://publications.parliament.uk/pa/cm/cmregmem/230109/230109.pdf

31 Robert Joyce, Matthew Mitchell and Agnes Norris Keiller, 'The cost of housing for low-income renters', Institute for Fiscal Studies, October 2017, available at: https://ifs.org.uk/sites/default/files/output_url_files/R132.pdf

32 For the parliamentary question see: 'Local Housing Allowance', TheyWorkForYou, 26 May 2022, available at: https://www.theyworkforyou.com/wrans/?id=2022-05-23.6683.h

33 Alexander Vasudevan, 'Berlin's vote to take properties from big landlords could be a watershed moment', *The Guardian*, 29 September 2021.

34 Linda McDowell, ed., *Undoing Place? A Geographical Reader*, Routledge, 1997.

35 bell hooks, 'Homeplace (a site of resistance)', in bell hooks, *Yearning: Race, Gender and Cultural Politics*, South End Press, 1990.

CHAPTER 2: THE HUNGRY TWENTIES

1 Glen Bramley et al., 'State of Hunger: Building the evidence on poverty, destitution, and food insecurity in the UK', Trussell Trust, May 2021, p. 11, footnote 2 and technical annex, available at: https://www.trusselltrust.org/wp-content/uploads/sites/2/2021/05/State-of-Hunger-2021-Report-Final.pdf

2 'Trussell Trust data briefing on end-of-year statistics relating to use of food banks: April 2021–March 2022', Trussell Trust, 2022, available at: https://www.trusselltrust.org/wp-content/uploads/sites/2/2022/04/EOY-Stats-2022-Data-Briefing.pdf

3 'Emergency food parcel distribution in the United Kingdom: April–September 2022', Trussell Trust, 2022, available at: https://www.trusselltrust.org/wp-content/uploads/sites/2/2022/11/MYS-UK-Factsheet-2022.pdf

4 See tabs for Round 10 and Round 11 of the Food Insecurity Tracking study, available at: https://www.foodfoundation.org.uk/initiatives/food-insecurity-tracking; for the autumn 2022 data, we deduce the '3 million or more' cited from the 6.0 per cent quoted on slide 6 of 15 for Round 11.

5 'Admissions for scurvy, rickets and malnutrition', NHS Digital, 21 October 2021, available at: https://digital.nhs.uk/supplementary-information/2021/admissions-for-scurvy-rickets-and-malnutrition-2007-08-to-2020-21

6 See tabs for Round 10 and Round 11 of the Food Insecurity Tracking study, available at: https://www.foodfoundation.org.uk/initiatives/food-insecurity-tracking

7 'Consumer price inflation, UK: September 2022', Office for National Statistics, 19 October 2022, available at: https://www.ons.gov.uk/economy/inflationandpriceindices/bulletins/consumerpriceinflation/september2022

8   'Tracking the price of the lowest-cost grocery items, UK, experimental analysis: April 2021 to September 2022', Office for National Statistics, 25 October 2022, available at: https://www.ons.gov.uk/economy/inflationandpriceindices/articles/trackingthelowestcostgroceryitemsukexperimentalanalysis/april2021toseptember2022

9   Michael Savage, 'UK food banks at breaking point urge Liz Truss to boost aid to poorest', *The Guardian*, 16 October 2022.

10 'Almost 1.3 million emergency food parcels provided in last 6 months', Trussell Trust, 10 November 2022, available at: https://www.trusselltrust.org/2022/11/10/almost-1-3-million-emergency-parcels-provided-to-people-across-uk-experiencing-hunger-over-past-six-months-as-cost-of-living-emergency-drives-tsunami-of-need-to-food-banks/

CHAPTER 3: COLD COMFORT: THE NEW STRUGGLE FOR HEAT

1   Brigid Francis-Devine et al., 'Research Briefing: Rising cost of living in the UK', House of Commons Library, 23 January 2023, available at: https://commonslibrary.parliament.uk/research-briefings/cbp-9428/

2   See the government's press release: 'Government announces Energy Price Guarantee for families and businesses while urgently taking action to reform broken energy market', 8 September 2022, available at: https://www.gov.uk/government/news/government-announces-energy-price-guarantee-for-families-and-businesses-while-urgently-taking-action-to-reform-broken-energy-market

3   Details of the change presented by Chancellor Jeremy Hunt to Parliament on 17 November 2022. Details available in: 'Autumn Statement 2022', HM Treasury, November 2022, available at: https://assets.publishing.service.gov.uk/government/uploads/system/uploads/attachment_data/file/1118417/CCS1022065440-001_SECURE_HMT_Autumn_Statement_November_2022_Web_accessible__1_.pdf

4   As reported in: Ross Hempseed, '"Situation is not sustainable or acceptable": Figures show Aberdeenshire, Shetland and Orkney paying among highest energy bills in UK', *Press and Journal*, 17 June 2022.

5   Calum Ross and Emma Morrice, 'Energy crisis hits hardest for 220,000 off-gas billpayers in northern Scotland', *Press and Journal*, 16 January 2023.

6   As reported in: Martin Williams, 'Revealed: Parts of Scotland have to pay nearly double Liz Truss's Energy Price Guarantee bills freeze', *Herald*, 9 October 2022.

7   Median household income is £533 per week, or £27,716 per year. See the Scottish government's latest release: 'Poverty and Income Inequality in Scotland 2017–20', gov.scot, 25 March 2021, available at: https://data.gov.scot/poverty/2021/#Income

8   Councillor Angus McCormack, chair of the Western Isles Poverty Action group, quoted (in English) in a report on the *Eòrpa* documentary in: 'Isles cost of living crisis comes under the Eorpa spotlight', *Stornoway Gazette*, 11 October 2022.

9   See the government's press release: 'Vital help with energy bills on the way for millions more homes across Great Britain and Northern Ireland', 19 December 2022, available at: https://www.gov.uk/government/news/vital-help-with-energy-bills-on-the-way-for-millions-more-homes-across-great-britain-and-northern-ireland

10 Hongde Zhao, Stephen Jivraj and Alison Moody, '"My blood pressure is low today, do you have the heating on?" The association between indoor temperature and blood pressure', *Journal of Hypertension*, 2019, Volume 37, Issue 3, pp. 504–12.

11 Jack Simpson, 'Awaab Ishak death: the coroner's verdict in full', *Inside Housing*, 16 November 2022.

12 One example dataset of the official death registrations that have been causing concern is: 'Deaths registered weekly in England and Wales, provisional: week ending 23 December

2022', Office for National Statistics, 5 January 2023, available at: https://www.ons.gov. uk/peoplepopulationandcommunity/birthsdeathsandmarriages/deaths/bulletins/ deathsregisteredweeklyinenglandandwalesprovisional/weekending23december2022. For actuarial analysis suggesting that NHS delays were responsible for more than 400 deaths in England through the autumn of 2022, rising to 500 plus on the basis of an update for the December 2022 ONS data, see: Stuart McDonald, Katja Grasic and Natalie Tikhonovsky, 'Are NHS waiting times contributing to excess deaths?', COVID-19 Actuaries Response Group, 2023, available at: https://covidactuaries.org/2023/01/11/ are-nhs-waiting-timescontributing-to-excess-deaths/

13 Amy Clair and Emma Baker, 'Cold homes and mental health harm: Evidence from the UK Household Longitudinal Study', *Social Science & Medicine*, Volume 314, December 2022.

14 G. Mohan, 'The impact of household energy poverty on the mental health of parents of young children', *Journal of Public Health*, Volume 44, Issue 1, March 2022, pp. 121–8.

15 Clair and Baker, 'Cold homes and mental health harm'.

16 Geoff Green and Jan Gilbertson, 'Warm Front Better Health: Health Impact Evaluation of the Warm Front Scheme, Sheffield Hallam University, May 2008, available at: http://shura. shu.ac.uk/18167/1/CRESR_WF_final+Nav%20(2).pdf

17 Katie Schmuecker and Rachelle Earwaker, 'Not heating, eating or meeting bills: managing a cost of living crisis on a low income', Joseph Rowntree Foundation, 29 June 2022, available at: https://www.jrf.org.uk/report/not-heating-eating-or-meeting-bills-managing-cost-living-crisis-low-income

18 Eve McLachlan, '"Our governments have failed": The crofters turning back to peat fuel amid cost-of-living crisis', *Press and Journal*, 12 January 2023.

19 Lauren Robertson, 'Orkney church to open heating hub for locals struggling with rising bills', *Press and Journal*, 29 August 2022.

20 Warm Welcome Campaign website available at: www.warmwelcome.uk

CHAPTER 4: PAY LATER? OF DEBT AND DREAD

1 Estimate from Citizens Advice on basis of Ofgem data, as detailed in: 'Kept in the dark: The urgent need for action on prepayment meters', Citizens Advice, January 2023, available at: https://www.citizensadvice.org.uk/about-us/our-work/policy/policy-research-topics/energy-policy-research-and-consultation-responses/energy-policy-research/kept-in-the-dark-the-urgent-need-for-action-on-prepayment-meters/. The report explains this is likely to be a 'conservative estimate' because it assumes that Ofgem's pending Q4 2022 data will record only the same number of moves to prepay as Q3, whereas in practice 'the higher price cap in Q4, and the need to use more energy in the winter, it is likely that the number of people moved to a prepayment meter for debt will be higher'.

2 Paul Morgan-Bentley, 'Exposed: How British Gas debt agents break into homes of vulnerable', *The Times*, 1 February 2023.

3 Ibid.

4 See the debate pack 'Self-Disconnection of pre-payment meters' prepared by the Commons Library after the Backbench Business Committee selected the subject for a debate opened by Anne McLaughlin MP on 15 December 2022. Available at: https://commonslibrary.parliament. uk/research-briefings/cdp-2022-0236/. See also the transcript of the debate in Hansard, available at: https://hansard.parliament.uk/commons/2022-12-15/debates/AEC02039-5470-4C5F-B84D-EEAA89F98E48/PrepaymentMetersSelf-Disconnection

5 'Kept in the dark', Citizens Advice.

6 'Greater Manchester Residents' Survey: Survey 3', Greater Manchester Combined

Authority, September 2022, available at: https://view.officeapps.live.com/op/view.aspx?src=https%3A%2F%2Fwww.greatermanchester-ca.gov.uk%2Fmedia%2F6662%2F20221004_gm-residents-survey3_fullreport_final.pptx&wdOrigin=BROWSELINK. Fieldwork was undertaken on a mixed sample of 1,677 online, telephone and 'river sampled' respondents who had replied to invitations to take part between 1 and 21 September.

7   Dean Kirby, 'Inside the courtroom where it takes minutes to force hundreds of people onto prepayment meters', *i*, 4 December 2022.

8   Dean Kirby, 'Only 72 out of 500,000 warrants by energy firms to enter homes refused in prepayment meters "scandal"', *i*, 18 January 2023.

9   Alex Lawson, 'Prepayment meters: magistrates told to stop allowing forced installations', *The Guardian*, 6 February 2023.

10 The interview was originally for this newspaper piece: Claer Barrett and Jennifer Williams, 'Harrowing plight of Britain's prepayment energy users left sitting in the dark', *Financial Times*, 10 June 2022.

11 The charity surveyed 6,411 of its members over thirty-six hours in September 2022, and partnerships director Jane Partington reported the results in an unpublished presentation for Greater Manchester's Challenge Poverty Week launch event, which was supplied to the author. 'Cost of Living Insights', Bread and Butter Thing, 2022.

12 The Bread and Butter Thing was highlighting comparisons with official numbers from late July 2022, but a later official release – covering the turn of 2022 and 2023 – suggests little change in the financial situation of households, with a marginal drop in the proportion reporting borrowing more than the year before (from 23 to 22 per cent) but a small rise (from 30 to 32 per cent) in the numbers saying that they would be unable to meet an unexpected expense of £850. See: 'Public opinions and social trends, Great Britain: household finances', Office for National Statistics, 2022, 2023, available at: https://www.ons.gov.uk/peoplepopulationandcommunity/wellbeing/datasets/publicopinionsandsocialtrendsgreatbritainhouseholdfinances

13 See in particular Figure 4.2 and surrounding pages in: Alex Davenport et al., 'Spending and saving during the COVID-19 crisis: evidence from bank account data', Institute for Fiscal Studies, October 2020, available at: https://ifs.org.uk/sites/default/files/output_url_files/BN308-Spending-and-saving-during-the-COVID-19-crisis-evidence-from-bank-account-data_2.pdf

14 Mike Brewer, Emily Fry and Lalitha Try, 'The Living Standards Outlook 2023', Resolution Foundation, January 2023, available at: https://www.resolutionfoundation.org/app/uploads/2023/01/Living-Standards-Outlook-2023.pdf

15 'Tracking the price of the lowest-cost grocery items, UK, experimental analysis: April 2021 to September 2022', Office for National Statistics, 25 October 2022, available at: https://www.ons.gov.uk/economy/inflationandpriceindices/articles/trackingthelowestcostgroceryitemsukexperimentalanalysis/april2021toseptember2022

16 Valentine Quinio, 'Cities in the North are still hit harder by the cost of living crisis', Centre for Cities, 18 August 2022, available at: https://www.centreforcities.org/blog/northern-cities-hit-harder-by-cost-of-living-crisis/

17 Harry Carr and Amelia Stewart, 'The Double Whammy: Mapping the UK's Personal Debt', Demos, February 2022, available at: https://demos.co.uk/wp-content/uploads/2022/02/Double-Whammy-Report.pdf. The Lowell's Financial Vulnerability Index used by this report is based on a mix of survey data and operational data on the firm's clients. The indicators it took into account include: the percentage of people in need of credit; the credit available; average credit scores; the area's level of benefit claimants; and the proportion of households already in debt, including those with high-cost loans. Full details of this index are available at: https://apps.urban.org/features/uk-financial-vulnerability-index/

18 'Cost of Living Insights', Bread and Butter Thing.

19 'Pay Later in 30 days Terms and Conditions', Klarna, 31 May 2022, available at: https://cdn. klarna.com/1.0/shared/content/legal/terms/0/en_gb/pay_after_delivery/

20 See: Raghuram Rajan, *Fault Lines: How Hidden Fractures Still Threaten the World Economy*, Princeton University Press, 2011.

21 StepChange commissioned a nationally representative YouGov online poll, with a sample size of 2,091 adults. Fieldwork was conducted between 29 and 30 November 2022. Results are available at: 'Proportion of those who say they can afford Christmas has nearly halved since last year', StepChange, 7 December 2022, available at: https://www.stepchange.org/media-centre/press-releases/xmas-spending-poll-2022.aspx

22 As reported in: Siddharth Venkataramakrishnan, 'Buy now, pay later demand soars among all age groups in the UK', *Financial Times*, 16 January 2023.

23 According to the latest numbers released at new year 2023, 'the annual growth rate for all consumer credit was little changed at 7.0 per cent in November. The annual growth rate of credit card borrowing rose from 11.5 per cent in October to 12.2 per cent in November.' From: 'Money and Credit – November 2022', Bank of England, 4 January 2023, available at: https://www.bankofengland.co.uk/statistics/money-and-credit/2022/november-2022

24 Siddharth Venkataramakrishnan, 'Klarna's valuation crashes to under $7bn in tough funding round', *Financial Times*, 11 July 2022.

25 See: 'Swimming with Sharks: Tackling illegal money lending in England', Centre for Social Justice, March 2022, available at: https://www.centreforsocialjustice.org.uk/library/swimming-with-sharks

26 Drawing on a mix of face-to-face and telephone interviews with low-income families at the turn of 2009/10, a report for the Department for Business, Innovation and Skills put the total number borrowing from illegal money lenders at 310,000 and noted that this already suggested an 'expanded' black market as compared to earlier government-sponsored work. See: Anna Ellison et al., 'Interim Evaluation of the National Illegal Money Lending Projects: Report prepared by POLICIS for Department for Business, Innovation and Skills', Department for Business, Innovation and Skills, October 2010, available at: https://assets.publishing.service.gov.uk/government/uploads/system/uploads/attachment_data/file/31888/10-1186-interim-evaluation-illegal-money-lending.pdf

27 'Swimming with Sharks', Centre for Social Justice.

28 Ibid.

29 'Public opinions and social trends, Great Britain: household finances', Office for National Statistics, 7 to 18 December 2022. See: Table 3 of the data release for those dates, available at: https://www.ons.gov.uk/peoplepopulationandcommunity/wellbeing/datasets/public opinionsandsocialtrendsgreatbritainhouseholdfinances

CHAPTER 5: A WINDOW ON FRAILTY: FROM DEPRIVATION TO DISEASE

1 'Changing life expectancy: new animation and report launched', Glasgow Centre for Population Health, 31 May 2022, available at: https://www.gcph.co.uk/latest/news/1037_changing_life_expectancy_new_animation_and_report_launched

2 'Life Expectancy in Scotland 2018–2020', National Records of Scotland, 23 September 2021, available at: https://www.nrscotland.gov.uk/statistics-and-data/statistics/statistics-by-theme/life-expectancy/life-expectancy-in-scotland/2018-2020

3 For ONS's UK-wide average for 2017–19 see: 'Health state life expectancies, UK: 2017 to 2019', Office for National Statistics, 25 January 2021, available at: https://www.ons.gov.uk/peoplepopulationandcommunity/healthandsocialcare/healthandlifeexpectancies/

bulletins/healthstatelifeexpectanciesuk/2017to2019; for ONS figures for individual cities for 2017–19, collated by the Health Foundation, see: 'Map of healthy life expectancy at birth', Health Foundation, 6 January 2022, available at: https://www.health.org.uk/evidence-hub/health-inequalities/map-of-healthy-life-expectancy-at-birth

4 Ibid.

5 For ONS's 2017–19 estimates see: 'Health state life expectancies, UK: 2017 to 2019', Office for National Statistics, 25 January 2021, available at: https://www.ons.gov.uk/peoplepopulationandcommunity/healthandsocialcare/healthandlifeexpectancies/bulletins/healthstatelifeexpectanciesuk/2017to2019; for ONS's 2018–20 estimates see: 'Health state life expectancies, UK: 2018 to 2020', Office for National Statistics, 4 March 2022, available at: https://www.ons.gov.uk/peoplepopulationandcommunity/healthandsocialcare/healthandlifeexpectancies/bulletins/healthstatelifeexpectanciesuk/2018to2020

6 Bruce Whyte, Mairi Young and Katharine Timpson, 'Health in a changing city: Glasgow 2021', Glasgow Centre for Population Health, August 2021, pp. 84–5, available at: https://www.gcph.co.uk/assets/0000/8225/Health_in_a_changing_city_Glasgow_2021_-_report.pdf

7 Ibid.

8 Ibid., p. 88.

9 Ibid.

10 Anne Case and Angus Deaton, *Deaths of Despair and the Future of Capitalism*, Princeton University Press, 2020.

11 For England and Wales time series see: 'Suicides in England and Wales: 2020 registrations', Office for National Statistics, 7 September 2021, available at: https://www.ons.gov.uk/peoplepopulationandcommunity/birthsdeathsandmarriages/deaths/bulletins/suicidesintheunitedkingdom/2020registrations; for 2018 and 2019 Scottish figures see: 'Deaths by suicide increased in 2019', Public Health Scotland, 24 November 2020, available at: https://publichealthscotland.scot/news/2020/november/deaths-by-suicide-increased-in-2019/

12 For alcohol figures for 2020 and 2021 for Scotland see: 'Alcohol-specific deaths', National Records of Scotland, 4 August 2022, available at: https://www.nrscotland.gov.uk/statistics-and-data/statistics/statistics-by-theme/vital-events/deaths/alcohol-deaths; for figures for England and Wales up to 2020 see: 'Alcohol-specific deaths in the UK: registered in 2020', Office for National Statistics, 7 December 2021, available at: https://www.ons.gov.uk/peoplepopulationandcommunity/healthandsocialcare/causesofdeath/bulletins/alcoholrelateddeathsintheunitedkingdom/registeredin2020

13 The England and Wales age-standardised rate of drug deaths for 2012 was forty-seven per million rising to eighty-four in 2019, see: 'Deaths related to drug poisoning in England and Wales: 2021 registrations', Office for National Statistics, 3 August 2022, available at: https://www.ons.gov.uk/peoplepopulationandcommunity/birthsdeathsandmarriages/deaths/bulletins/deathsrelatedtodrugpoisoninginenglandandwales/2021registrations

14 'Drug-related deaths in Scotland in 2021', National Records of Scotland, 28 July 2022, available at: https://www.nrscotland.gov.uk/files/statistics/drug-related-deaths/21/drug-related-deaths-21-report.pdf

15 'Life Expectancy in Scotland 2018–2020', op. cit.

16 Norman Silvester, 'Children living in Nicola Sturgeon's constituency are poorest in the UK as investigation reveals poverty rate at 69 per cent', *Sunday Mail*, 17 April 2022.

17 Sophie Parcell et al., 'Case study: Health and its determinants in West Central Scotland compared to the Ruhr area in Germany', GCPH, August 2011, available at: https://www.gcph.co.uk/assets/0000/2579/FINAL_for_web_case_study_RUHR.pdf

18   Gerry McCartney et al., 'Resetting the course for population health', GCPH and University of Glasgow, May 2022, available at: https://www.gcph.co.uk/assets/0000/8723/Stalled_Mortality_report_FINAL_WEB.pdf

19   Peter Walker and Rupert Neate, 'Truss to push ahead with low-tax economy despite calls for caution', *The Guardian*, 4 September 2022.

20   Stuart Adam and David Phillips, 'The Scottish Government's record on tax and benefit policy', Institute for Fiscal Studies, available at: https://ifs.org.uk/sites/default/files/output_url_files/BN324-The-Scottish-Government%252527s-record-on-tax-and-benefit-policy.pdf

CHAPTER 6: THE 'COST-OF-STAYING-ALIVE CRISIS':
DISABILITY TODAY

1   George Osborne, speech to Conservative Party conference, October 2012, full text available at: https://www.newstatesman.com/business/economics/2012/10/george-osbornes-speech-conservative-conference-full-text

2   Peter Walker, 'Benefit cuts are fuelling abuse of disabled people, say charities', *The Guardian*, 5 February 2012.

3   For derivation of the figure see: Anel Touchet and Marcello Morciano, 'The Disability Price Tag 2019: Technical report', Scope, February 2019, available at: https://www.scope.org.uk/campaigns/extra-costs/disability-price-tag/

4   Department for Work and Pensions, 'Households Below Average Incomes 2019/20', 25 March 2021, available at: https://www.gov.uk/government/statistics/households-below-average-income-for-financial-years-ending-1995-to-2020. Select 'Data tables' and then table 7_2tr of 'Disability trends': using the 'After housing costs' income measure shows 6.1 million disabled and 8.3 million non-disabled people in poverty, implying 42 per cent of those in poverty are disabled; using the 'Before housing costs' measure, the respective figures are 6.5 million, 5.2 million and an implied 44 per cent. NB: citing pandemic-related 'data quality issues', official statisticians declined to publish similar numbers in the 2020/21 dataset.

5   'UK Poverty 2022: The essential guide to understanding poverty in the UK', Joseph Rowntree Foundation, January 2022, pp. 57–8, available at: https://www.jrf.org.uk/report/uk-poverty-2022

6   Tom Clark and Peter Matejic, 'From disability to destitution', Joseph Rowntree Foundation, 26 July 2022, available at: https://www.jrf.org.uk/blog/disability-destitution

7   The comparable figures for non-disabled people were 40 per cent for difficulties with energy bills and 27 per cent for difficulties in paying rent or mortgage. All figures from ONS analysis of the 'Opinions and Lifestyle Survey', reported on the ONS website, headed 'Impact of increased cost of living on adults across Great Britain: June to September 2022', available at: https://www.ons.gov.uk/releases/impactofincreasedcostoflivingonadultsacrossgreatbritainjunetoseptember2022

8   Polling for Leonard Cheshire published in April 2022; full dataset available at: https://www.leonardcheshire.org/about-us/our-news/press-releases/rising-costs-are-catastrophe-disabled-people

9   See: Table 10 in Jamie Evans and Sharon Collard, 'Facing Barriers: Exploring the relationship between disability and financial wellbeing in the UK', Abrdn Financial Fairness Trust and University of Bristol, September 2022, available at: https://www.bristol.ac.uk/media-library/sites/geography/pfrc/documents/Facing%20barriers.pdf

10   Philip Alston, 'Visit to the United Kingdom of Great Britain and Northern Ireland: Report of the Special Rapporteur on extreme poverty and human rights', UN Human Rights Council, 23 April 2019, available at: https://documents-dds-ny.un.org/doc/UNDOC/GEN/G19/112/13/PDF/G1911213.pdf?OpenElement

11 Jonathan Portes and Howard Reed, 'The cumulative impact of tax and welfare reforms', Equality and Human Rights Commission, Research Report 112, 2018, available at: https://www.equalityhumanrights.com/sites/default/files/cumulative-impact-assessment-report.pdf

12 Frances Ryan, 'Pushing people to the brink of suicide: the reality of benefit assessments', *The Guardian*, 4 May 2017.

13 According to the official records as at September 2022, 'of the 5 million ESA claims with a start date between October 2013 and December 2021', 100,000 had been taken to a completed appeal, in which 34 per cent had the DWP decision upheld at hearing while the remaining 66 per cent were ruled in favour of the claimant. See: Department for Work and Pensions, 'National statistics ESA: Work Capability Assessments, Mandatory Reconsiderations and Appeals: September 2022', 8 September 2022, available at: https://www.gov.uk/government/statistics/esa-outcomes-of-work-capability-assessments-including-mandatory-reconsiderations-and-appeals-september-2022/esa-work-capability-assessments-mandatory-reconsiderations-and-appeals-september-2022

14 'People forced to use food banks at the start of the pandemic faced extreme poverty', Trussell Trust, 13 May 2021, available at: https://www.trusselltrust.org/2021/05/13/people-forced-to-use-food-banks-at-the-start-of-the-pandemic-faced-extreme-poverty/

15 Frances Ryan, '"Bedroom tax" puts added burden on disabled people', *The Guardian*, 16 July 2013.

16 See: Table 10 in Evans and Collard, 'Facing Barriers', available at: https://www.financialfairness.org.uk/docs?editionId=ed4ea324-d3fe-4f24-a7fa-e54658722477

17 After the abolition of the Social Fund crisis loans in 2012 legislation, Whitehall initially provided funding for replacement local welfare assistance schemes (LWAS) but on a time-limited basis. A 2018 report by Church Action on Poverty (available at: https://www.church-poverty.org.uk/wp-content/uploads/2019/06/Compassion-in-Crisis.pdf) recorded that by 2018/19, the funds that English councils had made available for LWAS were down by 72.5 per cent on 2013/14 and that at least twenty-eight councils had by this date axed such crisis relief completely.

18 'Consumer price inflation, UK: August 2022', Office for National Statistics, 14 September 2022, available at: https://www.ons.gov.uk/economy/inflationandpriceindices/bulletins/consumerpriceinflation/august2022#latest-movements-in-cpih-inflation

19 See: Chloe Kerr, 'IGNORING THE NEIGHSAYERS: Benefits scrounger octomom who gets £26,000 a year in taxpayers money has bought herself a horse costing more than £100 a month to help her beat depression', *The Sun*, 19 August 2017; and Neil Tweedie, 'The car scam that will drive you crackers: As the Lottery con grandmother is given this £20,000 car, we reveal how thousands are driving off in brand new vehicles paid for by YOU', *Daily Mail*, 11 May 2016.

20 The NatCen report itself can be read at: https://committees.parliament.uk/publications/8745/documents/88599/default/. Various details of the government's attempts to avoid release are available on the Commons Work and Pensions Committee website, including on this page: https://committees.parliament.uk/committee/164/work-and-pensions-committee/news/160750/disabled-peoples-experiences-of-the-benefits-system-committee-publishes-governmentcommissioned-research/

21 The research conducted by Censuswide, on behalf of the charity Sense, saw 2,008 disabled people and families across the UK surveyed between 1 June 2022 and 8 June 2022, as detailed here: https://www.sense.org.uk/media/latest-press-releases/disability-charities-write-to-future-pm-hopefuls/. The main findings of the survey are available at: https://www.sense.org.uk/media/latest-press-releases/rising-costs-in-the-uk-push-more-than-half-of-disabled-households-into-debt/

22 Of these 3.7 million, 2.2 million were deemed extremely vulnerable by dint of specific clinical conditions in spring 2020 and then another 1.5 million were advised to

shield on the basis of 'the COVID-19 population risk assessment'. See, for example, 'Coronavirus and clinically extremely vulnerable people in England: 17 May to 22 May 2021', Office for National Statistics, 8 June 2021, available at: https://www.ons.gov.uk/peoplepopulationandcommunity/healthandsocialcare/conditionsanddiseases/bulletins/coronavirusandclinicallyextremelyvulnerablepeopleinengland/17mayto22may2021

23 Information provided by DWP Minister David Rutley, in response to a parliamentary question in June 2022, available at: https://questions-statements.parliament.uk/written-questions/detail/2022-06-13/17006

24 In July 2022, the Work and Pensions Select Committee stated: 'Repayments should be paused and only restored gradually as the rate of inflation reduces, or when benefits have been uprated to reflect the current rate of inflation.' See: House of Commons Work and Pensions Committee, 'The cost of living: Second Report of Session 2022–23', available at: https://committees.parliament.uk/publications/23272/documents/169744/default/

25 During 2021, there were reports of multiple councils sharply increasing charges on disabled people for the services they provide, sometimes leaving working-age disabled people with as little as £3 a day for everything else. See: Robert Booth, 'English councils handing huge extra care bills to disabled and mentally ill adults', *The Guardian*, 8 April 2021.

26 See ongoing work at Nuffield Foundation, which started in 2021, available at: https://www.nuffieldfoundation.org/project/unpacking-the-disability-employment-gap

27 Glen Bramley et al., 'Counting the cost of UK poverty', Joseph Rowntree Foundation, 1 August 2016, available at: https://www.jrf.org.uk/report/counting-cost-uk-poverty

CHAPTER 7: DESTITUTE BY DESIGN:
TRAPPED IN THE IMMIGRATION SYSTEM

1 Suzanne Fitzpatrick et al., 'Destitution in the UK 2020', Joseph Rowntree Foundation, 9 December 2020, p. 15, available at: https://www.jrf.org.uk/report/destitution-uk-2020

2 'Migrants in the UK: An Overview', Migration Observatory, 2 August 2022, available at: https://migrationobservatory.ox.ac.uk/resources/briefings/migrants-in-the-uk-an-overview/

3 For example, an application for indefinite leave to remain – which Stella would hope to make at the end of her ten-year wait – currently costs £2,404. The estimated cost to the Home Office of processing an application is £491. See: Colin Yeo, 'Immigration and nationality fees for 2022/23', Free Movement, 7 April 2022, available at: https://freemovement.org.uk/immigration-nationality-application-fees-2022-23/

4 In 2022, councils were spending at least £64 million a year supporting 3,400 households with no recourse to public funds. See: NRPF Network, 'Social services' expenditure on households with no recourse to public funds reaches £64 million per annum', 30 November 2022, available at: https://www.nrpfnetwork.org.uk/news/nrpf-connect-data-report-2021-22

CHAPTER 8: ATOMISED, BUT NOT ALONE:
WORK AND RESISTANCE IN THE GIG ECONOMY

1 George Osborne, Budget speech, 2015, full text available at: https://www.gov.uk/government/speeches/chancellor-george-osbornes-budget-2015-speech

2 Penny Sukhraj, 'Deliveroo set for £8bn market cap on IPO as food orders surge', Financial News, 22 March 2021, available at: https://www.fnlondon.com/articles/deliveroo-set-for-8bn-market-cap-on-ipo-as-food-orders-surge-20210322

3 Arash Massoudi, Tim Bradshaw and Bryce Elder, 'Goldman Sachs bought £75m of Deliveroo shares to prop up IPO price', *Financial Times*, 6 April 2021.

4 The stock price was down 62 per cent year on year as of 12 December 2022, available at:

https://markets.ft.com/data/equities/tearsheet/summary?s=ROO:LSE; Christopher Akers, 'Deliveroo rides further into the red', Investors' Choice, 10 August 2022, available at: https://www.investorschronicle.co.uk/news/2022/08/10/deliveroo-rides-further-into-the-red

5   On fuel prices see: 'Behavioural impacts of rising automotive fuel prices on consumer fuel demand, UK: July 2021 to August 2022', Office for National Statistics, 2 September 2022, available at: https://www.ons.gov.uk/economy/economicoutputandproductivity/output/articles/behaviouralimpactsofrisingautomotivefuelpricesonconsumerfueldemandukjuly2021to
august2022/2022-09-02; Alexander Guschanski et al., 'Working for the economy: The economic case for trade unions', New Economics Foundation, 14 September 2014, available at: https://neweconomics.org/2014/09/working-for-the-economy

6   See, for instance, Wingham Rowan, 'A new kind of job market', TED Talk, 2013, available at: https://www.youtube.com/watch?v=v22SdEMzxO4

7   'Deliveroo: Chancellor Rishi Sunak hails "British tech success" as food delivery firm confirms London IPO pick', Sky News, 4 March 2021, available at: https://news.sky.com/story/chancellor-hails-british-tech-success-deliveroo-as-it-confirms-london-ipo-pick-12235393

8   Matthew Taylor, 'Good Work: The Taylor Review of Modern Working Practices', Independent Report, Department for Business, Energy and Industrial Strategy, July 2017, available at: https://www.gov.uk/government/publications/good-work-the-taylor-review-of-modern-working-practices

9   Uber BV v. Aslam [2021] UKSC 5, judgment available at: https://www.supremecourt.uk/cases/docs/uksc-2019-0029-judgment.pdf

10 Employment Rights Act 1996, available at: https://www.legislation.gov.uk/ukpga/1996/18/contents

11 'Taken for a Ride: Litigating the Digital Platform Model', International Lawyers Assisting Workers Network, March 2021, available at: https://www.ilawnetwork.com/issue-briefs-reports/taken-for-a-ride-litigating-the-digital-platform-model/; Alan Bogg, 'Taken for a Ride: Workers in the Gig Economy', Law Quarterly Review, 2019, Volume 135, pp. 219–26.

12 'Platform Work in the UK 2016–2019', Statistical Services and Consultancy Unit, University of Hertfordshire and Hertfordshire Business School, 2019, available at: https://feps-europe.eu/wp-content/uploads/downloads/publications/platform%20work%20in%20the%20uk%20
2016-2019%20v3-converted.pdf

13 Jamie Woodcock and Mark Graham, The Gig Economy: A Critical Introduction, Wylie, 2019.

14 The appeal was based on a 2018 judgment by the High Court, available at: https://www.lewissilkin.com/-/media/files/main/insights/eir/co8102018-r-iwugb-v-deliveroo-05122018-approved-004.pdf?la=en&hash=F1E966CB6A3A2E9A772C3A31A51C46214ADA632C; https://www.11kbw.com/content/uploads/R-IWGB-v-CAC-Interested-Party-Roofoods-Ltd-2021-EWCA-Civ-952.pdf

15 Julien Ponthus and Abhinav Ramnarayan, 'Deliveroo ticks up as retail investors join trading', Reuters, 7 April 2021, available at: https://www.reuters.com/business/deliveroo-ticks-up-retail-investors-join-trading-2021-04-07/

16 'IWGB Union takes Deliveroo to Supreme Court over bargaining rights months after company signs union partnership', Independent Workers' Union of Great Britain, 5 September 2022, available at: https://iwgb.org.uk/en/post/iwgb-takes-deliveroo-to-supreme-court/

17 'Deliveroo: Investor warns of workers' rights issues at firm', BBC News, 24 March 2021.

18 Queen's Speech, December 2019, Background Briefing Notes, available at: https://www.gov.uk/government/publications/queens-speech-december-2019-background-briefing-notes

19 'Trade Union Membership, UK 1995–2021: Statistical Bulletin', Department for Business, Energy and Industrial Strategy, 25 May 2022, available at: https://assets.publishing.service.gov.uk/government/uploads/system/uploads/attachment_data/file/1077904/Trade_Union_Membership_UK_1995-2021_statistical_bulletin.pdf

20 Sarah Butler and Jasper Jolly, 'Deliveroo workers protest as shares rise on first day of open trading', *The Guardian*, 7 April 2021.

21 Emiliano Mellino, Charles Boutaud and Gareth Davies, 'Deliveroo riders can earn as little as £2 an hour during shifts, as boss stands to make £500m', Bureau of Investigative Journalism, 25 March 2021, available at: https://www.thebureauinvestigates.com/stories/2021-03-25/deliveroo-riders-earning-as-little-as-2-pounds

22 Frank Field and Andrew Forsey, 'Delivering justice? A report on the pay and working conditions of Deliveroo riders', 2018.

23 *Uber BV v. Aslam*.

24 Sarah Butler, 'Deliveroo accused of "cynical PR move" with union deal for couriers', *The Guardian*, 12 May 2022.

25 Tony Wilson and Jonathan Buzzeo, 'Laid low: The impacts of the Covid-19 crisis on low-paid and insecure workers', Institute for Employment Studies, 22 January 2021, available at: https://www.employment-studies.co.uk/system/files/resources/files/The%20impacts%20of%20Covid-19%20on%20the%20low%20paid.pdf

26 'Consumer price inflation, UK: October 2022', Office for National Statistics, 16 November 2022, available at: https://www.ons.gov.uk/economy/inflationandpriceindices/bulletins/consumerpriceinflation/october2022

CONCLUSION: A FIX FOR BEING BROKE? FROM INSIGHT TO ACTION

1 Stalling overall life expectancy was evident by 2018, when official statistician Sophie Sanders commented, 'The slowdown in life expectancy improvements in the UK has continued, as 2015 to 2017 saw the lowest improvements in life expectancy since the start of the series in 1980 to 1982.' Quoted in 'National life tables, UK: 2015 to 2017', Office for National Statistics, 25 September 2018, available at: https://www.ons.gov.uk/peoplepopulationandcommunity/birthsdeathsandmarriages/lifeexpectancies/bulletins/nationallifetablesunitedkingdom/2015to2017#:~:text=In%202015%20to%202017%2C%20life,1983%20and%202015%20to%202017. The same year, and in reference to the same period, her ONS colleague Ben Humberstone commented, 'We've found a large fall in life expectancy at birth among women living in the most deprived areas in England.' Quoted in 'Health state life expectancies by national deprivation deciles, England and Wales: 2015 to 2017', Office for National Statistics, 27 March 2019, available at: https://www.ons.gov.uk/peoplepopulationandcommunity/healthandsocialcare/healthinequalities/bulletins/healthstatelifeexpectanciesbyindexofmultipledeprivationimd/2015to2017#:~:text=In%20England%2C%20the%20range%20in,females%20in%202015%20to%202017

2 The ONS records a rise from 47 to 84 per million people since 2012. See: 'Deaths related to drug poisoning in England and Wales: 2021 registrations', Office for National Statistics, 3 August 2022, available at: https://www.ons.gov.uk/peoplepopulationandcommunity/birthsdeathsandmarriages/deaths/bulletins/deathsrelatedtodrugpoisoninginenglandandwales/2021registrations. In Scotland, higher rates are reported per 100,000 residents instead. After the death toll more than doubled over the past decade, the latest numbers recorded that 'the age-standardised death rate in 2021 was 25 per 100,000 population', or 250 per million. See: 'Drug-related deaths in Scotland in 2021', National Records of Scotland, 28 July 2022, available at: https://www.nrscotland.gov.uk/files/statistics/drug-related-deaths/21/drug-related-deaths-21-report.pdf

3 Matthew Desmond, *Poverty, By America*, Allen Lane, 2023, pp. 13, 23.

4 Shadow Work and Pensions Secretary Jon Ashworth told *The Times* he wanted to end the situation whereby the 'awful rigmarole' of reapplying for benefits was putting some claimants

NOTES

off trying work. See: Henry Zeffman, 'Jobcentres should help over-50s back to work, says Labour', *The Times*, 9 January 2023.

5 For a critique of the social fund decision from the time, see: 'Shredding the ultimate safety net', *The Guardian*, 22 January 2012.

6 Official figures report '£217 billion paid out in benefits and pensions' by the Department for Work and Pensions in 2021/22. Department for Work and Pensions, 'DWP annual report and accounts 2021 to 2022', 28 July 2022, available at: https://www.gov.uk/government/publications/dwp-annual-report-and-accounts-2021-to-2022/dwp-annual-report-and-accounts-2021-to-2022. Total state support in England for debt advice is currently £76 million annually, but this includes business support services. Total grants for community-based debt advice are £30 million. (For full details, see: 'Money and Pensions Service update on debt advice commissioning: community-based debt advice in England', Money and Pensions Service, 29 September 2022, available at: https://moneyandpensionsservice.org.uk/2022/09/29/money-and-pensions-service-update-on-debt-advice-commissioning-community-based-debt-advice-in-england/. A recent freedom of information request from Damon Gibbons of the charity Centre for Responsible Credit established that the total budgeted £30 million regional grant for 2023/24 was down even in cash terms, from a budgeted £34 million in 2020/21. The official reply to the request is available at: https://static1.squarespace.com/static/5fc91d958b9551093cfd009d/t/6399c6953a0aa1474229e2df/1671022230209/FOI+205+Reply.pdf

7 The rumoured words of George Osborne at a 2013 Cabinet, reported in Andrew Grice, 'Inside Westminster: George Osborne's housing boom will echo into the future', *The Independent*, 9 October 2013.

8 During 2021/22, the proportion of Local Housing Allowance claimants with a shortfall was consistently a little above 50 per cent, and the average monthly shortfall on their rent among them was in the range £145–147. Official data provided to a parliamentary question in May 2022, available at: https://questions-statements.parliament.uk/written-questions/detail/2022-05-23/6683

9 Tom Clark and Andrew Leicester, 'Inequality and two decades of British tax and benefit reforms', *Fiscal Studies*, June 2004, Volume 25, Issue 2, pp. 129–58.

10 The supposedly automatic benefit inflation–indexation regime has been anything but since 2013, with a run of years where the adjustment was fixed at 1 per cent irrespective of what was happening to prices, followed by a run of outright freezes. For chapter and verse on these policies and how real rates of benefits were affected, see: Peter Matejic, 'Fifty years of benefit uprating', Joseph Rowntree Foundation, 13 April 2022, available at: https://www.jrf.org.uk/report/fifty-years-benefit-uprating

11 John Hills, *Good Times, Bad Times: The welfare myth of them and us*, 2nd edition, Policy Press, 2017.

12 John Curtice, 'Thermostat or weather vane? How the public has reacted to new labour government', in Alison Park et al. (eds), *British Social Attitudes: The 26th Report*, SAGE Publications Ltd, 2010, pp. 19–38.

13 On the 2015 tax credit U-turn, see: Sam Coates, 'Tax credit cuts abandoned but families still face sting in the tail', *The Times*, 26 November 2015. On the 2016 reversal on Personal Independence Payments, see: Nikki Fox, 'Relief and fear over U-turn on disability benefits', BBC News, 21 March 2016.

14 Increases in in-work benefits were announced in the then Chancellor's Autumn 2021 Spending Review, effected by a reduction in the 'taper' rate at which benefits are withdrawn as income rises. See: Richard Partington and Jessica Elgot, 'Budget 2021: Sunak softens universal credit cuts to tackle squeeze on families', *The Guardian*, 27 October 2021.

15 See: Desmond, *Poverty, By America*, especially pp. 131–3.

16 All four official poverty measures – before and after housing costs, absolute and relative – declined. See: Figure 3 in Department for Work and Pensions, 'Households below average income: an analysis of the income distribution FYE [Financial Year Ending] 1995 to FYE 2021', 24 May 2022, available at: https://www.gov.uk/government/statistics/households-below-average-income-for-financial-years-ending-1995-to-2021/households-below-average-income-an-analysis-of-the-income-distribution-fye-1995-to-fye-2021

17 Franklin D. Roosevelt, State of the Union address, 6 January 1941, available at: https://voicesofdemocracy.umd.edu/fdr-the-four-freedoms-speech-text/

18 For a thinker who used to be sceptical about the value of unions but has recently come to appreciate their value, see: Martin Wolf, *The Crisis of Democratic Capitalism*, Allen Lane, 2023.

19 See, for example, the government press releases 'Government introduces laws to mitigate the disruption of strikes on the public', 10 January 2023, available at: https://www.gov.uk/government/news/government-introduces-laws-to-mitigate-the-disruption-of-strikes-on-the-public and 'PM takes action to stop disruptive protests', 16 January 2023, available at: https://www.gov.uk/government/news/pm-takes-action-to-stop-disruptive-protests

20 Darren McGarvey, *The Social Distance Between Us: How Remote Politics Wrecked Britain*, Ebury Press, 2022.

21 Reported on Twitter, 7 November 2022, using Crick's dedicated account for covering parliamentary selections, @tomorrowsmps. Tweet available at: https://twitter.com/tomorrowsmps/status/1589552918788599808

22 On the rising numbers leaving the labour market on grounds of long-term sickness, see: 'Half a million more people are out of the labour force because of long-term sickness', Office for National Statistics, 10 November 2022, available at: https://www.ons.gov.uk/employmentandlabourmarket/peoplenotinwork/economicinactivity/articles/halfamillionmorepeopleareoutofthelabourforcebecauseoflongtermsickness/2022-11-10

RESOURCES

Throughout this book, the crucial, sometimes even life-saving, support of community groups and charities has been a constant. Mindful that some readers may need somewhere to turn themselves, and that others might be moved to donate time or money, we offer this short directory. Many of the groups reported on are small, grassroots initiatives of limited relevance beyond a particular locale, so, without attempting to be comprehensive, we have also dropped in a number of nation-wide organisations concerned with the main themes of the book.

COLD

Warm Welcome Campaign – equips and supports thousands of free, warm and welcoming spaces across the UK, providing an online map for those in need

Website: https://www.warmwelcome.uk/
Email: info@warmwelcome.uk

DEBT SUPPORT

StepChange – the UK's largest provider of free debt advice, online or over the phone

Address: 123 Albion Street, Leeds LS2 8ER
Tel: 0800 138 1111
Website: https://www.stepchange.org/

Visit from the Stork CIC – helps parents in Greater Manchester feel informed and listened to, with peer support groups covering topics such as debt and money worries. The organisation also delivers baby essentials to families in hardship

Address: 6th Floor, Suite 17–18, St James House, Pendleton Way, Salford M6 5FW; Emmanuel Church, 174 Langworthy Road, Salford M6 5LH
Tel: 07402630671
Website: https://www.visitfromthestork.co.uk/

DRUG SUPPORT

Scottish Drugs Forum – a national resource of expertise on drugs and related issues in Scotland, fighting to improve Scotland's response to problem drug use, working with policymakers as well as people who use or have used services

Address: 91 Mitchell Street, Glasgow G1 3LN
Tel: 0141 221 1175
Website: https://www.sdf.org.uk/

FOOD AID

The Bread and Butter Thing – brings nutritious, affordable food and everyday essentials to those in need across the north of England

Website: https://www.breadandbutterthing.org/

The Community Food Hub, Tottenham – provides food and crisis management for vulnerable people in Tottenham, including delivery services, with no referral necessary

Address: Tottenham Town Hall, Town Hall Approach Road, London N15 4RY
Website: https://www.freedomsark.org/community-projects/the-community-food-hub/

Drumchapel Foodbank – provides food parcels to those facing immediate food poverty and financial crisis in Drumchapel

Address: Ladyloan Place, Unit 9, KCEDG, Main Reception, Drumchapel, Glasgow G15 8LB
Tel: 0141 944 3335

Website: https://www.drumchapelfoodbank.com/
Email: contact@drumchapelfoodbank.com

The Felix Project – rescues fresh, nutritious food that cannot be sold and would otherwise go to waste and delivers it to charities, schools and holiday programmes throughout London

Address: Unit 6, Kendal Court, Kendal Avenue, England W3 0RU
Tel: 020 3034 4350
Website: https://thefelixproject.org/
Email: info@thefelixproject.org

The Food Foundation – a think tank challenging food policy and business practice across the UK to ensure everyone can afford and access a healthy and sustainable diet

Address: International House, 6 Canterbury Crescent, London, SW9 7QD
Tel: 020 3086 9953
Website: https://foodfoundation.org.uk/
Email: office@foodfoundation.org.uk

Independent Food Aid Network – a UK network of independent, grassroots food aid providers, including independent food banks, working to ensure food security for all

Address: 71–75, Shelton Street, Covent Garden, London, WC2H 9JQ
Website: https://www.foodaidnetwork.org.uk/
Email: admin@foodaidnetwork.org.uk

Tottenham Foodbank – a Trussell Trust-accredited food bank providing emergency food parcels for individuals and families in Tottenham

Address: Tottenham Town Hall, Town Hall Approach Road, London N15 4RY
Tel: 020 8493 0050
Website: https://tottenham.foodbank.org.uk/
Email: info@tottenham.foodbank.org.uk

The Trussell Trust – supports a UK-wide network of food banks providing food parcels, based on referrals, and campaigns to end the need for emergency food

Address: United Reformed Church, Church House, 86 Tavistock Place, London, WC1H 9RT; Unit 9 Ashfield Trading Estate, Ashfield Road, Salisbury, Wiltshire, SP2 7HL
Tel: 01722 580 180
Website: https://www.trusselltrust.org/
Email: enquiries@trusselltrust.org

HOMELESSNESS AND HOUSING

Crisis – national charity for people experiencing homelessness, providing direct help and campaigning for the changes needed to eradicate homelessness altogether

Address: 66 Commercial Street, London E1 6LT
Tel: 0300 636 1967
Website: https://www.crisis.org.uk/
Email: enquiries@crisis.org.uk

Shelter – defends the right to a safe home, providing information, support and advice to people facing homelessness and experiencing unfit and unsafe housing throughout the UK

Address: 88 Old Street, London EC1V 9HU; 4th floor, Scotiabank House, 6 South Charlotte Street, Edinburgh EH2 4AW
Tel: 0344 515 2000
Website: England: https://england.shelter.org.uk/; Scotland: https://scotland.shelter.org.uk/; Wales: https://sheltercymru.org.uk/; Northern Ireland: https://www.housingadviceni.org/
Email: info@shelter.org.uk

Simon Community Scotland – provides information, care and accommodation to people experiencing, or at risk of, homelessness in Glasgow, Edinburgh, Perth and North Lanarkshire

Address: 22 Holyrood Road, Edinburgh EH8 8AF; 389 Argyle Street, Glasgow G2 8LR
Tel: Edinburgh: 0808 178 2323; Glasgow: 0141 552 4164 or 0800 027 7466
Website: https://www.simonscotland.org/
Email: hello@simonscotland.org

TENANTS' RIGHTS

Generation Rent – fights to stop renters being unfairly evicted from their homes in the UK, making the voice of private renters heard by landlords, putting pressure on policymakers and politicians to do the right thing for renters

Address: c/o Read Milburn, 71 Howard Street, North Shields NE30 1AF
Tel: 07498 926134; 07753 369555
Website: https://www.generationrent.org/
Email: info@generationrent.org

Renters' Reform Coalition – a coalition of organisations campaigning to reform the private rented sector, pushing for safe, secure and affordable homes for all in the UK

Website: https://rentersreformcoalition.co.uk/

MIGRANTS' RIGHTS

GYROS – helps migrants and culturally and linguistically diverse communities across East Anglia, providing free information, advice and advocacy on matters including immigration, education and housing

Address: 43 North Quay, Great Yarmouth NR30 1JE
Tel: 01493 745260
Website: https://www.gyros.org.uk/

Leeds Asylum Seekers' Support Network – supports refugees and asylum seekers in Leeds, providing temporary housing, English lessons and a befriending project, helping people feel settled in the city

Address: 22/23 Blayds Yard, Leeds LS1 4AD (visit via appointment only)
Tel: 0113 373 1759
Website: https://lassn.org.uk/

Praxis – provides support to migrants and refugees in London through immigration advice, housing and peer support groups

Address: Pott Street, London E2 0EF
Tel: 020 7729 7985
Website: https://www.praxis.org.uk/

The No Accommodation Network – holds a list of more than 140 frontline organisations that work to end destitution among refugees, asylum seekers and other migrants denied access to public funds. The British Red Cross also offers support services around the country

Website: https://naccom.org.uk/projects/; https://www.redcross.org.uk/get-help/get-help-as-a-refugee

WELL-BEING AND COMMUNITY SUPPORT

GalGael – offers activities, such as woodworking courses, in Glasgow to help people reclaim skills, agency and sense of worth

Address: 15 Fairley Street, Glasgow G51 2SN
Tel: 0141 427 3070
Website: https://www.galgael.org/
Email: mail@galgael.org

GENERAL

Citizens Advice – offers free and impartial advice concerning matters such as debt, housing and immigration across the UK

Website: England: https://www.citizensadvice.org.uk/; Scotland: https://www.citizensadvice.org.uk/scotland/; Wales: https://www.citizensadvice.org.uk/wales/; Northern Ireland: https://www.citizensadvice.org.uk/about-us/northern-ireland/

ACKNOWLEDGEMENTS

This book would not exist without the generous support of the Joseph Rowntree Foundation (JRF), with special thanks due to its chief executive, Paul Kissack, together with directors Graeme Cooke, Frank Soodeen and Sophia Parker for throwing their weight behind it.

I'm hugely grateful to Sarah Chalfant at the Wylie Agency for seeing the urgency and potential of reportage on the poverty crisis at this moment and for taking on what is, in terms of the book trade, a rather unusual multi-author volume. Both Sarah and Jessica Bullock, also at Wylie, greatly sharpened the proposal, and Jessica then worked tirelessly and efficiently to represent the book and find it an ideal home at Biteback Publishing. Together with Wylie colleague Nanae Hart and Tracey Preece of the JRF, Jessica also worked hard to ensure that the royalties could be passed to Leeds Asylum Seekers' Support Network.

At Biteback, Olivia Beattie proved to be the ideal publisher to work with, playing a part in everything from the final commissioning decisions to the ironing out of infelicities in the text. She also commissioned Steve Leard to produce the book's powerful cover. Thanks to Ella Boardman for her close eye in copyediting, to Namkwan Cho for typesetting, to Suzanne Sangster for energetic work in publicising the book and to Nell Whitaker for her imaginative efforts in doing the same on social media.

Every one of the seven commissioned writers – Jem Bartholomew, Cal Flyn (and her researcher Laura Beveridge), Dani Garavelli, Frances Ryan, Samira Shackle, Daniel Trilling and Jennifer Williams – has put their heart into the task and not merely put up with but responded with generosity and patience to my endless nit-picking to get the text as clear as possible and the endnotes in good order. I'd like to thank each of them individually for that, and also Kerry Hudson and Joel Goodman, who threw themselves into writing the foreword and producing the photographs with exactly the same passion.

Last, but certainly not least, I'd like to thank those dozens of people on the wrong end of the poverty crisis who agreed to talk so candidly to this book's reporting team. One lesson from the testimony in these pages is just how difficult it can be to open up about the realities of being broke. The decision to speak up and be counted is always a brave one. I hope that the power of these pages is sufficient that those interviewed will also feel that it has been worthwhile.

Tom Clark
March 2023

CONTRIBUTORS

Jem Bartholomew is an award-winning freelance reporter for outlets including *The Guardian*, *The Economist* and the *Wall Street Journal*. He was a Fulbright scholar and was a reporting fellow at the Tow Center at Columbia University 2022–23. His investigation into the UK prison system won Best Newcomer at the State Street Press Awards 2019.

Tom Clark is an award-winning journalist and a contributing editor at *Prospect* magazine. He previously worked at *The Guardian*, in Whitehall and at various think tanks, including the Joseph Rowntree Foundation, where he was a fellow from 2021 to 2023.

Cal Flyn is a bestselling non-fiction writer whose reportage has been published in the *Wall Street Journal*, the *Telegraph* and *The Times*. Her most recent book, *Islands of Abandonment*, was shortlisted for the Baillie Gifford Prize and the Royal Society of Literature's Ondaatje Prize and won the *Sunday Times* Charlotte Aitken Young Writer of the Year Award.

Dani Garavelli is a feature writer who has been honoured three times in a row as Feature Writer of the Year at the Scottish Press Awards, in 2019, 2020 and 2021, and in 2021 won the inaugural Anne Brown Essay Prize at the Wigtown Book Festival.

Joel Goodman is a renowned photojournalist whose work has been published in press and on television around the world.

Kerry Hudson is the award-winning author of *Lowborn*, a prize-winning novelist and a fellow of the Royal Society of Literature. She has written for *The Guardian*, *The Observer* and the *Big Issue*, among others, and has also created scripts for the BBC.

Frances Ryan is an award-winning *Guardian* columnist whose work has appeared everywhere from the front page of the *New York Times*, to Channel 4, to *British Vogue*. She has twice been highly commended at the National Press Awards. She is the author of *Crippled* (2019) and the upcoming *Who Wants Normal?* (2025).

Samira Shackle is a multi-award-winning journalist based in London and a regular contributor to the *Guardian* Long Read. Her first book, *Karachi Vice*, is a work of narrative non-fiction that tells the story of five ordinary citizens in Pakistan's largest city. It was picked as a Radio 4 Book of the Week.

Daniel Trilling is a reporter and author based in London who writes on migration, nationalism and human rights. He is the author of *Lights in the Distance*, based on years of reporting on the experiences of refugees in Europe, and *Bloody Nasty People*, a history of Britain's far right. His chapter for *Broke*, republished in *Prospect* magazine, was shortlisted for the 2023 Orwell Prize for Reporting Homelessness.

Jennifer Williams is the northern correspondent at the *Financial Times* and previously worked at the *Manchester Evening News* for eleven years, including as politics and investigations editor. She was the Feature Writer/Long Form Journalist of the Year winner at the Regional Press Awards in 2018 and has been nominated for the Orwell Prize four times.